296.4
Gol

GOLDIN, HYMAN E.
  A treasury of Jewish
  holidays

5128

296.4
Gol

5128

A Treasury of Jewish Holidays

Twenty-year Calendar o[f]

	5,712 1951-2	5,713 1952-3	5,714 1953-4	5,715 1954-5	5,716 1955-6	5,717 1956-7	5,718 1957-8	5,719 1958-9	5,720 1959-6
ROSH HASHANAH Tishri 1-2	Oct 1-2	Sep 20-21	Sep 10-11	Sep 28-29	Sep 17-18	Sep 6-7	Sep 26-27	Sep 15-16	Oct 3-4
FAST OF GEDALIAH Tishri 3	Oct 3	Sep 22	Sep 12	Sep 30	Sep 19	Sep 8	Sep 28	Sep 17	Oct 5
YOM KIPPUR (Yizkor) Tishri 10	Oct 10	Sep 29	Sep 19	Oct 7	Sep 26	Sep 15	Oct 5	Sep 24	Oct 12
SUKKOT (first 2 days) Tishri 15-16	Oct 15-16	Oct 4-5	Sep 24-25	Oct 12-13	Oct 1-2	Sep 20-21	Oct 10-11	Sep 29-30	Oct 17-1
HOSHANAH RABBAH Tishri 21	Oct 21	Oct 10	Sep 30	Oct 18	Oct 7	Sep 26	Oct 16	Oct 5	Oct 23
SHEMINI ATZERET (Yizkor) Tishri 22	Oct 22	Oct 11	Oct 1	Oct 19	Oct 8	Sep 27	Oct 17	Oct 6	Oct 24
SIMEHAT TORAH Tishri 23	Oct 23	Oct 12	Oct 2	Oct 20	Oct 9	Sep 28	Oct 18	Oct 7	Oct 25
HANUKKAH Kislev 25-Tebet 2	Dec 24-31	Dec 13-20	Dec 2-9	Dec 20-27	Dec 10-17	Nov 29 Dec 6	Dec 18-25	Dec 7-13	Dec 26 Jan 2
	1952			**1955**			**1958**		**196[0]**
ASARAH BETEBET (fast) Tebet 10	Jan 8	Dec 28	Dec 16	Jan 4	Dec 25	Dec 14	Jan 2	Dec 21	Jan 10
		1953	**1954**		**1956**	**1957**		**1959**	
HAMISHAH ASAR BISHEBAT Shebat 15(Arbor Day)	Feb 11	Jan 31	Jan 19	Feb 7	Jan 28	Jan 17	Feb 5	Jan 24	Feb 13
TAANIT ESTHER (fast) Adar 13	Mar 10	Feb 28	Mar 18	Mar 7	Feb 25	Mar 16	Mar 5	Mar 23	Mar 12
PURIM Adar 14	Mar 11	Mar 1	Mar 19	Mar 8	Feb 26	Mar 17	Mar 6	Mar 24	Mar 13
SHUSHAN PURIM Adar 15	Mar 12	Mar 2	Mar 20	Mar 9	Feb 27	Mar 18	Mar 7	Mar 25	Mar 14
PASSOVER (Pesah) Nisan 15-22 Yizkor, Nisan, 22	Apr 10-17 Apr 17	Mar 31 Apr 7	Apr 18-25 Apr 25	Apr 7-14 Apr 14	Mar 27 Apr 3	Apr 16-23 Apr 23	Apr 5-12 Apr 12	Apr 23-30 Apr 30	Apr 12 Apr 19
ISRAEL-INDEPENDENCE DAY Iyyar 5	Apr 30	Apr 20	May 8	Apr 27	Apr 16	May 6	Apr 25	May 13	May 2
LAG BAOMER Iyyar 18	May 13	May 3	May 21	May 10	Apr 29	May 19	May 8	May 26	May 1
SHABUOT Sivan 6-7 Yizkor, Sivan 7	May 30-31 May 31	May 20-21 May 21	Jun 7-8 Jun 8	May 27-28 May 28	May 16-17 May 17	Jun 5-6 Jun 6	May 25-26 May 26	Jun 12-13 Jun 13	Jun 1- Jun 2
SHIBEAH ASAR BETAMMUZ Tammuz 17 (fast)	Jul 10	Jun 30	Jul 18	Jul 7	Jun 26	Jul 16	Jul 5	Jul 23	Jul 12
TISHEAH BEAB Ab 9 (fast)	Jul 31	Jul 21	Aug 8	Jul 28	Jul 17	Aug 6	Jul 26	Aug 13	Aug 2

5,721 1960-1	5,722 1961-2	5,723 1962-3	5,724 1963-4	5,725 1964-5	5,726 1965-6	5,727 1966-7	5,728 1967-8	5,728 1968-9	5,730 1969-70	5,731 1970-1
ep 22-23	Sep 11-12	Sep 29-30	Sep 19-20	Sep 7-8	Sep 27-28	Sep 15-16	Oct 5-6	Sep 23-24	Sep 13-14	Oct 1-2
ep 24	Sep 13	Oct 1	Sep 21	Sep 9	Sep 29	Sep 17	Oct 7	Sep 25	Sep 15	Oct 3
ct 1	Sep 20	Oct 8	Sep 28	Sep 16	Oct 6	Sep 24	Oct 14	Oct 2	Sep 22	Oct 10
ct 6-7	Sep 25-26	Oct 13-14	Oct 3-4	Sep 21-22	Oct 11-12	Sep 29-30	Oct 19-20	Oct 7-8	Sep 27-28	Oct 15-16
ct 12	Oct 1	Oct 19	Oct 9	Sep 27	Oct 17	Oct 5	Oct 25	Oct 13	Oct 3	Oct 21
ct 13	Oct 2	Oct 20	Oct 10	Sep 28	Oct 18	Oct 6	Oct 26	Oct 14	Oct 4	Oct 22
ct 14	Oct 3	Oct 21	Oct 11	Sep 29	Oct 19	Oct 7	Oct 27	Oct 15	Oct 5	Oct 23
c 14-21	Dec 3-10	Dec 22-29	Dec 11-18	Nov 30 Dec 7	Dec 19-25	Dec 8-15	Dec 27 Jan 3	Dec 16-23	Dec 5-12	Dec 23-30
		1963			**1966**		**1968**			**1971**
c 29	Dec 17	Jan 6	Dec 26	Dec 15	Jan 2	Dec 23	Jan 11	Dec 31	Dec 19	Jan 7
1961	**1962**		**1964**	**1965**		**1967**		**1969**	**1970**	
1	Jan 20	Feb 9	Jan 29	Jan 18	Feb 5	Jan 26	Feb 14	Feb 3	Jan 22	Feb 10
r 1	Mar 19	Mar 9	Feb 26	Mar 17	Mar 5	Mar 25	Mar 13	Mar 3	Mar 21	Mar 10
r 2	Mar 20	Mar 10	Feb 27	Mar 18	Mar 6	Mar 26	Mar 14	Mar 4	Mar 22	Mar 11
r 3	Mar 21	Mar 11	Feb 28	Mar 19	Mar 7	Mar 27	Mar 15	Mar 5	Mar 23	Mar 12
r 1-8 / 8	Apr 19-26 Apr 26	Apr 9-16 Apr 16	Mar 28 Apr 4	Apr 17-24 Apr 24	Apr 5-12 Apr 12	Apr 25 May 2	Apr 13-20 Apr 20	Apr 3-10 Apr 10	Apr 21-28 Apr 28	Apr 10-17 Apr 17
21	May 9	Apr 29	Apr 17	May 7	Apr 25	May 15	May 3	Apr 23	May 11	Apr 30
4	May 22	May 12	Apr 30	May 20	May 8	May 28	May 16	May 6	May 24	May 13
21-22 / 22	Jun 8-9 Jun 9	May 29-30 May 30	May 17-18 May 18	Jun 6-7 Jun 7	May 25-26 May 26	Jun 14-15 Jun 15	Jun 2-3 Jun 3	May 23-24 May 24	Jun 10-11 Jun 11	May 30-31 May 31
1	Jul 19	Jul 9	Jun 27	Jul 17	Jul 5	Jul 25	Jul 13	Jul 3	Jul 21	Jul 10
22	Aug 9	Jul 30	Jul 18	Aug 7	Jul 26	Aug 15	Aug 3	Jul 24	Aug 11	Jul 31

A Treasury of
JEWISH
HOLIDAYS

HISTORY · LEGENDS · TRADITIONS

by Hyman E. Goldin

ILLUSTRATED BY RESKO

TWAYNE PUBLISHERS · NEW YORK

Designed by Sidney Solomon

Foreword

THE JEWS have always enjoyed their Sabbaths and Festivals, observing them with great devotion and joy. They treasure these festive days, because they remind them of their lofty ideals and religious beliefs. On such days, Jews dispersed in every land recall the great historic events of their past. The celebration of these holy days has helped them to survive terrible persecutions by giving them new hope and courage; and by uniting their present-day lives with their glorious past, they have served as a promise that some day they would again rebuild their homeland in the Holy Land, and once more be an independent people.

And this proved to be no false hope, no empty dream. After almost two thousand years, the ideals symbolized by our Sabbaths and Festivals have become a reality. We have lived to see the actual rebuilding of Eretz Yisrael, as a Jewish State, the State of Israel. Its flag, the White and Blue, is now waving in glory with the flags of sixty other nations of the world. The Festivals are now an actual part of an established national existence, and they no longer serve merely as symbols of hope.

The Jews in Israel now observe their Passover as a Festival symbolizing not the freedom their forefathers won when they were redeemed from the land of Egypt, but the new freedom wrested from their modern oppressors. They celebrate Shabuot, not as a symbol of their bygone days when their ancestors used to gather their last crop of the cereal harvest in the land of their promise, and bring to the Temple their first ripe fruits as a *bikkurim* offering, to give thanks to the Almighty; they actually till the soil in the Land of Israel and bring their *bikkurim* on Shabuot as an offering, not to the Temple as yet, but rather as gifts for the purpose of obtaining more soil for the State of Israel, thus helping to support the tens of thousands of immigrants from every corner of the earth who desire to settle as free men in the Holy Land. Sukkot is now observed as a real *hag haasiph,* harvest festival, and they are actually pitching numberless tents, like their ancestors of old in the wilderness, as temporary shelters for the thousands of immigrant families who are still without homes.

The rebirth of Israel has created new Festivals, and has lent renewed significance to the old. May we continue to cherish them as we have for so many centuries, for in them is enshrined the living spirit of our culture and traditions.

HYMAN E. GOLDIN

Contents

Contents

Contents

Sabbath

THE JEWISH DAY OF REST

SIGNIFICANCE OF THE SABBATH. The Fourth of the Ten Commandments, given by the Almighty on Mount Sinai, reads:

"Remember the Sabbath-day to keep it holy. Six days shalt thou labor, and do all thy work; but the seventh day is a Sabbath to the Lord thy God; in it thou shalt not do any manner of work, thou, nor thy son, nor thy daughter, nor thy man-servant, nor thy maid-servant, nor thy cattle, nor the stranger that is within thy gate; for in six days the Lord made heaven and earth, the sea, and all that in them is, and rested on the seventh day; therefore the Lord blessed the Sabbath-day, and hallowed it."

The Almighty tires not and needs no rest. However, the Biblical account of the six-days' creation and the seventh day of rest, has a deeper meaning for us. It conveys to us the great religious truth that the world is the work of the Almighty. The six days signify epochs or stages in the evolution of the world; the Sabbath, as the completion of the creation, symbolizes the sublime peace and bliss to be enjoyed after the end of each week.

God gave us the Sabbath to permit us to enjoy the needed bodily rest and recreation after six days of toil, worry, and care. And this rest is to be enjoyed equally by all our fellow beings, the servant as well as the master, and the hired laborer as well as his employer who lives in ease. Even the beast in our employ is to have rest.

Thus the Sabbath implies that all men are free and equal before God. And it specifies that creatures under man's dominion shall also be treated with regard.

"Six days shalt thou labor, and do all thy work." The Almighty commanded us to work, so that we might preserve all those beautiful things that have been provided for us. Work is not only necessary for our happiness, but it is made holy by God. Man's duty is to labor and by his industry to add to the wealth, comfort, and happiness of the world. Idleness is sin. Sings the Psalmist (CXXVIII:2):

> When thou eatest the labor of thine hands;
> Happy shalt thou be, and it shall be well with thee.

The Sabbath also reminds us of the deliverance of the Jews from the land of Egypt, where they were held in bondage and were given no rest (Deuteronomy V:15): "And thou shalt remember that thou wert a servant in the land of Egypt, and the Lord thy God brought thee out thence by a mighty hand and by an outstretched arm; therefore the Lord thy God commanded thee to keep the Sabbath day."

Ancient civilization was founded on slavery. The Jewish Sabbath first proclaimed liberty to man: every man is to enjoy the bliss of peace and rest.

HOLINESS OF THE SABBATH. But besides material needs, man also has spiritual wants. The Fourth Commandment therefore ordains: "Remember the Sabbath-day to keep it holy." That is, we should set aside the seventh day of the week as a day of rest consecrated to God and the higher purposes of life. While abstaining from labor, we should keep the Sabbath holy, and devote a great part of the day to those things which draw us nearer to God, our family, and our fellowmen.

Thus, the Sabbath was instituted by God with a two-fold purpose: first, to give us a regular day of rest from our usual toil and care; secondly, to give us an opportunity for learning about Him and what He desires from us.

From very ancient times, the Sabbath has been celebrated as a day of religious devotion and instruction. This day of rest has been set aside to permit us to learn the sacred Jewish rites and religious customs, and to meditate on the Law of Moses. Josephus states (Ant. XVI, ii, 4): "And the seventh day we set apart from labor; it is dedicated to the learning of our customs and laws."

It is therefore the sacred duty of all Jews to attend religious services on the Sabbath, and to listen to the divine word of God, read and expounded to the worshiping assembly.

The Sabbath is also designed to lend special joy and sanctity to the home. It is a day for family reunion. The members of the family gather around a table offering finer and more festive food than on weekdays, in an atmosphere of joy and thanksgiving in honor of the day. The Sabbath thus fills our hearts with cheer and comfort, and greatly strengthens the ties of mutual affection, understanding, and loyalty in the family circle.

The Jew is therefore ordered by the Fourth Commandment to keep the Sabbath holy by refraining from manual work and from everyday activities. Some Jews, especially in the United

States of America, are forced by circumstances to profane the Sabbath. While this is most unfortunate, it does not follow that they should neglect the Sabbath entirely. They can find a way of preserving the gift of the Sabbath, which from the earliest times was precious and meaningful in the life of the Jewish people.

The Sabbath is the time to think of ideas, of improving our lives as individuals and as members of a larger community. The Jewish family has the responsibility of making the Sabbath a day of happiness, an occasion for a happy family reunion, perhaps reading books of Jewish interest. Further why shouldn't the family go to the synagogue for late Friday evening services and participate in the discussion of important topics bearing upon the spiritual life of the Jewish people?

Women and children certainly are free to attend the synagogue. If the father comes home late, the candles can be lit at the proper time in honor of the Sabbath just the same. The father can spend the Sabbath eve with his family singing *zemirot* (Sabbath hymns), in the true Sabbath spirit. If the father works only till noon on Saturday, he can spend the rest of the day in a manner befitting the Sabbath spirit. We can form clubs and family circles to meet in the afternoons. We can say farewell to the Sabbath with *Habdalah* on Saturday evening, or attend an *oneg shabbat* late in the afternoon.

IMPORTANCE OF THE SABBATH. Our sages say that when God was about to give the Fourth Commandment to the Jews, he said to Moses: "I have a precious gift stored away in My treasures, and its name is *Sabbath*. I desire to give this gift to Israel. Go and apprise them of it."

The Sabbath is, indeed, the most beautiful gift Israel has received from God. In time past, after a week of toil, privation, and even persecution, the Jew, surrounded by his family, enjoyed the holy Sabbath. On this blessed day, he banished mourning, weeping, and sadness, and he forgot his trials and tribulations. Joy, freedom, and holiness permeated his home, his synagogue, and even his street. During the past three thousand years, thousands and thousands of Jews have given up their lives rather than break the holy Sabbath.

As far back as the days of the early prophets, the observance of the Sabbath was considered to be of prime importance in the life of the Jewish people. All the prophets, from Isaiah and Jeremiah to Nehemiah, eloquently urged the Jewish people to keep the Sabbath faithfully.

Later on in Jewish history, the leaders of Jewish thought, the Talmudic authorities, came to consider the observance of the Sabbath as the foundation of the Jewish faith. Two major volumes of the Talmud—Shabbat and Erubin—are devoted exclusively to the laws of the Sabbath; and numerous legends, proverbs, laws, and stories about this day of rest are scattered throughout the other treatises of the Talmud and the Midrash.

The following are some quotations from the Talmud concerning the Sabbath:

"Great is the Sabbath, for it outweighs all the other commandments of God."

"Whosoever keeps the Sabbath-day holy is protected against temptation to sin."

"Jerusalem was destroyed by the enemy for no other reason than that the Jews desecrated the Sabbath."

"If the Jews were to observe two Sabbaths properly, they would at once be redeemed; even if only one Sabbath were rightly kept, the Messiah would appear."

"On the Sabbath, man is endowed with an additional soul, which is taken away from him at the conclusion of the Sabbath."

SABBATH THE BRIDE. A poetic and beautiful idea about the Sabbath was conceived by our Talmudic sages. They said that the Jews were wedded to the Sabbath, the Jews being the bridegroom and the Sabbath the bride. They describe how the wedding between the Jews and the Sabbath took place:

"When the seventh day of the creation was consecrated by God as the Sabbath, the Holy Day of rest, it complained: 'O mighty Lord, every day of the week is associated with another: Sunday is associated with Monday; Tuesday with Wednesday; and Thursday with Friday; but I stand alone, without an associate.' God replied: 'I have provided an associate for you: a true bridegroom.' 'Who may that be?' asked Sabbath. 'None other,' replied God, 'than My people Israel. You shall be the bride, and My people the bridegroom.' "

Every Jew should therefore rejoice with the coming of the Sabbath. The mere expectation of a distinguished guest would make him active in setting his house in order; how much more so when that guest is the Sabbath! In expectation of the Sabbath, the pious Jewish woman busies herself with many chores on Friday. She polishes the silverware and other utensils to be used for and on the Sabbath; she puts fresh coverings on the beds, arranges the household furniture, and covers the table with a fresh, white cloth, which remains on the table till the end of the Sabbath.

In honor of the Sabbath, everybody must wash his face and hands, and if facilities are available, his whole body in warm water. Our sages say that everybody should try to wear fine clothes especially set aside for the Sabbath, and, if possible, not to wear the same clothes as on weekdays.

Note how our sages of old received the Sabbath-bride: Rabbi Haninah used to wrap himself in his festive cloak and stand ready, on Friday toward evening, saying: "Come ye, and let us go forth to meet Queen Sabbath." Rabbi Yannai would put on his best Sabbath clothes and would say: "Come, O bride; come, O bride!"

In the sixteenth century a beautiful poem was composed by Rabbi Solomon Alkabiz, entitled *"Lekah Dodi"* (Come My Beloved), which was incorporated in our Friday evening services. This poem, opening with an invitation to friends to welcome the bride Sabbath, is full of courage and hope for the oppressed Jewish people.

PREPARING FOR THE SABBATH. "And thou shalt call the Sabbath *oneg* (pleasure)," are the words of the Almighty through His prophet Isaiah. And our sages ask: "How is the Sabbath to be observed as a day of pleasure?" And they reply: "With good food and drink, with clean and becoming clothes, with joy and entertainment; and for this you will receive reward from Heaven."

It is therefore the duty of everybody not to hesitate in making the purchases necessary for a worthy celebration of the Sabbath. The more one spends, the greater the merit. No one should stint in making preparations for the Sabbath, but should procure choice meat, fish, dessert, and good wine, in accordance with one's means.

Even a poor man should economize the whole week in order to save up enough money to buy food in honor of the Sabbath. If necessary, one should borrow money, and even pledge one's personal property as security, in order to provide for the Sabbath. Our Rabbis say: "The Holy One, blessed be He, said to the Israelites: 'My children, borrow for My sake and sanctify the holy day; and have confidence in Me that I will repay it.'"

Our Talmudic sages also maintain that expenses incurred for a joyful Sabbath celebration do not impoverish, but on the contrary enrich those who spend beyond their means to enjoy it. To prove this, the sages handed down a beautiful story of a certain man who was known to the people of his town as "Joseph, the Honorer of the Sabbath." He was called that because he used to live in extreme poverty all week, saving all his meagre earnings until the Sabbath, when he would spend it all for food in honor of that day.

"Joseph had an extremely rich non-Jewish neighbor, who was as superstitious as he was rich. One day Joseph's neighbor consulted a fortune-teller, and was told that all his wealth would one day become the property of Joseph. He was so frightened by the fortune-teller's words that he couldn't sleep, but sat up nights thinking of how to avoid the calamity foretold him. He finally hit upon a scheme which he thought would be efficacious and safe.

"He sold all his possessions, and with that money he bought the most costly gem that could be found in the whole world. This precious gem he carefully sewed up in the lining of his turban.

" 'Now,' said he with a self-satisfied smile, 'my Jewish neighbor can never possess my wealth.'

"Once, as the proud owner of the precious gem was crossing a bridge, a strong gust of wind carried off the turban into the stream, where it sank to the bottom. After many hours of futile search for the turban, the loser of the gem consoled himself: 'My loss is great; I am now poor and penniless, but at least I am certain that my wealth will not fall into the hands of the Jew.'

"Time passed, and the precious gem became loosened from the lining of the turban and was swallowed by a fish. Late one Friday afternoon, some fishermen, on drawing up their net from the stream, found it empty but for one beautiful fish which they brought to town for sale. 'Who will buy this beautiful fish from us?' inquired the fishermen from the passers-by. 'Because it is late in the afternoon, we are ready to sell it at a sacrifice.'

"No one paid attention to the fishermen's offer, because everybody had already been fully prepared for the Sabbath. At last one of the passers-by suggested to the fishermen: 'Go to the house of Joseph, the Honorer of the Sabbath; he never refuses to buy anything offered to him on Friday with which he can honor the Sabbath.'

"Accordingly, the fishermen went and offered the fish to Joseph, who bought it from them at their price. On cutting the fish open, the pious man was greatly surprised by the presence of the precious gem. The Sabbath over, he sold the gem for a huge sum of money.

"Joseph was afterwards met by an old man (said to be the

prophet Elijah) who said: 'Him who lends to the Sabbath, by incurring additional expenses in honoring the Sabbath, the Sabbath will repay.' "

Although it is a meritorious act to enjoy good food on the Sabbath, yet it is even more important to provide the poor with all that they may require for the Sabbath. If one can afford to help the needy in this way, but fails to do so, and merely makes an elaborate meal for one's family in honor of the Sabbath, this consuming of good food is no longer considered a *mitzvah*, a fulfillment of God's will, but mere gluttony.

The Talmudic sages say that Ezra, upon returning from the Babylonian captivity (459 B. C. E.), instituted many important ordinances for the good of the Jewish people. One of these ordinances instructs the Jewish woman to rise early on Friday morning and bake bread to supply the poor with *hallot*, white loaves of bread, for the Sabbath.

No matter how many servants one may have, it is the duty of every man and woman personally to honor the Sabbath. Even our great scholars, in Talmudic times, themselves did some work in honor of the Sabbath. Rab Hisda, for instance, so the Talmud records, used to cut the vegetables very fine for the Sabbath. Rabbah and Rab Joseph used to chop wood for the Sabbath cooking. Rab Zera was in the habit of lighting the fire over which the Sabbath food was cooked. Rab Nahman used to put the house in order, bringing in all the utensils needed for the Sabbath and putting away the things used only during weekdays.

THE LIGHTING OF THE CANDLES. While it is still daylight, the table is set for the evening meal with the best cutlery and tableware in the house. In the middle of the table is placed the Sabbath *menorah*, or candlesticks, provided with candles. Near the candlesticks is generally placed a bottle of sparkling wine, with a silver goblet over which the *kiddush* (Sanctification Prayer) is to be chanted. Two *hallot* (white loaves of bread) covered with a napkin often especially embroidered for the purpose, are placed before the seat of the master of the house.

The two *hallot* are known as *lehem mishneh* (double bread). It recalls how the Israelites, while in the wilderness on their way to the Promised Land, gathered on Friday a double portion of the *manna* to last them for two days, because on the Sabbath they were not permitted to gather the food that descended to them from the skies. The napkin that covers the *hallot* is reminiscent of the dew which covered the *manna* every morning. (See Exodus XVI:11:36.)

The Sabbath begins on Friday evening before sundown, and ends on Saturday at nightfall, when at least three stars become visible to the naked eye, or about a half-hour after sunset.

All—men as well as women—are responsible for the lighting of the Sabbath candles in honor of the Sabbath. However, inasmuch as the woman is at home and attends to household matters, the fulfillment of this duty is usually left to her, and by her lighting the candles she exempts all other members of the household from doing so.

No less than two candles are lit for the occasion. The candles must be lit before sunset, in the room and on the table where meals are served. To avoid error, it is best to light them about a half-hour before sundown.

SABBATH EVE. Before sundown, the father and all other male members of the family go to the synagogue to welcome the Sabbath with public prayer, known as *kabballat shabath* (welcoming the Sabbath), and to pray the *maarib* (evening service). The *hazan* (cantor) chants the *kiddush* at the conclusion of the prayer, for the sake of those who have no families and cannot say it at home.

When the services are concluded, greetings are exchanged either in Yiddish, *gut shabbos,* receiving the reply *gut shabbos, gut yohr;* or, in Hebrew, *shabbat shalom* (a Sabbath of peace), receiving the reply, *shabbat shalom uverakha* (a Sabbath of peace and blessing). If there are strangers in town who cannot celebrate the Sabbath at their own homes, they are invited by some of the worshipers to go home with them and enjoy the Sabbath meal.

Especially on the holy day of Sabbath, it is necessary that harmony and peace reign in the Jewish home. Our Talmudic sages say that on the Sabbath eve every man is escorted to his home by two angels sent down from heaven. One is the angel of goodness, gracious and beautiful; the other is the angel of evil, dark and with an evil, somber face. If the house is spick and span, the Sabbath candles lighted, and the table set for the Friday evening meal, and if the mistress of the house is friendly and kind, the good angel exclaims in delight: "May the next Sabbath, in this house, be enjoyed in just such fashion," and the evil angel is forced to respond "Amen." But if the house is still in weekday disorder, the table undecked for the Sabbath meal, and the mistress of the house unfriendly and quarrelsome, the evil angel declares in triumph: "May the next Sabbath, in this house, be like this one"; to which the good angel is forced to murmur a sad "Amen."

Entering the house, the father warmly greets the members of the family with *gut shabbos,* or *shabbat shalom.* Then the entire family chants the hymn *shalom alekhem* (peace be unto you, angels of peace). After that the father recites Proverbs, Chapter XXI, verses 10-30. In these poetic verses, King Solomon praises the valiant, God-fearing woman whom the husband must love, cherish, and admire above all earthly treasures.

KIDDUSH (SANCTIFICATION). Our Rabbis of old decreed that the Sabbath should be sanctified, or inaugurated, by reciting the *kiddush,* a prayer said over a goblet of wine at the coming of the Sabbath. In honor of the occasion, God-fearing Jews obtain the best wine they can afford.

Some Jewish families are unable to procure wine for the *kiddush,* and as no other beverage may be used for this purpose, they recite the *kiddush* over two whole *hallot,* white loaves of bread especially baked for the Sabbath either at home or by a baker. In some Jewish homes two small *hallot* are baked for each male member of the family.

While the *kiddush* is recited, whether over wine or over *hallot,* the *hallot* must remain covered. The *kiddush* is recited in the room where the evening meal is served.

Every member of the family listens attentively to the recital of the *kiddush,* and responds *Amen* after each benediction. Everyone present tastes some of the wine over which the *kiddush* has been recited, without saying the benediction.

THE SABBATH MEALS. After *kiddush,* the hands are washed and the proper benediction for hand-washing is recited. Then the father breaks bread, pronouncing *hamotzi* over it. If each member of the house is not provided with his own *hallot,* the father distributes a slice of his own loaf to each member of the family, who likewise recites the *hamotzi* over it.

Now, the meal is served. Stuffed fish has long been a favorite dish for this occasion, and there are many other Sabbath favorites. Between courses, the father chants *zemirot* (special Sabbath hymns). Everybody merrily joins in the singing. The meal is concluded by the recital of Grace.

During the Sabbath-day, every Jew must eat three meals— one on the Sabbath eve, and two during the day. The third meal generally known as *seudah shelishit,* is eaten late in the afternoon.

HABDALAH CEREMONY. *Habdalah* (separation) is a term used for the ceremony and prayer by means of which a distinction is made between the Sabbath and the work-day. The Jewish law requires that a formal separation be made between holy and profane times, and prohibits the resumption of ordinary work after the Sabbath or a Festival until that division has been made. This ceremony is performed over a goblet of wine, or any other beverage except water. In the *habdalah* are included benedictions over spices and the creation of light.

At the appearance of the stars on Saturday evening, the mother bids the Sabbath farewell by chanting a beautiful prayer, beginning with, "God of Abraham, Isaac, and Jacob." In this prayer she offers thanks to the Almighty for His gift, the holy Sabbath, and prays for the health and happiness of her own family and for all Israel.

When the father returns from the synagogue, the family gathers around him for the *habdalah* ceremony. One member of the family holds the lit, twisted candle, especially made for this occasion, another holds the *besamim* (spice) box. The father raises the goblet of wine or other beverage as he chants the *habdalah* prayer, pronounces one benediction over the beverage, another benediction while inhaling the spices, and still another thanking the Almighty for creating light. The father first closes his hands, bringing them close to the light, bending his fingers to make a shadow, and opens them while reciting the last benediction. The ceremony concluded, the father greets the family with the greeting *gut woch,* happy week, and the family sings a song about the prophet Elijah and the Messiah.

MELAVEH MALKAH. Some Jews known as *hasidim,* observe an additional ceremony later in the evening which is called *melaveh malkah* (farewell to the queen). They usually gather at the rabbi's home, where they eat and drink, tell stories from Jewish lore about great hasidic leaders, sing songs, and dance hasidic dances. The rabbi addresses them on subjects from the Torah and on the teachings of the great hasidic rabbis.

Rosh Hodesh

NEW MOON

ROSH HODESH OF OLD. *Rosh Hodesh,* the beginning of the month, had always been considered a semi-holiday among the Hebrews. On this occasion special sacrifices were offered in the Temple at Jerusalem, and trumpets were blown by the Levites. As far back as the days of Saul, the first Jewish king, *Rosh Hodesh* was celebrated with a family feast.

The New Moon Day had to be accurately fixed by the Jews so that the festival days might be exactly determined. During the existence of the Second Temple, the calendar was regulated by direct observation. The Sanhedrin, the highest court at Jerusalem, consisting of seventy one members, sent witnesses to observe the first appearance of the new moon. A special court, called Bet-Yazek, was established in Jerusalem to hear and examine the witnesses. After the testimony of at least two witnesses had been accepted by the court, the ceremony of announcing the new month was observed by that judicial body in the following manner. The President of the court said: "The new month is proclaimed," and all present said after him, "Proclaimed, proclaimed."

That night, torches and bonfires would be lit on the highest peak near Jerusalem, as signals to the nearby towns and villages that the new month had been officially declared. The people on the other peaks, farther away, would in turn light torches and bonfires as signals to more distant settlements. Thus the fire signals carried the news to all the inhabitants of Palestine. Even the Jews in Babylonia were informed of the New Moon by relays of torches and bonfires. The following day was celebrated as *Rosh Hodesh,* the beginning of the month.

ROSH HODESH NOW. After the destruction of the Temple by the Romans, the offering of sacrifices ceased, and special prayers were adopted instead. On the Sabbath before *Rosh Hodesh,* the coming of the new moon is announced. The congregation is informed of the exact time when the new moon is to appear (*molad*). Then a special prayer is offered, expressing the hope that the new month will be a time of blessing and good for all Israel, a period characterized by reverence for God and dread of sin.

The Jewish month, which is in accordance with the lunar and not the solar calendar, consists either of twenty-nine or thirty days. When the previous month has twenty-nine days, only one day of *Rosh Hodesh* is observed. When the preceding month has thirty days, two days of *Rosh Hodesh* are observed, the first day of which is the thirtieth day of the previous month. Very religious Jews consider the day before *Rosh Hodesh* as *yom kippur katan*, minor day of atonement. They fast on that day and pray for forgiveness.

In the synagogue, special prayers are recited on *Rosh Hodesh*. Immediately after the *shaharit*, half of *hallel* is recited. A portion of the Bible is read, at which four persons are called up to recite the benediction over the Torah. After that the *musaf* service takes place. A special *shemone esreh*, silent prayer, is read for this occasion. At home, the mother abstains from sewing and from doing any other work which can be postponed. The meal is also more festive than on weekdays.

KIDDUSH HALEBANAH. Between the third and fourteenth day of the new month, the ceremony of *kiddush halebanah*, Sanctification of the Moon takes place. It is performed outdoors, on a clear night and in full view of the moon. Special prayers have been adopted for this occasion. This ceremony is still observed by thousands of Jews in all parts of the world.

Rosh Hashanah

THE JEWISH NEW YEAR
(TISHRI 1 AND 2)

MEANING OF ROSH HASHANAH. Unlike all other Jewish Festivals, Rosh Hashanah is neither connected with great historical events nor with the festivities of the soil. It is purely a religious holiday devoted to prayer and serious thought, a

time when Jews contemplate their ideals and their deeds of the past.

In the Bible, *Rosh Hashanah* is mentioned as *Yom Teruah*, the Day of Sounding the Trumpet. The Talmudic authorities know it by three additional names: *Yom Hazikaron*, Day of Memorial; *Rosh Hashanah*, New Year; and *Yom Haddin*, Day of Judgment. It is the beginning of the Jewish civil New Year.

THE SOLEMN SEASON. During their long history, the Jews have found need for a period of solemn contemplation, prayer, and self-examination. They have set aside a period of forty days for this purpose, beginning with the first day of the month of Elul and ending with the day of *Yom Kippur* (Day of Atonement).

On the second day of the New Moon of the month of Elul, this solemn season is proclaimed by the blowing of the *shofar* (ram's horn) in the synagogue after the morning service. This *shofar* blast is repeated every morning during that month, with the exception of the Sabbaths and the day before *Rosh Hashanah*. These *shofar* soundings serve to remind the people that the great Holy Days, at times called *Yamin Noraim* (Days of Awe), are approaching, and urge them to begin taking stock of their religious conduct and their relations with their fellowmen.

On the Sabbath evening before *Rosh Hashanah*, either after midnight or at early dawn, the first *selihot* service takes place in the synagogue. The term *selihot* denotes a special prayer book containing prayers of repentance and forgiveness, and selections recalling the hardships of the exile and of the persecution and martyrdom which the Jews have endured. When *Rosh Hashanah* occurs on a Monday or Tuesday, the *selihot* services begin on the Saturday night of the preceding week.

A comparatively new custom now prevails among Jews—exchanging *shanah tobah* greeting cards. Cards, bearing good wishes for a happy new year, are sent to relatives and friends.

Many people extend their New Year greetings to their friends in local Jewish papers or magazines.

The *selihot* read on the morning preceding *Rosh Hashanah* are much longer than those read on other days. After the morning service, religious Jews remain in the synagogue for the ceremony of *hatarat nedarim* (release of vows). If a person has made a vow during the past year and unwittingly violated it, he seeks now to be absolved from the vow. At this ceremony he makes a declaration before a court consisting of three laymen, to the effect that he failed to carry out a vow or vows, and they absolve him from his promise by reading a special formula provided for in the Talmud for this occasion. This, however, does not mean that a man can thus nullify any vow he makes to his fellow man or to his God.

A SOLEMN FESTIVAL. The Jew does not spend his New Year's Day in boisterous merrymaking and riotous festivity, but welcomes this day in a spirit of awe and reverence. He spends his *Rosh Hashanah* quietly, considering it as a day of reckoning with his God and his fellowman. He solemnly contemplates his moral and religious conduct of the past year, repenting and resolving in his heart to let the teachings of the Almighty, as contained in His Torah, guide his acts during the coming year.

A DAY OF JUDGMENT (*Yom Haddin*). The Jew believes that *Rosh Hashanah* is a day of judgment, when the Almighty sits as Judge, so to speak, and unfolds the records of every person's life, decreeing the destiny of each person for the year just begun. All the destinies of mankind, individual and national, are recorded in heaven for the New Year in the Book of Life and in the Book of Death. At once the righteous are inscribed for life, the wicked are sentenced to death, and the indifferent are given ten days' time in which to repent.

On *Rosh Hashanah,* the Jew wholeheartedly prays for mercy and forgiveness. He pours out his soul in prayer before his Father in Heaven, convinced that the Almighty Judge, in His mercy and lovingkindness, will answer his prayer and will inscribe the congregation of Israel in the Book of Life, Health, and Happiness.

A FESTIVAL OF REST. The two days of *Rosh Hashanah* are to be strictly observed as a festival. All laws pertaining to other festivals must be observed: no manual labor is permitted except that which is necessary for the preparation of food for human beings (See Erub Tabshilin, page 40, below).

TIME OF THE FEAST. Rosh Hashanah was, according to the Law of Moses, to be observed on only one day, the first day of the month of Tishri. However, for the reason given below (page 45), the sages extended it to the second day of Tishri; hence, *Rosh Hashanah* is observed for two days. The sages consider the two days of *Rosh Hashanah* as making up one long day.

ROSH HASHANAH EVE. The mother officially ushers in the holy day by lighting the festival candles, pronouncing the usual blessing and adding the benediction *sheheheyanu*. The father and the other male members of the family proceed to the synagogue for the *maarib* (evening) service, at which the *kiddush* is recited over a cup of wine. At the conclusion of the service, the worshipers exchange the traditional *Rosh Hashanah* greeting in Hebrew, *leshanah tobah tikatebu* (may you be inscribed for a happy year), in a spirit of friendship, joy, and hope.

Upon returning home from the synagogue, the father greets his family with a joyful *leshanah tobah* (for a happy year), and the table is set for a festive meal. Although this Festival is of a solemn nature, it is, like other holidays, celebrated with much joy and happiness. Rich meats and confectionery are provided, and the meals are even more elaborately served than on other festivals.

The evening meal is preceded by the *Rosh Hashanah kiddush* (sanctification), either over wine or over two *hallot* (white loaves of bread), baked in the shape of a ladder or twist, symbolizing the hope that our prayers will go up to heaven. The ladder also reminds us that on *Rosh Hashanah* men are judged: some are destined to climb and prosper, others to descend and fail in their attempt.

At the evening meal, it is customary to symbolize the sweetness of the new year by dipping a slice of the *hallah* in honey after saying the *hamotzi* benediction. After eating this honey-dipped *hallah*, it is customary to say: "May it be Thy will, O Lord our God, to renew unto us a happy and pleasant year." A special effort is made by pious Jews to secure fish for the evening meal, because fish symbolize fruitfulness and plenty. The head of the family is served the head of the fish to symbolize our wish and hope that every one be "a head rather than a tail," that is, a leader among his fellows.

THE MORNING SERVICE. The morning services at the synagogue bear a character of extreme piety and holiness. The great poems included in the prayers make one understand the meaning of the Holy Day, and its effect upon our lives. The *shofar* ceremony makes a great impression upon worshipers of all ages. The special intonation of the reading of the Torah, the Rabbi's sermon, and the special traditional melodies adopted in ancient times for the chanting of prayers, all lend beauty and meaning to the service.

THE SHOFAR. The *shofar* ceremony which takes place immediately after the reading of the Torah is the most impressive part of the morning service. A sacred hush descends on the worshipers. Men, women, and children who crowd the synagogue stand waiting for the man clad in a white *kittel* (robe) to pronounce the benedictions over the blowing of the *shofar*. The plaintive notes of the ram's horn call to mind important historical events, sublime ideals, and hope and trust in God. The ram's horn commemorates the readiness with which Abraham prepared to sacrifice his only son Isaac before he was told to sacrifice a ram instead.

The blowing of the *shofar* calls upon Israel to rally to its God and exhorts it to a spirit of self-analysis. The great Maimonides says that the notes of the *shofar* loudly call to the Jews: "Awake, ye that are sleepy, and ponder your deeds; remember your Creator, and go back to Him in penitence. Be not of those who miss reality in their hunt after shadows, and waste their years in seeking after vain things which can neither profit nor deliver. Look well to your souls and consider your deeds; let each one of you forsake his evil ways and thoughts, and return to God, so that He may have mercy on you."

The *shofar* recalls how the children of Israel received the Ten Commandments at Mount Sinai to the accompaniment of *shofar* blasts. The Jew is further reminded by the plaintive notes of the *shofar* of the tragic destruction of the Temple in Jerusalem, and of the centuries of suffering that followed. But it also recalls to the Jewish heart the promise of redemption, the time when the prophet Elijah will appear to announce the arrival of the Messiah, and from the top of the mountains will sound the mighty *shofar* of freedom and equality for mankind.

The *shofar* ceremony commences with the reading of Psalm 37, which is repeated seven times in succession. This beautiful Psalm tells us that God's sovereignty over *all* the people will some day be proclaimed with the blowing of the *shofar*. The one who blows the *shofar*, clad in the kittel, pronounces the proper benedictions, and then sounds the horn. Another person, who is familiar with the rules regarding the blowing of the *shofar*, stands near and calls out chantingly *tekiah*, and a long note is sounded on the *shofar*; he keeps on calling the notes to be sounded until the required number of sounds is attained. The notes sounded are: *tekiah*, one long note; *shevarim*, three shorter notes; and *teruah*, which consists of nine quick, sharp notes. These are repeated during the *musaph* (additional) service several times in different sequences.

The *shofar* may not be sounded on the Sabbath.

THE MUSAF SERVICE. The *musaf* service consists of the *amidah* (silent prayer), which contains a prayer that God's glory and sovereignty may become manifest to all mankind, and that wickedness may disappear from the earth and all mankind seek after the true God whose glory fills the universe. We pray that all nations may form a single band to perform the will of the Almighty.

A big section of the *musaph* service is devoted to three groups of prayers representing three fundamental ideas in Jewish religion. These are: *malkiyot* (kingship), which speak of God as King of the universe, and of the day when all mankind will accept His kingship over them; *zikhronot* (remembrances), in which God is described as remembering the world and its creatures, and as the Creator who passes judgment upon man; *shofarot* (ram's horns), which contain prayers concerning the Torah and Zion, because the *shofar* is associated with both. The Torah was given on Mount Sinai to the sound of the *shofar*, and Elijah will sound the *shofar* to announce the arrival of the Messiah. After each group of prayers the *shofar* is sounded.

UNETANEH TOKEF. The High Holiday prayerbook, known as *mahzor*, contains selections from the Bible and the Talmud, and some *piyutim*, poems and hymns of praise, composed by poets and sages over many centuries. Some of these *piyutim* were composed by such celebrated poets as Eliezer Kalir, Judah Halevi, and Solomon ibn Gabirol.

One of the best known prayers in the *mahzor* is *unetaneh tokef*, composed by Rabbi Amnon of Mayence, Germany, in the Middle Ages. Rabbi Amnon composed this prayer under the most extraordinary circumstances.

It has been reported that the Bishop of Mayence made many efforts to convert Rabbi Amnon to Christianity, and finally succeeded in extracting a promise from the Rabbi that he would give him an answer within three days. But the moment Rabbi Amnon made the promise, he realized what a grave sin he had committed in indicating even a remote possibility that he might abandon the faith of his fathers. He spent the three days in fasting and praying. When he was brought before the Bishop, he said, "Pray cut out my tongue which spoke blasphemy and falsehood." The Bishop, instead, had the Rabbi's fingers and toes amputated.

This happened a few days before *Rosh Hashanah*. When the Holy Day arrived, Rabbi Amnon requested that he be carried to the synagogue, with his severed fingers and toes beside him. When the *hazan* (cantor) and the congregation had finished the *kedushah* of the *musaf*, he requested permission to offer a special prayer which began with the Hebrew words *unetaneh tokef*. At the conclusion of this prayer the Rabbi passed away. This prayer was subsequently incorporated in the *mahzor*, and is read on *Rosh Hashanah* and *Yom Kippur* by the Jews all over the world with great awe and reverence.

Unetaneh tokef is a religious poem which tells of the greatness of God and the littleness of man. God is the great Shepherd before whom all human beings pass for judgment on *Rosh Hashanah* and *Yom Kippur*. On these days it is determined who may live and who shall die, who will prosper and who grow poor, who will have rest and peace and who is destined to wander and suffer. "Repentance, prayer, and charity can change an adverse verdict," says the author. For God does not want man to die but rather to mend his ways and live on. "What is man?" asks the Rabbi. "He comes from dust and to dust he returns. He is like a fragile potsherd, a fleeting shadow, a dream that vanishes. But God is the living, everlasting King."

TASHLIKH. After the *minhah* (afternoon) service, orthodox Jews go to the bank of a river, or to some other body of fresh water to perform the *tashlikh* ceremony. They recite certain prayers, and then shake the corner of their garments to indicate that it is in man's power to shake himself free of sin and to correct his ways. The ceremony takes place near fresh water where fish thrive, to indicate that man is compared to fish. Just as fish are apt to be caught in a net, so can man get himself into trouble if he does not watch his conduct. Fish also symbolize fruitfulness and plenty.

THE TEN DAYS OF REPENTANCE. The first day of *Rosh Hashanah* ushers in a period of penitence which ends with *Yom Kippur,* the Day of Atonement. These ten days are known as *aseret yeme teshubah* (The Ten Days of Repentance), and are observed with awe and solemnity both in the synagogue and at home.

According to the Jewish belief, the wicked and the indifferent are given ten days' time within which to repent. On *Rosh Hashanah* the destiny of all mankind is recorded and written down, while on *Yom Kippur* the seal is attached to the decree. If the wicked repent before *Yom Kippur,* the decree is changed, and they are granted a good and happy New Year.

SHABBAT SHUVAH. The Sabbath between *Rosh Hashanah* and *Yom Kippur* is called *shabbat shuvah* (the Sabbath of Repentance). The *haftorah* (prophetic portion) for this Sabbath is Chapter 14 of Hosea, which begins with the words: *"Shuvah Yisrael ad adonai elohekha"* (return, O Israel, unto the Lord thy God). The Rabbi of the synagogue delivers a sermon on this Shabbat dealing with the subject of repentance.

Fast of Gedaliah

TISHRI 3

The third day of Tishri is a fast which commemorates the assassination of Gedaliah, the son of Ahikam. After the destruction of the First Temple, the Babylonian king Nebuchadnezzar left a small number of farmers in the land of Judah, and appointed Gedaliah as their governor. These farmers, under the leadership of the prophet Jeremiah and the Governor Gedaliah, began to rebuild the ruined land. Unfortunately, Gedaliah was assassinated by traitors, and the remnant of the Jews left in Judah were either exiled or slain by the Babylonians.

For a full description of this historical event, see pp. 244-246, below.

Yom Kippur

DAY OF ATONEMENT (TISHRI 10)

MEANING OF YOM KIPPUR. This very solemn and holy day,
Yom Kippur (Day of Atonement), is observed on the tenth
day of the month of Tishri. On this day, the destiny of all
mankind, as written down on *Rosh Hashanah,* is sealed by the
Heavenly Court. The deeds of every man are considered and
weighed. If his good deeds outweigh the bad, the man is
declared deserving. If his bad deeds outweigh the good, the
man is considered undeserving. Sins, however, are forgiven

by our merciful Father after sincere repentance, prayer, and charity. Therefore, the whole day of *Yom Kippur* is spent at the synagogue, repenting, praying, and donating to charitable institutions.

Yom Kippur is a day of self-retrospection. Every Jew must solemnly contemplate his past conduct, repent, and resolve to improve and follow the ways of God in the future.

This holy day, then, teaches us the following sublime principles of the Jewish religion:

1. No priest and no mediator is necessary to obtain forgiveness of sin; man himself can obtain such forgiveness from his Creator by solemnly repenting of his actions, and beginning a new life of virtue and goodness.

2. Sin is not an evil power ruling over man and plotting his downfall; sin is merely a weakness of man, always subject to his control, if he but make an earnest endeavor to overcome it.

3. As a child of God, man is always certain that the Father will receive him in favor and forgive his sins, as soon as he returns solemnly to him.

WHAT SINS ARE FORGIVEN. According to our Rabbis, *Yom Kippur* teaches another sublime principle of the Jewish religion: We must be reconciled with our neighbors before we ask forgiveness from our Father in heaven.

Repentance, prayer, and charity on the Day of Atonement obtain mercy and forgiveness from the Almighty for sins committed against Him, but they do not atone for the transgressions committed against a fellow man. Such sins will be forgiven by the Almighty only when we conciliate the person we have wronged. If, therefore, we have a money dispute with our fellow man, we must notify him, on the day before *Yom Kippur*, that immediately after *Yom Kippur* we will submit the case to the proper tribunal for decision, and that we will honestly and sincerely abide by the decision of that tribunal. Even if we have sinned against our fellow man by slander or by talebearing, it is our duty to go to him and ask his forgiveness. Otherwise the Almighty will not forgive our sins committed against Him, no matter how fervently we pray, or how solemnly we repent of our actions.

If any one seeks our forgiveness for having wronged us, we must not cruelly refuse him, but must grant him forgiveness willingly and wholeheartedly. We must follow the ways of the Lord our God, by being slow to anger and easily appeased. Even if we have been grievously wronged, we should not seek vengeance, nor bear a grudge against the one that wronged us. It is the way of the truly pious to forgive all those who have wronged them during the year, whether or not such persons ask their forgiveness. If we harbor enmity in our hearts, our prayers will not be heard in heaven on *Yom Kippur;* but if we are magnanimous and forgiving, all our sins will be forgiven by the Almighty.

EREB YOM KIPPUR. The day before *Yom Kippur* is considered a semi-holiday. It is a *mitzvah* (religious duty) to prepare a sumptuous feast and to fare generously on this day. In fact, our sages say that it is so virtuous to feast well on *ereb* (the day before) *Yom Kippur* that it is equivalent to fasting on *Yom Kippur* itself. It is a *mitzvah* to serve fish at the midday meal. The *hallot* are baked in the shape of a ladder, as on *Rosh Hashanah,* to express the hope that the *Yom Kippur* prayers will reach heaven.

Some orthodox Jews ask some one, generally the *shamesh* (sexton) of the synagogue, to strike them thirty-nine times with an old *tephilin* strap. This is a self-inflicted punishment for sins committed for which one renders oneself liable to the punishment of lashes.

At the *Minhah* (afternoon) service at the synagogue, everyone drops coins in the charity plates on a table at the entrance. At the end of the *shemoneh esreh* (silent prayer) of the *Minhah, al het* (a list of sins committed) is read. Many people bring large candles to the synagogue, which are lit in memory of departed persons.

KAPPAROT. During the existence of the Temple at Jerusalem, the Jews sacrificed animals as a substitute for their own lives. On every *Yom Kippur,* a scapegoat (*azazel*) was sent from the Temple into the desert, to carry away the sins of the people. With the destruction of the Second Temple by the Romans, the sacrificing of animals ceased, and as a means of offering a ransom, the custom of *kapparot* was introduced. They chose for their ransom (*kapparah*) a chicken, or any other fowl, upon the head of which each man laid his sins. Men generally select roosters and women hens; they swing the fowl above their heads three times, reciting: "This fowl is my substitute and my ransom, and shall be killed that I may survive for a long and peaceful life." Some people prefer white fowl, because white symbolizes purity and innocence. The fowl is killed and cooked, and served at the fast meal on the eve of *Yom Kippur.* Persons unable to procure a live fowl substitute for it a few coins which they swing above their heads and recite: "This coin is my substitute and my ransom, and shall be given for charity that I may survive for a long and peaceful life." The *kapparot* ceremony is performed either in the morning or on the night before *Yom Kippur.*

Many famous Rabbis, among them the great Maimonides, were strongly opposed to the custom of *kapparot,* yet it still survives.

THE FAST MEAL. About an hour before sunset on the day before *Yom Kippur,* we partake of the fast-meal, which marks the end of all eating and drinking until after the appearance of the stars on the following evening. Everyone is expected to fast, except children under thirteen and sick persons. Either at this meal or at the midday meal, some people are accustomed to serve soup containing *kreplach*—small pieces of noodle-dough folded in triangular form and stuffed with ground meat. As on *Rosh Hashanah,* it is customary to dip a piece of the *hallah* in honey. It is customary not to serve fish on this occasion. Food which is easy to digest is eaten at this meal. Eating spicy food is avoided, as neither water nor food may be had after concluding the Grace at the end of the meal. If the meal is finished long before sunset, and one intends to eat or drink after the final meal, one must either expressly say so or bear it in mind before saying the Grace after the meal.

BLESSING THE CHILDREN. It is customary with some fathers and mothers to bless their children before going to the synagogue on *Yom Kippur* eve, because the holiness has already become effective and the gates of mercy are already open to our prayers. In this blessing, the parents pray that their children may be granted a happy life, and that their hearts may be firm in the fear of God. The following is an appropriate prayer for the occasion:

May the Lord render you like Ephraim and Manasseh. (For daughters: May the Lord render you like Sarah, Rebecca, Rachel, and Leah.)

Merciful Father, aid my children to see and understand that sin is folly and virtue is wisdom, and that "the beginning of wisdom is the fear of God." Create in them a pure heart, and renew a right spirit within them.

Almighty God, help my children to see sin as weakness, and yielding to temptation as lack of power of will. Bestow upon them a new strength, a heavenly spiritual strength, so that they can overcome and destroy the enemy, the evil inclination, within their hearts.

O God, grant them understanding to know and perceive that the selfish, the idle, and the shirker do not live. The soul that sins dies. He alone lives who lives worthily and abides by Thy holy commandments; for he who findeth Thee findeth life. May they always choose the path of life.

Inscribe us all in Thy book of life, health, and happiness. Amen.

As on the Sabbath eve, about a half-hour before sundown the candles are lit, and the proper benedictions are recited by the mother. After that everybody goes to the synagogue for the evening service.

A DAY OF AFFLICTION. Because the Almighty decreed that *Yom Kippur* shall be a "day of affliction" to us, our sages said that on this day, even when it occurs on the Sabbath, we must abstain from eating, drinking, bathing, anointing (massaging), and wearing shoes.

Only bathing and washing for pleasure is forbidden, but if one is ill, one may wash oneself on *Yom Kippur.* The same is true of massaging.

Only leather shoes are forbidden on *Yom Kippur,* but shoes of other material may be worn. One who is even slightly indisposed, however, or one who has a bruised foot, may wear leather shoes on *Yom Kippur.*

Persons dangerously sick, or women in confinement, should at their request be given food on *Yom Kippur,* lest fasting impair or endanger their health. Even if many physicians agree that fasting will not harm them but on the contrary will help them, nevertheless, their request for food must be complied with, because in eating and drinking the judgment of the sick is held more reliable: the sufferer is the best judge of his condition.

A child less than nine years old should not be permitted to fast even part of the day, because it may undermine his health. A child fully nine years old and in good health should be trained to fast gradually. He may at first be made to abstain from food a few hours beyond his regular eating time.

A DAY OF REST. *Yom Kippur* is a holy day to the Lord our God, and on that day everybody must abstain from doing any sort of manual labor and from transacting any business. In this respect, all laws effective on the Sabbath must be observed on *Yom Kippur.*

KOL NIDRE EVE. Men, women and children gather in the synagogue for the evening service. Seeking forgiveness of one's wronged neighbors is done before the beginning of the service of *Kol Nidre* which starts before sunset.

Before the *kol nidre* service, men put on the *tallit* (fringed garment). Pious men generally put on white robes (*kittel*), which stand for purity and innocence. The *kittel* also serves as a reminder of humility to soften arrogant hearts, because white robes are also used for burial. On the *kittel* they put the *tallit*. The women too are as a rule dressed in white. At the synagogue the scrolls of the Torah are draped in white mantles, and the Ark in which the scrolls are contained is adorned with white curtains; the tables are decked with white covers, and many lights are lit.

It is a holy evening. With solemn faces, all await the opening of the service. Now the curtains from the Ark are drawn, the congregation rises, the Scrolls are taken out, and the *hazan* (cantor) sings that inspiring traditional melody, *kol nidre*. Thrice he chants it, while the congregation listens attentively.

KOL NIDRE is in reality not a prayer, but a declaration voiding and nullifying in advance all vows and promises to Almighty God, which men are apt to utter inconsiderately and hastily in the emergencies of sorrow or passion in the year to come. Promises and responsibilities undertaken by a person under normal circumstances cannot be voided by reciting a formula. Some authorities claim that this *kol nidre* formula was primarily introduced for the benefit of those who, under coercion on the pain of death, were forced to accept Christianity or the faith of Islam. Those victims outwardly lived as Christians or Mohammedans, but secretly they continued to observe the laws of their own religion. *Kol nidre* nullifies the vows made by those unfortunate Jews whose hearts were filled with remorse and bitterness for having been forced to bow to the will of oppressors.

APPEAL FOR DONATIONS. The Rabbi now appeals to the worshipers to be mindful of the great importance of the Holy Day of *Yom Kippur*. He exhorts them to return to their God, their Torah, and their culture. In most American synagogues, appeals are made at this time for funds, either for the congregation itself or for some other worthy Jewish cause, such as Hebrew schools, hospitals, the Jewish National Fund, the United Jewish Appeal, and the like. Generous pledges are made by the worshipers to be paid after *Yom Kippur* in order to help maintain Jewish institutions.

After that the *hazan,* together with the congregation, begins the *maarib* (evening) service, which includes the *amidah,* or *shemoneh esreh* (silent prayer) of *Yom Kippur* containing a special prayer known as *al het* (confessions). This confession contains a list of sins arranged in a double alphabetical order that might have been committed during the year, sins of arrogance, slander, gluttony, dishonesty, disrespect for parents, treachery, haughtiness, stubbornness, and the like; and they pray to the Almighty for forgiveness. This prayer is repeated eight times during *Yom Kippur,* twice at the evening service, and six times during the day services. It was also recited once at the afternoon service (*minhah*) the day before *Yom Kippur.*

YOM KIPPUR DAY. Religious Jews spend the whole day of *Yom Kippur* at the synagogue, fasting, praying, and liberally responding to appeals made for various charitable and national institutions. A large prayer book, called the *mahzor,* contains four distinct services for the day of *Yom Kippur*: *shaharit* (morning or forenoon) ; *musaf* (additional) ; *minhah* (afternoon) ; and *neilah* (closing).

During the *shaharit* service, *al het* is read twice; once in the silent prayer, and again when the *hazan* repeats the silent prayer before the congregation. Immediately after the *shaharit,* six persons are called up to recite the benediction over the portion of the Torah read on *Yom Kippur.* Thereafter one is called up for the *maftir,* the reading from the prophets, which is from Isaiah LVIII, on this occasion.

MEMORIAL SERVICES. On *Yom Kippur,* memorial prayers (*yizkor*) are said for the departed, because remembrance of the dead breaks a man's stubborn pride and humbles his heart. Another reason for having memorial prayers on *Yom Kippur* is that the dead too need atonement, and therefore offerings of charity are made for their souls. By giving charity and praying, the living are able to lighten the judgment of the dead in the world to come, and in return the pious souls of the departed plead for the living ones who remember them.

In many congregations it is customary to offer a memorial prayer for Jewish martyrs who have lost their lives because of persecution, or in defense of Jewish communities, and for the heroic defenders and fighters in Israel.

MUSAF. The *shemoneh esreh* is then read silently by the congregation and again the *al het* is recited. The *hazan* repeats the silent prayer to the traditional *Yom Kippur* melody. During this service, the *Unetaneh Tokef* is recited, and many other *piyutim* (poems and hymns of praise). Some begin each verse with a letter of the alphabet, in their fixed order; some are acrostics, spelling out the name of the author. One prayer tells of the story of the Ten Martyrs executed by the Romans during the Bar Kokhba revolt. (See Lag Baomer, pp. 188-204.)

An impressive part of the *musaf* is the one describing the *abodah* (sacred service) in the Temple in ancient Jerusalem. It tells of the ceremonies in the Temple on the Day of Atonement when the High Priest entered the Holy of Holies, where no one but he could penetrate—once a year on *Yom Kippur*. The *hazan* chants this prayer with the intonation of the traditional melody, and when he reaches the part of the prayer describing the kneeling down of the High Priest, he too kneels with his face to the ground. He is then helped to his feet by two men. This ceremony is repeated three times.

MINHAH. At the *minhah* (afternoon) service, a scroll of the Torah is taken out of the Ark, and three persons are called up to recite the benedictions. For the *haftorah* the Book of Jonah is read, where it is recorded that the prophet Jonah boarded a ship for a distant land to escape the ordeal of bringing a message from God to the people of Nineveh. But he soon discovered that no one can escape from the Almighty because He is everywhere. The Book of Jonah teaches that the God of Israel is a universal God, whose loving kindness extends to all peoples and all lands.

NEILAH. After the *minhah* service, the congregation reads the final service of the day, *neilah* (closing service). It is so called, because during the whole day of *Yom Kippur,* the gates of heaven are open to receive and accept prayers and supplications. While the sun is reddening the tops of the trees, the gates of mercy slowly close. At the time of the closing of the Heavenly gates, we beg for special mercy and favor, and with more fervor than ever supplicate the Almighty.

The *hazan* (cantor) chants the *kaddish* with its beautiful traditional melody before the *neilah* service, and after that the congregation reads the silent prayer. Then the Ark is opened and stays thus until the end of the *neilah* service. Religious Jews remain standing during the entire service.

At the very end of the service, during the recitation of the *kaddish* by the cantor, one long note is sounded by the *shofar,* and the congregation calls out in unison, *Leshanah habaah birushalayim,* next year in Jerusalem, and with this the Holy Day is brought to a close.

MAARIB. Now the *maarib* (evening) service is chanted. At the end of the service the *habdalah* ceremony is performed over a goblet of wine. Outside the synagogue, the *kiddush halebanah* ceremony is performed (see page 15) if the moon is visible.

Before leaving the synagogue, greetings are exchanged with the traditional words *gemar hatimah tobah* (a favorable final sealing, or verdict).

At home a light meal is eaten, and everyone is cheerful and happy, confident that the New Year will bring happiness, health, and salvation for Israel. Many Jews make a start, that very evening, in building the *sukkah* for the joyous Festival which is to follow four days after Yom Kippur.

Sukkot

FEAST OF BOOTHS (TISHRI 15-23)

ERUB TABSHILIN. On a Festival no food may be prepared from one day to the other. If, however, the two days of a Festival occur either on Friday and Saturday or Thursday and Friday, and food must be prepared on one of the Festival days for the Sabbath, then it is necessary to perform the ceremony of *erub tabshilin*, meaning *combination of dishes*, which sanctions the preparation of food for the Sabbath during the Festival. The ceremony is performed as follows:

On the afternoon preceding the Festival, before sundown, the master of the house takes a piece of bread together with some cooked or roasted food which is generally eaten with bread, such as eggs, meat, or fish, and pronounces the necessary benediction concerning the observance of the *erub,* and then recites the formula given in all prayer books.

HAG SAMEAH (a happy holiday). Because the word *rejoicing* is mentioned by the Lord our God in connection with the Festivals, the meals on such days are more sumptuously prepared than on the Sabbath. The Festival garments are also costlier than those of the Sabbath.

To do honor to the Festival, a Jew must not be miserly, but he must spend as lavishly as his means permit, to provide meat, wine and other gala dishes. It is also the duty of every Jew, particularly on a holiday, to bring joy and happiness to his wife, his children, and all his dependents, in the manner appropriate to each. The women and children, for instance, are to receive new apparel and dainty food bought especially for the Festival. From this injunction there developed various customs: for instance, the one observed before Passover when parents provide their children with a supply of nuts for the Festival, and when the children indulge in playing various games with nuts as stakes.

But our own happiness and gaiety does not constitute real Jewish happiness. Jews must share their happiness with those who are less fortunate than themselves. When they are about to enjoy good food and drink on the Festival, they do not neglect the orphan, the widow, and others who are in need. They provide them with food, drink, and clothing, so that they too may enjoy their Festival and be happy. To enjoy good food and drink on a Festival together with one's family, and to refuse to help provide for the poor and those whose souls are embittered, is mere gluttony. To such gluttons our holy sages apply the Biblical verse: "Their sacrifices shall be unto them as the bread of mourners; all that eat thereof shall be polluted; for their food is only for their appetite." (Hosea IX:4.)

SPIRITUAL DEVOTION. Although eating dainty food and drinking good wine on a Festival is considered a *mitzvah,* a meritorious act, nevertheless we do not spend the whole day in eating and drinking. We go to the synagogue in the evening, morning, and afternoon to pray and to listen to the Rabbi's explanations of the importance of the Festival, or to discussion of other Jewish concerns. We devote about half our time on Festivals to spiritual matters, as we do on the Sabbath.

MEANING OF SUKKOT. The feast of *Sukkot* (booths) is commemorative of the pioneer days of the Jewish people. When our ancestors in ancient times left Egypt, they wandered for forty years in the wilderness before they were allowed to come to the promised land, pitching tents or building booths wherever they stopped. The Almighty, therefore, commanded that the Jewish people, throughout all generations, should celebrate the Feast of Booths. For seven days, from the fifteenth through the twenty-first day of the month of Tishri, they are to dwell in booths (*sukkot*).

The *sukkah,* in which we dwell during this Festival, is a little tabernacle or booth built of wood or canvas, and it is covered with branches of trees and plants in such a manner that the heavens and the stars are still visible overhead. As this Festival also commemorates the fruit harvest in Israel, the interior of the *sukkah* is decorated with flowers, and ripe fruits are suspended from the ceiling of leaves and branches.

During the Festival, the *sukkah* is considered as a temporary residence, and all meals are served there. Some pious Jews even sleep there overnight.

The mother and the children help the father to decorate the *sukkah,* and at times they even help him build it. They try to make it attractive-looking and pleasant. It is a happy occasion for the children to suspend bunches of grapes and juicy fruits from the ceiling of the *sukkah.*

SUKKOT IN ISRAEL. Now that the Jews have their own homeland, Israel, hundreds of thousands of Jews from many lands are being brought into the country by the Israeli Government. They have brought in all those Jews who were being held in camps on Cyprus by the British. Tens of thousands of Jews were brought from many European countries and from the Displaced Persons Camps in Germany and Austria. Still more thousands came from China and South and North Africa. Almost the entire Jewish population of Yemen was brought to Israel by planes. From very distant lands, Jews seeking a home were flown to Israel, as if "on eagles' wings."

The Israeli Government was unable to provide homes for all the Jews that immigrated into Israel in such a short time. Tens of thousands of men, women, and children were accommodated by the Government in temporary dwellings, tents, and booths. Thus, like our ancestors of old, many of our brethren now in the State of Israel live in *sukkot,* booths. In Israel the festival of *sukkot* no longer commemorates the days of old, but is a living reality.

THE FESTIVAL CANDLES. The *sukkah* is maintained by everybody with respect and honor. Mother never washes dishes in the *sukkah,* and no menial work is performed there. She brings into the *sukkah* the festival *hallot* (white bread), shaped like a ladder, which she has baked or bought especially for the occasion, and sets them on a clean, white tablecloth. She also brings along the candlesticks and the candles; she lights the Festival lights, pronouncing two benedictions over them, and then she recites a beautiful special prayer for the occasion.

AN AGRICULTURAL FESTIVAL. *Sukkot* is also known as *hag haasiph,* the Harvest Festival. It was really a Festival of thanksgiving. The agricultural year was over at this time, particularly the fruit harvest. The grapes were made into wine, and the olives pressed into oil. All the other products of the soil had been gathered, and the Palestinian Jews, who were closely attached to the soil, celebrated the event with merriment and festivity, and rendered thanks to the Lord for the prosperous season.

The harvest festival is now celebrated in Israel, the new Jewish State, with joy, pomp, and splendor. Now that their wanderings of almost two thousand years have come to an end, and their fond hopes of rebuilding their homeland of Israel have been realized, the citizens of Israel celebrate their harvest with merriment and praises to the Almighty.

The Israelis are an agricultural people again in their own homeland. They are again dependent on the soil, crops, and water for their livelihood. They look to Heaven for the bounties of nature, and ardently pray for the safety of their homeland and their people whom they so dearly love and cherish.

THE FOUR SPECIES. To show their appreciation for the Lord's bounty, the Jews were commanded to take four things—the *etrog* (citron), the *lulab* (branch of a palm tree), myrtle branches, and willows of the brook—and "rejoice before the Lord their God for seven days," when celebrating the harvest festival.

Every morning during the first seven days of *Sukkot,* except on the Sabbath, before eating or drinking, the Jews take these four species, and recite the necessary benediction over them. The one who is fortunate enough to have an *etrog* and *lulab* of his own, brings them into the *sukkah* and every member of the family pronounces the blessing over them. Those who possess no *etrog* and *lulab,* pay the *shamesh* (sexton) from the synagogue to bring the synagogue *etrog* to their homes every morning. Men perform this ceremony in the synagogue, either with their own *etrog* and *lulab* or with the ones belonging to the synagogue.

The benediction over the four species is recited while standing holding the *lulab* in the right hand and the *etrog* in the left with the peduncle (the end that was attached to the stalk) upward and the end where the flower grew downward. As soon as the benediction is concluded, the *etrog* is reversed with the peduncle downward, and with the *etrog* held close to the *lulab* (so as to make them appear a unit), they are waved together slightly so that the *lulab* rustles.

Our sages say (Midrash Rabbah, Lev. xxx, 11): "the four species symbolize the Jewish people: Just as the *etrog* has both taste and fragrance, so do some of the Jews possess both knowledge of the Torah and good deeds; just as the fruit of the date-palm has taste but no fragrance, so do some of the Jews possess knowledge of the Torah but no good deeds; just as the myrtle has fragrance but no taste, so do some of the Jews possess good deeds but no knowledge of the Torah; just as the willow of the brook has neither taste nor fragrance, so do some Jews possess neither knowledge of the Torah nor good deeds. And what does the Holy One, blessed be He, do? To destroy them is impossible. And so He says: 'Let them all be tied together with one band of brotherhood, and let one procure forgiveness for the other.'"

In the synagogue, the *hallel* is chanted, *lulab* and *etrog* in hand. After the *musaf* service, the holy Ark is opened and the ancient processional ceremony is enacted. The *hazan* (cantor) goes first, then the Rabbi, followed by all those who have an *etrog* and a *lulab,* and they march either around the *bimah* or down the aisles. The *hazan* chants the *hoshanah* prayer to the traditional melody. This ceremony is repeated on each of the first seven days.

A PILGRIM'S FESTIVAL. *Sukkot* was the last of the three Festivals on which pilgrims from all over Palestine and — during the existence of the Second Temple—from neighboring lands as well, marched into the Holy City, Jerusalem, to celebrate the Festival of Thanksgiving. The Festival was designated by our Lord God as *the season of rejoicing.* Jerusalem was at this Festival crowded with happy pilgrims, rejoicing before the Lord by offering sacrifices and participating in the ceremonies in the Temple, while the Levites played musical instruments.

TIME OF THE FEAST. Moses, at the command of God, ordained that on Passover and *Sukkot* only the first and the last
days are to be observed as a strict festival on which no manual
work may be performed. *Shabuot* and *Rosh Hashanah,* according
to the Biblical law, were to be observed for only one day each.
However, the changing conditions of Jewish life before the
fall of Jerusalem were responsible for the introduction of an
extra day in the feast.

Until the middle of the fourth century C. E., no calendar
had yet been established, and the dates for the observance of
the Festivals were fixed by the Sanhedrin, the Supreme Court
at Jerusalem. Because of the persecution of the Jews by the
Roman Caesars, the decision of the Sanhedrin could not readily
be conveyed to the distant Jewish settlements. The communities
outside Palestine were therefore instructed to add an extra
day to each Festival, to make certain that the Festival would be
observed on the proper day as required by the Law of God.
Passover was then extended to eight days instead of seven, and
Sukkot to nine days instead of eight, the first two and the last
two days of which were observed as a strict Festival. *Shabuot*
and *Rosh Hashanah* were given one additional day each.

In 360 C. E., Hillel II framed a permanent calendar, the
principles of which hold good to this day, and fixed precisely
the dates of the various holidays. The dates no longer being
in doubt, the Rabbis of Babylonia wished to drop the extra
day of the Festivals, but they were advised by the Palestinian
authorities not to break an established custom. Even today,
therefore, orthodox Jewry observes this long-established custom.

The Jews of Palestine, however, were not compelled to add
an extra day to the Festivals, because the Sanhedrin at Jerusalem had always been in a position to fix the exact dates. In
Israel, therefore, the Jews observe the Festivals in accordance
with the rules as laid down in the Law of Moses.

DAYS OF REST. According to the Law of Moses, a Festival
must be observed as a day of rest and happiness. The first two

days of *Sukkot* are to be observed as strict holidays, during which no manual labor may be performed. The only work permissible is that which is needed to supply food for human beings. And one may prepare only the food needed for the same day, but one may not prepare food on one day of the Festival for use on another.

We are permitted to kindle the fire which may be needed either for cooking, baking, or lighting the house on the Festival.

On the eve of *Sukkot,* as on all Festivals, the father and all other male members of the house go to the synagogue to join in the *maarib* service. At the conclusion of the service, the *hazan* (cantor) chants the *kiddush* (sanctification prayer). After that greetings are exchanged either in Yiddish—*gut yom tov* (happy holiday), and the response is, *gut yom tov, gut yohr* (happy holiday, happy year)—or in Hebrew—*hag sameah* (happy holiday). Arriving home, the father greets the members of the house with a cheerful *gut yom tov,* or *hag sameah,* and everybody goes into the *sukkah.* There the Festival candles burn brightly, the table is decorated with silverware and china, and a bottle of sparkling wine stands in the center. The meal begins with the *kiddush.* The *hamotzi* (piece of *hallah*) is dipped in honey, and then the family enjoys the festive meal, singing new Palestinian songs of the soil and harvest between the courses.

SIMHAT BET HASHOEBAH. When the Temple was in existence in Jerusalem, at the morning service on each of the seven days of *Sukkot* a libation of water was made together with the pouring of wine. The water for this occasion was drawn from the Pool of Siloam in a golden pitcher. It was carried in solemn procession to the water-gate of the Temple, and the train halted while the *shofar* (ram's horn) was blown. The ceremony of the water libation developed into an extremely impressive and joyous ceremony known as *simhat bet hashoebah,* feast of water-drawing.

It is told in the Talmud that on the night of the first day of

Sukkot, the outer court of the Temple was brilliantly illuminated with four golden lamps, each containing one hundred and twenty *lugs* of oil, in which were burning the old girdles and garments of the priests. These lamps were placed on high pedestals, which were reached by ladders. Special galleries were erected in the court for the accommodation of women, while the men below held torches in their hands, sang hymns, and danced. On the fifteen steps of the Gate of Nicanor stood the Levites, chanting the fifteen "songs of degrees" in the Psalms, to the accompaniment of their musical instruments, of which the most important was the flute. The illumination, which was like a sea of fire, lit up every nook and corner of Jerusalem. The festival was celebrated throughout the night with songs, music, shouting, clapping of hands, jumping, and dancing.

Nowadays a special celebration commemorating the *simhat bet hashoebah* of old is held in many synagogues on the night of the second day of *Sukkot*. After chanting the Psalms of Ascent, the evening is spent in singing, partaking of refreshments, and general merriment. Some Jewish organizations arrange special parties on this evening, which they call *simhat-bet-hashoebah* gatherings.

HOL HAMOED. The first two days of strict holiday are followed by four days of *hol hamoed,* semi-holidays. At the morning service in the synagogue, the *hallel* prayers are recited, and the procession with the *lulab* and the *etrog* is repeated daily. At home these days of *hol hamoed* are observed with recitation of the benediction over the *lulab* and the *etrog* and by eating in the *sukkah.*

It is customary to read Ecclesiastes in the synagogue, when one of the days of *hol hamoed* occurs on the Sabbath, before the reading of the portion in the Torah. Ecclesiastes, or as it is known in Hebrew, *Kohelet* is one of the Biblical books of wisdom.

HOSHANAH RABBAH. The seventh day of *Sukkot* is likewise

observed as a semi-holiday, but with much more solemnity than the other days of *hol hamoed*. This day is known by the special name of *Hoshanah Rabbah*, literally meaning *great salvation*. During the seven days of *Sukkot*, after the *musaph* (additional) prayer, while marching with the *lulab* and the *etrog*, special prayers are read daily, called *hoshanot*, because they begin with the word *hoshanah* (pray, save). On *Hoshanah Rabbah*, the *hoshanot* are much longer.

According to tradition, the season of judgment, which began with *Rosh Hashanah*, ends on *Hoshanah Rabbah*. Pious Jews therefore stay up most of the night chanting Psalms, and reading Deuteronomy and other sacred books. Some even wear the *kittel* (white robe) in the synagogue as on the Day of Atonement. The procession with the *lulab* and the *etrog* is repeated seven times, while the *hoshanot* are chanted. In addition, little willow branches, called *hoshanot*, are held and beaten during the morning service at the synagogue. This commemorates that during the existence of the Temple, a solemn procession of people carried large branches around the altar on this day.

SHEMINI ATZERET. The eighth day of *Sukkot* is a new Festival, and is known as *Shemini Atzeret* (the Eighth Day of Solemn Assembly). The *lulab* and the *etrog* are no longer used, and there is no processional in the synagogue. Eating in the *sukkah* is not obligatory, although observed by many people.

During the morning service at the synagogue, memorial services (*yizkor*) for the departed are read. An important feature of the service is the prayer for rain, called simply *geshem* (rain). Jews in every part of the world have prayed that God send rain in the ancient homeland at this season. Now that the Jewish homeland, Israel, is a reality, the prayer has practical significance. In Israel there is no rain at all during the summer, and it is called the dry season. It rains only during the winter, and the water thus obtained is saved and stored for use during the dry season. Though far away from their homeland, Jews everywhere pray for rain in the land of their ancestors. No work may be done on *Shemini Atzeret*. The meal at home is of a festive character.

SIMHAT TORAH. The ninth day of *Sukkot* is the jolliest. It is a new Festival, known as *Simhat Torah* (Rejoicing of the Law). It is a Torah Festival. On Shabuot the Jews commemorate the great event on Mount Sinai, when the Almighty gave the Ten Commandments to their ancestors. *Simhat Torah* is the day on which reading of the Torah is concluded and re-commenced.

Every Saturday a portion of the Torah (the *sidrah*) is read at the synagogue during the morning services. A part of this portion is also read at the Sabbath *minhah* (afternoon) service and during the morning service on Mondays and Thursdays. In this manner the Five Books of Moses are read during the year. On *Simhat Torah* we conclude the reading of the Torah with the last *sidrah* in *Debarim* (Deuteronomy), and the reading is resumed again by reading the first chapter in *Bereshit* (Genesis). Jews have been so happy in the Torah, that they consider this event as the most important in their private and national lives, and therefore celebrate this Festival with great merriment and joy.

Men, women, and children flock to the synagogue, the children carrying little flags made especially for this occasion, and bearing the inscription in Hebrew: "Be joyful and rejoice in the Rejoicing of the Torah." Nuts, candies, and cakes are distributed to the children by the members of the synagogue, and everybody is in a happy, jolly mood. Individual verses from a prayer known as *atta hareta* are chanted by various readers and repeated by the congregation.

THE HAKAFOT. Next comes the procession (*hakafot*) with the Torah scrolls and the small *megilot,* prophet scrolls, called *nebiim.* All the scrolls are taken out of the Ark. The Torah scrolls are given to male adults, and the prophet scrolls are given to boys. The *hazan* (cantor) marches in front, followed by the Rabbi and other men carrying the scrolls and boys carrying the *nebiim*. In the rear march the children with their flags. The *hazan* chants as he marches certain verses imploring the Almighty to help the Jewish people, and these are repeated by the congregation. They march through the aisles and everybody kisses the Torah scrolls as they are carried by. Arriving at the starting point in front of the Ark, the marchers break out with singing and dancing. Then another group takes the scrolls, and then still another, until the ceremony is repeated seven times. Each round is concluded by singing and dancing. The *hakafot* ceremony is repeated at the morning services.

During the morning services, everyone is called up to recite the benediction for the reading of a portion of the last *sidrah* in the fifth book, *Debarim* (Deuteronomy). The person called up for the reading of the last part of this *sidrah,* is called *hatan torah* (the bridegroom of the Torah), because he has the great honor of concluding the reading of the Five Books of Moses. Then another person is called up for the reading of the first chapter in Genesis, and he is called *hatan bereshit* (the bridegroom of Genesis), because he has the honor of being the one to commence the reading of the Torah all over again.

Before, the *hatan torah* and the *hatan bereshit* are called up, one person has the honor of reading a part of the Torah *im kal hanearim* (with all the children). All boys under the age of thirteen come up to the Torah, the very small ones with their fathers, and the person called up reads the benediction very slowly so that the small children can repeat it after him. The reader, the children, and the fathers stand under a large *tallit* spread out like a canopy, while this ceremony takes place. Thus even the small boys have the honor on *Simhat Torah* of reciting a benediction over the Torah.

Refreshments—wine, cake and other dainties—are distributed to everybody at the synagogue during the morning services. The rest of the day is spent in merriment and happiness, and thus the Festival of *Sukkot* comes to an end.

Hanukkah

FESTIVAL OF LIGHTS
(KISLEV 25—TEBET 2)

1. CELEBRATION OF HANUKKAH

WHAT IS HANUKKAH? In Hebrew, *hanukkah* means dedication. It is the name of a festival that recalls the triumph of the Jews over the Syrians and Greeks. These heathen nations had forcibly taken possession of God's Temple in Jerusalem and dedicated it to their god Zeus. The Jewish people, whose numbers were small in comparison with the mighty Grecian armies, fought many stubborn and brave battles against their enemies, and drove them out of Jerusalem, once more dedicating the Holy Temple to the God of Israel. They then celebrated the festival of dedication for eight days by illuminating the Temple and their homes.

All this happened over two thousand years ago (165 B. C. E.), but the Jews in every land, year after year, still celebrate the festival of *Hanukkah* with great merriment and joy. For eight days, beginning with the twenty-fifth day of the month of Kislev, the Jews in every home light the *Hanukkah* lamp with its eight small candles. The children and the grown-ups as well indulge in all sorts of games, and offer special prayers of thanksgiving to the Almighty.

These tiny candles, despite their feeble light, reveal a wonderful story of God's salvation of the Jews from ruin and destruction. They bring to mind the story of the heroes, under the leadership of the unforgettable Maccabean family, who fought and died for freedom of worship and religion. They teach that those who have faith in God never fail, and that right prevails over might.

THE MEANING OF HANUKKAH TODAY. Recently, *Hanukkah* has become even more important as a Festival. The Festival of Lights brings, not only to Jews but to all people, a message of idealism, courage, and hope. In spite of the fearful persecution and hatred which the Jew has suffered through the ages, he still lives on, adhering to the teachings and ideals of his fathers. The miracle of the Jewish people is told by the tiny candles that are lit on Hanukkah. Their weak glow tells the story of the eternal people.

The Jews settling in the State of Israel are urged on by Maccabean courage and hope. In spite of obstacles, they keep on with the task of rebuilding their homeland. Ceaselessly and tirelessly they keep on improving and cultivating the land of

Israel, not for themselves alone, but for future generations. These settlers are indeed imbued with the spirit of God, and inspired by superhuman courage.

THE HANUKKAH SPIRIT. In his feasting and celebrating the Jew is never selfish. He does not keep the joy for himself alone but shares it with others less fortunate than himself. During the eight days of *Hanukkah,* when he is happy, he liberally donates charity to the poor and needy of his community.

As the main object of the Grecian oppressors was to undermine and destroy the Jewish religion and the Law of God, there has developed among the Jews the beautiful custom of giving liberal gifts for the special purpose of supporting and maintaining poor students engaged in the study of the holy Law. And for the same reason it has become the custom for pupils to make gifts to their Hebrew teachers during the *Hanukkah* festival. These gifts are called in Yiddish *Hanukkah gelt* (*Hanukkah* money).

But these are not the only ones to receive *Hanukkah gelt.* On the first night of *Hanukkah,* the children drop a gentle hint to their parents, that there is something due them. The father, smiling, opens his purse and hands each one several coins, *Hanukkah gelt.* The children receive *Hanukkah* gifts from their mothers, brothers and friends.

HANUKKAH CEREMONIES. Unlike all other Jewish festivals, *Hanukkah* is marked by no special feasting. No elaborate meal is prescribed by law or custom for the occasion. The only special dish introduced by custom of long standing is *Hanukkah latkes,* potato or other pancakes, which are eaten during the eight days of *Hanukkah.*

In some localities, it is also customary to prepare meals of dairy foods, in which cheese predominates. This is done to commemorate the story of Judith, a brave Jewish woman who risked her life to save a Jewish community.

HANUKKAH LAMP. *Hanukkah* is the festival of lights, to indicate that light—the symbol of wisdom, understanding, right, and justice—prevails over darkness, ignorance, injustice, and intolerance.

In every synagogue and in every Jewish home, the *Hanukkah* lamp is prepared for the lighting of candles on the eve of the twenty-fifth day of the month of Kislev. The lamp is of metal —usually copper—and is, as a rule, decorated with such symbols as lions, eagles, vines, and pomegranates. It has eight branches for the eight candles to be lit during *Hanukkah,* and one special branch to hold the *shamesh.* The *shamesh,* or the servile candle, is lit first by the one officiating, and is used to light the other candles over which the benedictions are pronounced. Some *Hanukkah* lamps are oil-burning and are provided with wicks instead of candles.

WHO LIGHTS THE HANUKKAH LAMP? Every man and every woman must observe the commandment of lighting the *Hanukkah* lamp, because all, men as well as women, were benefited by the miracles of *Hanukkah.* Even children, provided they are old enough to be trained for this duty, must be taught to light the *Hanukkah* lamp.

In some communities, it is customary for every member of the household to light the *Hanukkah* lamp, and pronounce the benedictions over it. In others, the head of the family alone lights the lamp, pronouncing the benedictions, while all the members of the household gather around and listen attentively, saying *Amen* at the end of each benediction. The entire family then chants in chorus *Hanukkah* hymns.

WHEN THE LAMP IS LIT. Late in the afternoon of the twenty-fourth day of Kislev, every Jew goes to the synagogue to witness the lighting of the *Hanukkah* lamp. Immediately after nightfall and the appearance of the stars, the *Hanukkah* lamp is lit. The time for the lighting of the *Hanukkah* lamp must not be deliberately delayed.

Returning from the synagogue after *maarib* (evening) service, the master of the house finds the *Hanukkah* lamp all prepared for the occasion. A holiday spirit pervades the house and all is cheerful and gay.

During the eight days of *Hanukkah* all kinds of work may be done, although it is customary to do no work after the Hanukkah lamp has been lit.

On the Sabbath eve, the father first lights the *Hanukkah* lamp, and then the mother lights the Sabbath candles.

At the close of the Sabbath, the *habdalah* ceremony is performed before the *Hanukkah* lamp is lit.

SIZE OF CANDLES. Candles for the *Hanukkah* lamp should be large enough to burn at least half an hour. During this half-hour, it is forbidden to make use of the light shed by the *Hanukkah* candles, either for reading or working. The lights are to serve solely for the celebration of *Hanukkah*.

On the Sabbath eve, when the *Hanukkah* candles are lit earlier than on weekdays, it is necessary that the *Hanukkah* candles be large enough to keep burning for no less than thirty minutes after the appearance of the stars, as otherwise the benedictions pronounced over them are of no value.

HOW THE CANDLES ARE LIT. On the first evening of *Hanukkah,* one candle is lit over which the benedictions are pronounced; on the second night, two candles; on the third, three; and thus one more is added each evening, until the eighth, when all the eight candles are lit. The order of arranging and lighting the candles is as follows: On the first evening the candle to be lit is placed at the right end of the *Hanukkah* lamp. On the second evening one is added towards the left; and on every succeeding evening one candle is added always towards the left. The newly-added candle must be lit first, immediately after benedictions are pronounced, and then the lighting of the rest of the candles is continued towards the right.

On the first evening of *Hanukkah,* whoever lights the *Hanukkah* lamp recites three benedictions before lighting it. On the other evenings, only the first two of those three are pronounced.

ORDER OF LIGHTING THE HANUKKAH LAMP. The following three benedictions are pronounced before lighting the *Hanukkah* lamp on the first evening of *Hanukkah,* of which only the first two are recited thereafter:

"Praised be Thou, O Lord our God, Ruler of the world, who hast sanctified us by Thy commandments, and hast bidden us to kindle the *Hanukkah* lights."

"Praised be Thou, O Lord our God, Ruler of the world, who didst wondrous things for our fathers at this season in those days."

The following benediction is recited on the first night only:

"Praised be Thou, O Lord our God, Ruler of the world, who hast granted us life, and hast sustained us to celebrate this joyous festival."

After kindling the *Hanukkah* lamp, the following is recited:

"We kindle these lights on account of the miracles, the deliverance and the wonders which Thou didst for our fathers, through Thy holy priests. During all the eight days of *Hanukkah* these lights are sacred, and we are not permitted to make profane use of them, but we are just to look at them, in order that we may give thanks to Thy name for Thy miracles, Thy deliverance, and wonders."

HANUKKAH GAMES. The religious Jew generally looks with disfavor upon the playing of games of chance. On *Hanukkah,* however, he allows the playing of games, provided they are not played for money. During *Hanukkah,* after the evening meal, people usually indulge in playing such games as checkers, chess, dominoes, cards, and one special game known as *kautowes.* The last game consists of arithmetic riddles and puzzles, the answer to which must always be forty-four, the total number of lights lit during the eight days of *Hanukkah.*

The younger children play with the *Hanukkah draidel,* a revolving die, on the four sides of which are marked the Hebrew letters: *nun, gimmel, he, shin.*

These four letters stand for the four Hebrew words: *nes gadol hayah sham,* there was a great miracle.

These four letters also indicate the result of each game. If after the die is spun by one of the players the letter *nun* comes out on the top, the spinner gets nothing, because the *nun* stands for the Yiddish word *nichts,* "nothing." If the letter *gimmel* comes out on the top, the player takes all, because *gimmel* stands for *gantz,* "all." If it is *he,* the player gets half, because the *he* stands for *halb,* "half." If it is the letter *shin,* the player must add to the stakes, because this letter stands for *stell,* "place" or "add."

HANUKKAH IN AMERICA. In former years, Hanukkah was primarily a home festival. But today, especially in America, it is gradually becoming a community festival.

The spirit of *Hanukkah* is felt in Jewish and Hebrew schools and clubs. Almost every Hebrew school has a *Hanukkah* play in which many young pupils participate. Many schools have special assemblies, public entertainments and classroom parties. Youth clubs generally present *Hanukkah* plays, and make collections for the Jewish National Fund.

II. THE STORY OF HANUKKAH

1. *Alexander the Great in Jerusalem*

During one period, the Jewish people were in their own land in Palestine, and the Holy Temple still existed in Jerusalem, but the Jews were not entirely an independent people. For several centuries they had enjoyed security and peace, first under the rule of Persian kings, and then under the dominion of Alexander the Great. In the year 336 B. C. E., when the latter became king of Macedonia, he gathered a mighty army, and, hoping to conquer and rule the world, he crossed over into Asia from his native Greece. His victorious army defeated Darius, king of Persia, and Alexander the Great became ruler of the Persian empire, which included Syria, Palestine, and Egypt.

Most of the countries and fortified cities surrendered without battle at the approach of Alexander's army. Those few fortified towns that offered resistance were easily conquered by Alexander. Having been told that the Jews of Jerusalem would also resist and would not surrender peacefully, Alexander led his army to Jerusalem with the intention of laying siege to that city. But upon nearing Jerusalem, he was met by a long procession of men who had come from the Holy City to greet him and to offer him peace. At the head of the procession marched the venerable high priest Simeon. He was dressed in his priestly robes, with the glittering breastplate on his chest, and with the beautiful mitre on his head. With him came the heads of the priestly families in their robes, and the leaders of the people.

The Rabbis have preserved in the Talmud a beautiful story about Alexander's visit to Palestine. It relates that, when Alexander saw the procession headed by the high priest, he dismounted from his horse, and bent low before him. Alexander, the mighty king, had never before bowed down to any living person, and the generals and commanders who accompanied him were greatly astonished at their king's behavior. Alexander, noting their surprise, said to them: "Once, upon laying siege to one of the strongly fortified cities, I saw, in a dream of the night, a man of venerable appearance riding on a white horse, who addressed me thus: 'You will conquer the whole world, and no power shall be able to withstand you.' The man whom I had seen in my dream had exactly the same appearance as the venerable man who is now heading the procession to meet me and offer me greetings of peace. It is for this reason that I have paid him this honor."

The king of Macedonia was then led into the Temple, where

he was shown how the Jews worshiped their God. The mighty king, being favorably impressed, promised to protect the Jews and to give them freedom of worship. On his departure, he took with him a number of Jews whom he had led into Egypt. There he founded a new town in his name, known to this day as Alexandria, where he settled the Jews, and where they enjoyed all the rights of citizens and prospered for many centuries.

The Rabbis further relate that before leaving Jerusalem, Alexander asked the high priest that a statue in his image might be erected in the Temple, as a memorial of his visit. The high priest explained to the king that the putting up of statues or images of any kind in the Temple was forbidden by the Law of God. "But," said the high priest, "I shall erect a living memorial to remind the Jewish people of the mighty king's kindness to them. Every male child born during the year of the king's visit to Jerusalem shall bear the king's name, Alexander." The king was pleased. And upon Alexander's return from his successful campaign in Egypt, the high priest gathered together all the new-born children, and pointing to the multitude of infants, he said to the king: "This is the living memorial I have erected in the king's honor. Every one of these infants bears the name Alexander; thus will the king's name be perpetuated among the Jews."

2. The Pious and the Hellenists

Alexander the Great reigned only for a short time. Before his death he divided his vast empire among three of his foremost generals; Palestine fell to the rule of General Seleucus. Thus it came to pass that the customs and manners of the Greeks spread all over Syria and Palestine.

The Greeks were pagans; they did not believe, as did the Jews, in one spiritual God in heaven, but in many gods of their own fancy. They represented their gods in the image of man and with the faults of man. The gods shed blood, made war, attacked their fellow gods in order to steal their wives, hated one another, and so forth. These gods were divided into three groups, one of which dwelt on the top of Mount Olympus, another of which inhabited the surface and the interior of the earth, and a third of which ruled the seas.

Many years passed, and most peoples who came under the influence of the Greeks abandoned gradually their old-established religions and customs. They stopped speaking their own languages and adopted the language of their Greek conquerors. They gave up the traditions of their forefathers and supplanted them with those of the Greeks. The large majority of the Jewish people, however, would not be misled by the Greeks, and refused to be assimilated. They remained faithful to their own religion and worshiped the only true God in heaven. The Greeks, made proud by their victories, insisted upon making their rule and their manner of living universal, and they therefore hated the Jews who refused to accept their beliefs.

There were unfortunately many Jews, especially among the rich, who wished to gain the friendship of their Syrian and Greek neighbors. They therefore thought it best to stop speaking the Hebrew language, which was their mother tongue, to cease observing their own laws and customs, and to adopt the language, customs and habits of the Greeks and the Syrians. These feeble-spirited Jews were known as the *Hellenists,* because they wished to become Hellenized, to ape the Greeks in all things. These Hellenists were bent upon destroying the very foundation of the Jewish religion.

The Hellenists decided to educate the Jewish youth after the fashion of the Greeks. They built gymnasiums for men and youths, and hired Greek teachers to train them. Young Jews thus began to compete in Olympic games, which consisted of foot-races, jumping, wrestling, discus-throwing, and boxing. They abandoned their study of the Torah and flocked to the gymnasium to take part in sports. Young priests neglected their holy services at the Temple to participate in the exercises at the stadium.

The faithful Jews looked with hatred and contempt upon the Hellenists who sought to break away from their own people and from the religion of their fathers. They looked with horror at this attempt to train the Jewish youth in the customs of the heathens. They therefore organized themselves to oppose the Hellenists, and to preserve the Jewish religion, laws, and customs. They formed the Society of the Pious, Hasidim. Thus there arose two parties in Judah, the Pious and the Hellenists. The pious despised the Hellenists; and the latter ridiculed the Pious by mocking everything they held dear and sacred.

The Society of the Pious was, at that time, headed by the high priest Onias III; the Hellenists were led by Joshua, or, as he preferred to be known by his Greek name, Jason, the brother of Onias. Onias was hated by the Hellenists because he held them in check and thwarted their schemes. His chief enemies were the three brothers, Simon, Menelaus, and Lysimachus, prominent members of the Hellenist party. These three brothers caused untold misery to their own people.

3. *The Temple Cannot be Robbed*

One of these three brothers, the worthless Simon, merely to wreak vengeance upon the high priest Onias, leader of the Society of the Pious, hit upon a shameful scheme to bring disgrace upon the Jewish people, his own brethren, who had remained faithful to their God and their country. He one day went to Apollonius, the military commander of the Greeks and the Syrians, and informed him that vast treasures of gold and silver were held in the Temple in Jerusalem for safekeeping. The traitor then added. "The great treasures do not belong to the Temple, but belong to private people; therefore they ought to be confiscated for the king."

The military commander at once sent this information to the Syrian king, Seleucus IV, who was then in urgent need of money. Rome had at that time already risen to power, and the Syrian king was forced to pay a yearly war indemnity to the

Romans. The king therefore welcomed this opportunity of securing the necessary funds, and he at once ordered his treasurer Heliodorus to hasten to Jerusalem to take the treasure from the Temple. When Heliodorus arrived in Jerusalem and demanded the treasures, the high priest Onias refused to deliver them, saying: "Most of the treasure belongs to poor orphans and widows, who have put them there for safekeeping; I dare not surrender them." Heliodorus, in obedience to the king's command, ignored the words of the high priest, and forced his way into the Temple. But something unforeseen happened that prevented Heliodorus from seizing the treasures. What really happened, no one knew. But legend has preserved the following remarkable story of this incident:

"When Heliodorus forced his way into the Temple to take possession of the treasure for the Syrian king, he beheld there an old man astride a powerful steed. Mounted on the steed with him were two angel-faced lads holding whips in their hands. The great horse kicked Heliodorus and felled him to the ground. Thereupon, the old man gave the command to the lads: 'Strike, strike the intruder without mercy.' The two lads whipped the helpless Heliodorus into unconsciousness, and the priests dragged him out of the Temple.

"A deep sleep then overcame Heliodorus, and he dreamt that the two lads, by whom he had been beaten so cruelly, said to him: 'The just high priest Onias prayed to his God that your life be spared. God has hearkened to his prayers, and preserved your life. Rise, now, and pay him your respects.'

"Heliodorus rose with a start, tried to recover his senses, and was very happy to discover that he was still alive. He presented the high priest with gifts of gold and precious stones and took a hurried leave.

"King Seleucus was furious when his treasurer Heliodorus returned from the Temple at Jerusalem empty-handed. He turned to him and asked: 'Tell me, then, whom shall I send now to take possession of the treasures for me?'

" 'O sire,' replied Heliodorus, 'if you have an enemy in
your realm whom you wish to be rid of, entrust him with the
mission of confiscating the treasures for you; for he will surely
receive his just reward.' "

4. The Traitor Menelaus

Soon after, Seleucus IV, king of Syria, was murdered by
a courtier. The murdered king's younger brother Antiochus
Epiphanes, who had just escaped from Rome after having
spent twelve years there as a hostage, succeeded to the throne
of Syria. The Jews now became subjects of Antiochus Epiphanes, the monster who was nicknamed "Epimanes," the
"Madman."

Now the Hellenists began to carry out their evil designs
against their enemy, the high priest Onias III. Onias' own
brother, Jason, leader of the Hellenists, promised to pay the
new king a large sum of money if he would take away the
priesthood from his brother and transfer it to him. King
Antiochus, being in need of money, at once appointed Jason
to the high-priesthood in place of his brother. The deposed
Onias feared his brother Jason, and he fled to Antioch, the
capital city of the Syrian king.

But Jason's victory was short-lived. Menelaus, a brother of
that same Simon who had suggested to the Syrian military
commander Apollonius that the Temple be robbed of its
treasures, aspired to the high priesthood himself, and he began
to plot against Jason. Every year Jason had to pay the Syrian
king a large sum of money in order to retain the office of high
priest, and this sum he used to send to the king through Menelaus. Once, when Menelaus brought this annual tribute to the
king, he said: "Sire, would it please you to appoint me high
priest in the place of Jason, I should pay into the royal treasuries
a much larger sum of money than was paid by him." "The high
priesthood belongs to the highest bidder," said the king; and
thus Menelaus became the high priest in place of Jason.

The king knew that Menelaus would meet with opposition upon his arrival at Jerusalem to assume the priesthood, and he said to Menelaus: "I send to Jerusalem along with you a company of my trustworthy soldiers to drown in blood any opposition to the new high priest; these soldiers will likewise collect from the Jews the sum of money you promised to pay into the royal treasury." The Syrian soldiers were placed by Menelaus in the fortress Acra, near the Temple, and were ordered to hold the people in check while Jason's removal as high priest was announced. Jason fled from Jerusalem for fear of Menelaus.

The anger among the people of Jerusalem was great. According to the Law of Moses, the office of high priest could be held only by the members of the priestly family, the descendants of Aaron of the tribe of Levi. The holding of the office was considered the highest honor among the Jews. And now it was defiled. The new high priest appointed by the king, the Hellenist Menelaus, was not a member of the priestly family, but of the tribe of Benjamin. This incident roused the people to fury; but they were compelled to remain silent for fear of the Syrian soldiers at the disposal of Menelaus.

The new high priest was unable to raise the large sum of money he had promised, and the king summoned him to Antioch for an explanation. Menelaus thereupon sent for his brother Lysimachus and said: "Look, brother, I must present myself before the king at Antioch. Take charge of the Temple in my stead while I am away." Menelaus gathered many sacred vessels of gold and other holy articles belonging to the Temple and carried them away with him to Antioch. He intended to sell them to raise the money he had promised to the king.

When Menelaus arrived at Antioch, King Antiochus was absent from the capital, and the government had been left to the care of his personal representative Andronicus. The aged Onias III, who was still living at Antioch, heard with great anguish and grief of the robbery of the Temple, and openly accused Menelaus of the shameful deed. Even among the Greeks, temple robbery was regarded as a grave crime deserving of severe punishment. Because Menelaus feared the anger of the king, he bribed Andronicus with a large sum to get Onias out of the way. Andronicus agreed to kill Onias; but Onias, learning of the plot, fled for protection to the temple of Apollo in Daphne, near Antioch. According to the law of the Greeks, no man could be killed at a shrine. Andronicus persuaded Onias to leave the temple with a promise that no harm would befall him. But no sooner had the aged Onias left the temple than he was murdered by Andronicus on the spot. Even the Greeks were greatly displeased with the murder of the aged high priest. When king Antiochus returned to Antioch, a complaint was lodged with him against Andronicus, the murderer of Onias. The king was forced to bow to the will of the people, and he imposed the sentence of death upon his friend Andronicus.

Menelaus was still in Antioch, and he needed large sums of money with which to placate the king. He sent word to his wicked brother Lysimachus, whom he had left in charge of the Temple at Jerusalem, to deliver to him at once vessels from the Temple that were still more costly than those which he had already taken. Lysimachus did not hesitate a moment, but at once entered the Temple, and looted it of all the best and costliest vessels.

The second robbery of the Temple so enraged the people that they rioted openly against Menelaus, the high priest, and his brother Lysimachus. Jews from towns outside Jerusalem flocked to the capital to wreak vengeance upon the robbers of the Temple. Lysimachus had three thousand soldiers at his disposal, but the angered people attacked them with stones and sticks, blinded them with ashes, and routed them. Many of the soldiers were killed and trampled under foot. The furious mob dragged Lysimachus out of his hiding place, and put him to death in front of the Temple treasury which he had looted.

Menelaus appeared before the king and complained: "O Sire, the Judeans have revolted against the king in Jerusalem; they have murdered my brother and slain many of the king's faithful soldiers." To this complaint the king replied: "I shall hold a court of inquiry at Tyre, and punish the guilty as they deserve." The king then commanded the Jews to defend their acts of violence before him at Tyre.

The Jews sent three wise elders as their representatives to appear before king Antiochus. These elders said to the king: "Menelaus and Lysimachus looted our holy Temple at Jerusalem, and this shameful crime led to the bloody riots, because it enraged the people against the robbers. The people of Judah had no intention of revolting against the king."

The king then seemed inclined to punish the high priest Menelaus for having looted the Temple. But the shrewd Menelaus, dreading the anger of the king, bribed a certain officer high in the king's favor. This officer counselled the king against punishing Menelaus, who had always been faithful to him, and advised him to punish instead the three elders who had come to accuse Menelaus. Swayed by this counsel, king Antiochus declared Menelaus innocent and condemned the three elders to death. The people of Tyre were displeased with the king's judgment, and in protest took part in the funeral procession held in honor of the three martyrs.

Menelaus now realized that the entire people of Judah were his enemies, and he began to plan new crimes against them. He sought to poison the ears of the king against the entire people of Judah. He one day appeared before the king and complained: "O Sire, it grieves me to state the candid truth about my own people. But my loyalty to your majesty and to Syria outweighs the love and the loyalty I bear to my own people, and the statement I desire to make in accusing my own people will prove of benefit to the throne. The people of Judah are friendly to the Egyptian court, and they persecute and hate me because I am faithful to Syria."

Encouraged by the evident impression his infamous complaint had made upon the king, the wicked Menelaus decided to go a step further. He told the king the shameful lie that "The Law of Moses, which the Jews hold in great esteem, teaches them to hate and despise all men. Such a law must be destroyed."

From the very beginning of his reign, king Antiochus looked upon the Jews with disfavor, for the simple reason that they refused to accept the idol-worship of the Greeks, and remained faithful instead to their own God and religion. On many occasions he sought to injure the national pride of the Jews, and even persecuted them. The Jews, in turn, feared and hated the Syrian ruler. Now, because of the foul slander of the traitor Menelaus, Antiochus' disfavor towards the Jews turned into distrust and bitter hatred.

5. Antiochus the Monster

King Antiochus was eager to extend his power and his empire, and he therefore decided to conquer the land of Egypt. He raised a large sum of money with which he hired troops in order to wage war against Egypt. But he delayed his attack until the Romans—who, he feared, might come to the aid of the Egyptians—became involved in a war with Perseus, king of Macedonia. Antiochus, now free from the danger of Roman interference, sent his troops across the Egyptian border.

The Jews anxiously watched the progress of the war. Should Egypt be victorious and Antiochus defeated, his rule over the land of Judah would come to an end. The Egyptians had always been friendly to the Jews. The Egyptian court had always received with open arms all those Jews who, to escape the tyranny of Antiochus, had fled from their own land and sought safety in Egypt. Suddenly the report spread in Jerusalem that the tyrant Antiochus had fallen in battle. The Jews, overjoyed at the fall of the "madman," openly declared their hatred for the rule of the Syrian king.

But king Antiochus had met with no resistance at all in Egypt, and had already left that country rich with booty. When he learnt of the action of the Jews at Jerusalem, his anger burst forth in fury. Without warning he fell upon the people of Jerusalem, and for three days massacred men, women, and children, without distinction between friend or foe. He entered the Temple and the Holy of Holies, the place where no man was permitted to enter, save only the high priest on the Day of Atonement. The king did this, he said, to show his contempt for the God of Israel. He removed everything of value from the Temple: the golden altar, the candelabra, the table, and the golden vessels, and in words of scorn Antiochus the madman then blasphemed the God of Israel. And the traitor Menelaus acted as the king's guide.

To excuse the murder of the innocent and the robbery of the Temple, Antiochus spread abroad malicious lies about Judaism. He spread the report that he had found in the Holy of Holies the stone image of a man with a long beard seated on a donkey, and holding a book in his hand. The image, he said, represented Moses who gave the Jews the abominable laws that taught them to hate all men.

Antiochus circulated also another abominable lie to blacken the Jews among the nations. In the Temple, he said, he had found a Greek lying on a bed who pleaded to be set free. The Greek had told him, so Antiochus' false story goes, that it was an annual Jewish custom to fatten a captured Greek, then kill him and eat his intestines, while the Jews took an oath of hatred and destruction of the Greeks.

The Romans were still involved in the war against Perseus, king of Macedonia, and Antiochus thought it safe to attack Egypt a second time. He invaded that country without meeting resistance, and penetrated to the neighborhood of Alexandria. The king of Egypt had, meanwhile, sent ambassadors to Rome to plead for help against Antiochus. The Romans, having at last defeated the Macedonians whose king Perseus had fled, could turn their attention to Egypt. Three Roman legates betook themselves to the camp of king Antiochus, and handed him an ultimatum from the Roman Senate to leave Egypt. "You must give me time to think the matter over," said Antiochus to the Roman legates. Thereupon, Popilius Lanenas, one of the Roman legates, drew a circle in the dust, and said: "I shall not leave this circle before the Syrian king decides whether he is for peace or for war with Rome." Antiochus feared the power of Rome, and he decided to leave Egypt at once. He returned to his capital Antioch disappointed, angry, and humiliated.

The enraged Antiochus vented his anger upon the defenseless Jews. Speaking words of friendship, he sent Apollonius, one of his princely subjects, at the head of fierce troops of soldiers, on what was supposed to be a mission of peace to Jerusalem. Suddenly, on a Sabbath day, the bloodthirsty soldiers threw themselves upon the unsuspecting inhabitants of Jerusalem, killed men and youths, and carried away women and children to be sold as slaves. Many of the houses of Jerusalem were destroyed by fire, and the walls of the city were torn down. The Temple itself was spared, but its wooden gates were burned, and its halls were destroyed with axe and hammer. Now only Syrian and Greek soldiers and other foreigners moved about the ruined places. Jerusalem and the Temple were deserted. The only activity displayed in the city was at the fortress Acra where the king's soldiers were stationed.

6. Antiochus' Evil Designs

The work of destruction, however, grew painful even to the wicked Menelaus, who had been the cause of it. It was profitless to be the high priest of a Temple that had no worshipers, or to be the head of a people that had turned their backs upon their chief. He therefore hit upon a new, even more shameful scheme: Telling the king that the Jewish religion was the source of all trouble, he advised Antiochus to destroy the Jewish religion root and branch. Antiochus was well pleased with the suggestion.

Antiochus took it as a personal insult that the Jews still trusted in the God of their fathers. Despite bloody persecutions, these proud Jews still hoped that their God would destroy him, Antiochus. The mad king therefore resolved to conquer the God of Israel, to prove to the Jews that he was mightier and more powerful than their God. He would undo what their God had done. He issued a decree which was carried by messenger to all the cities of Judah, that all the Jews must cease to follow the law of their God, and must pray and offer sacrifices only to Greek gods. For that purpose, altars and statues were erected everywhere to the Greek gods, and the officers of the king were given the power to punish with death any one disobeying the king's command. This decree struck terror and dismay into the hearts of the Jews. On whom could they now rely? Who would come to their aid? But the faithful Jews raised their eyes heavenward and fervently prayed that the Almighty would plead their cause, and save His people from the hands of the bloodthirsty Antiochus.

The Greeks began with the Temple at Jerusalem. Antiochus sent a powerful army from Antioch to Jerusalem to dedicate the Temple of the God of the Jews to Olympia and Zeus, the gods of the Greeks. To conquer the God of Israel in His own Temple—such was the plan of Antiochus! A pig was offered on the altar of the Temple; its blood was sprinkled upon the altar and in the Holy of Holies; its meat was cooked and its broth poured upon the Scrolls of the Law. The Scrolls of the Law were then burnt to show Antiochus' contempt for the God of Israel. The statue of Zeus was placed upon the altar. The Temple of Jerusalem, the holy shrine dedicated to the worship of the one God in heaven, was thus defiled by Antiochus and dedicated to the worship of heathen idols.

In their helplessness, some of the Jews yielded to the decree of the king. Outwardly they offered sacrifices to the Greek gods, and denied their own faith. But many were the faithful who resolved not to yield to the king's decree and to give their lives for their God and His Law.

In Antioch, Eleazar, an aged and venerable Jew, was summoned by the king. The king's officers said to the old man in the presence of the monster Antiochus: "It is the will of our mighty king Antiochus that you eat of the swine meat which was sacrificed to our god Zeus. If you do the king's bidding, your life will be spared, and the king will make you rich and powerful. Should you disobey our mighty king's command, you shall die a horrible death."

"Silver and gold mean naught to me, and torture and death hold no horrors for me," calmly replied Eleazar; "I will remain faithful to my God and His Law to the very day of my death."

The chief officer took pity on the aged Eleazar, and in a kindly tone said to him: "Old man, I am moved to compassion and pity; I know you will suffer torture and a horrible death; therefore, I will do this for you: I will give you meat which is not forbidden by your Law; you will eat this meat in front of Zeus, and the rest of the people, thinking you are eating of the forbidden meat, will follow your example."

"What! you would have me mislead my people and induce them to worship the despicable idols of the Greeks?" exclaimed Eleazar indignantly. "No, it shall not be. I will not deceive my people, even if I were to die a thousand horrible deaths."

The king's officers admired the heroism of the old man, and were moved to pity by his old age. But the wicked king knew no pity. He ordered that Eleazar be tortured to death for his stubbornness, so that all Jews might be terrified into submission to his royal decree.

7. Hannah and Her Seven Sons

The sages have preserved a very sad but wonderful story about a Jewish woman named Hannah, and her seven sons who lived in Syria. One day they were summoned before the king. In the presence of a large gathering of officers and spectators, the king said to Hannah's eldest son: "By my royal will and pleasure, you must bow to these images, mine and that of Zeus."

The fearless youth calmly replied: "But your majesty, the Lord our God who is in heaven commanded us in His Law: 'Thou shalt not have any other gods; thou shalt not bow to them, neither shalt thou serve them.' How then can I disobey the will of the Supreme King in order to obey your command?"

"Dare to disobey me," said the king in a firm voice, "and you shall suffer death at my hands; the Supreme King you speak of will not be able to save you from my hand."

"I am ready to die for the sake of my God," replied the brave young Jew.

The king grew angry, and turned to his officers: "Fetch hither pans filled with hot burning coals; cut off the young rebel's hands and cut out his blasphemous tongue, and roast them on the coals in the pans in the presence of his mother and brothers. Let them see with their own eyes the horrible death of this young man, and learn obedience to my command."

After the eldest son had been horribly tortured to death, the king turned to the second son and said to him: "Do the will of your king and bow to these statues, and you will spare yourself torture and death."

"Bring on your fire and sword," said the second son, "and do with me as you see fit."

"Cut off his ears, nose, the fingers of his hands and the toes of his feet," shouted the mad king; "put his body on the hot coals and let him die."

"Heartless king!" exclaimed the second son. "We are helpless, and you can do with us as you please. You can torture us, you can put us to death and destroy our bodies, but you cannot destroy our souls. Our souls shall be taken up to Heaven by the One who gave them to us, and there they shall enjoy everlasting bliss; but your spirit shall descend to the infernal regions, and your memory shall be a curse and a disgrace for ever and ever."

The second son died a more horrible death than the first. Now the king turned to the third son, and spoke to him in a kindlier voice: "You have seen the horrible fate of your two older brothers. Obey me and your life will be spared."

"O king, you may double the tortures and take my life," said the third youth bravely, "but I will not disobey my Father in Heaven."

King Antiochus, seeing the brave demeanor and strong determination of the youth, feared lest he be insulted by him in the presence of his own officers and subjects. He therefore turned to the executioners and commanded: "Take this ungrateful rebel from my sight and remove his head without delay." Thus did the third son meet his death.

Then the king said to the fourth son: "Bow but once to these two images, and you will escape death."

"I will worship God, the Lord of the heavens and of the earth," said the fourth youth. "To Him alone will I bow, and to no mortal." Thereupon the fourth son was also put to death by the order of the king.

When the fifth son was brought before the king and ordered to bow to the images, he said: "O merciless king! You think that by killing us, defenseless youths, you will acquire for yourself a great name, and that you will go down in history as a great hero. No, on the contrary, your name and memory will be cursed by all generations to come; for they will say: 'Indeed, there has never arisen a more tyrannous king than Antiochus.' "

Incensed at the audacious words, the king exclaimed: "Remove him at once from my presence, and put an end to his speech for ever!" And thus did the fifth son meet his death for his loyalty to the God of Israel.

Thereupon the sixth son was brought before the king, and the boy said: "O king, listen to my words. We have sinned against our merciful Father in heaven, and He delivered us into your hands. But you have tortured us far more than was the will of our God. Know you, therefore, O king, that in the end you will suffer for your untold cruelty, and that you will have to endure terrible tortures for your heartlessness."

The king ordered that this youth, too, be removed quickly from his presence. And thus perished the sixth son.

At last the youngest son was brought before the king. The king's haughty heart was for once moved to pity upon beholding the child. The murderer turned to the unfortunate mother, who had been looking on without complaint or murmur, and said: "Six of your sons have already given their lives; wherefore shall this one die too? He is so young and innocent. Mad mother, persuade him to obey my command, and I will make him the happiest man in my kingdom. And your life, too, O woman, will be saved."

The wretched mother embraced her youngest and last son, kissed him and said: "My child! Heed not the word of this tyrant who has killed your six brothers. Rely not upon his promise, for he himself knows not what may happen to him tomorrow. By listening to the king, you will lose everlasting life. Die for the sake of our God, as your six brothers have died, and our Father in heaven will give you eternal life in the world to come."

The king, abashed at being unable to persuade even a small child to do his bidding, said to the seventh son: "You are young and you want to enjoy the pleasures of life. Here, I will drop this ring near you, and you will simply stoop to raise it from the ground. The people will then believe that you have bowed to these images, and you will save me disgrace. By doing this you will commit no crime against your God, and your life will be saved."

"O heartless king," said the child, "you think that our God will allow your cruel acts to pass by unnoticed and unpunished. Behold, a day will come when you will be punished many

times over for your cruelty. You will die the death of a
wretch."

Disappointed with himself, the king shouted: "Take him
away from here. Let this brat suffer tortures more terrible than
any of his six brothers have received. Show no mercy."

Hannah, the most unhappy of mothers, thereupon went to
the roof of her house and prayed: "O Lord God! Abraham our
father was ready to do Thy bidding and to sacrifice one son for
the sake of Thy name, and I have sacrificed seven sons for the
sake of Thy great name. Pray, take my soul, for I loathe to fall
into the hands of these tyrants." The bereft mother, having
nothing to live for, threw herself down. Her soul flew up to
heaven with a smile, and a voice resounded from Heaven,
saying: "The mother and the children rejoice; they have now
entered everlasting bliss."

8. *More Persecutions*

Antiochus, full of anger and hatred toward the Jews and
their religion, decided that if the Jews continued to oppose his
will, he would wipe them from the face of the earth. To prove
to the Jews that their God was powerless, he determined to
challenge and defeat the God of Israel. And Antiochus issued
another decree, which was sent forth to all the towns of Judah,
commanding the people on pain of death to renounce the Law
of their God and to offer sacrifices only to the Greek gods.

Day after day, in the whole land of Judah innocent blood
was shed. The officials appointed by king Antiochus to carry
out his orders now turned their attention to the country towns
to which the inhabitants of Jerusalem had fled. They erected
altars everywhere and called upon the people in the name of
the king, on pain of death, to offer swine to Zeus, and to partake of the forbidden meat. The greater part of the population
fled into the mountains, and either hid themselves in the caves
and hollows, or sought refuge in the desolate regions of the
Dead Sea.

The resistance of the Jews infuriated king Antiochus still more. He ordered his officials to take more drastic measures, and the officials redoubled their persecutions. Scrolls of the Law that fell into their hands were burned, and any one caught in the act of reading such a scroll was put to death. All synagogues and schools were destroyed.

All these cruelties, however, instead of frightening the people into yielding to Antiochus, made them more determined in their resistance. Death had lost its horror for them. They preferred death to violating the Law of God. This steadfastness and admirable courage were inspired by the pious Jews. Some of these loyal Jews left their hiding places by secret bypaths, and, like the prophets of old, went from town to town, village to village, calling upon the people to remain loyal to the God of their fathers. Their fiery addresses had a tremendous influence upon the people.

The Syrian officials of Jerusalem soon learned of the activity of the pious men of Judah and discovered their hiding places. Philippus, the commander of the Syrian soldiers at Jerusalem, set out with his men to locate the place of refuge. One Sabbath day, he ordered his soldiers to surround the caves where a thousand men, women, and children were hiding. He commanded the pious men to step forth, and promised to spare their lives if they submitted to the decree of the king. They answered with one accord: "We shall not come forth; we shall not obey the king and profane the Sabbath."

Thereupon Philippus ordered his men to make an attack upon the caves. The pious men offered no resistance; they made no attempt even to stop up the entrances to the caves with stones. They considered such labor as forbidden on the Sabbath. With firm hearts they looked on, and called heaven and earth to witness that though innocent they were being delivered to death. The Syrian soldiers threw firebrands into the openings and crevices of the caves. Flames and smoke filled the caves. Nearly all the men, women, and children perished: some were burnt to death, and others died of suffocation.

The terrible death of these martyrs struck deep sorrow and grief into the hearts of the Jewish people. Even the most courageous despaired. What was to be the outcome of it all? No visible sign from heaven was given them to inspire them with hope. There was no prophet to console them and foretell an end to their suffering.

9.   *Mattathias Maccabee*

In the midst of their despair, there arose one who inspired the Jews with new hope and courage. In the small town of Modin, about thirteen miles north of Jerusalem, dwelt the priestly family of the Maccabees: the aged Priest Mattathias and his five heroic sons, Johanan, Simeon, Judah, Eleazar and Jonathan. They had left Jerusalem because of the defilement of the Temple by the Syrian officials. The aged priest was profoundly grieved at the plight of his people, and he resolved to deliver them, or die for the cause of his God and His Law.

When Appelles, one of the Greek officials, arrived at Modin, he erected an altar to Zeus in the middle of the market place and demanded that the inhabitants worship the Greek gods. Mattathias, as the leader and most respected citizen of Modin, was called upon to be the first to worship the idol, and thereby set an example to the others. His five sons and their followers were present when the aged priest replied with firm determination: "Though all the nations that are under the king's dominion obey him and fall away from the faith of their fathers, yet will I and my sons abide by the covenant of our fathers. God forbid that we should forsake the Law to depart from our faith either to the right or to the left."

At that very moment, an unfaithful Jew approached the altar in the sight of all to offer a sacrifice to Zeus. Mattathias could contain himself no longer; he fell upon the traitor and killed

him near the altar, in the presence of the Greek officials. His
five sons, armed with long knives, fell upon Appelles and his
troops, killed them and destroyed the altar.

Mattathias immediately raised the standard of rebellion.
"Whosoever is zealous for the Law of God, let him follow
me," became his battle-cry. The people of Modin and the neighboring towns joined him, and he withdrew with them to a safe
retreat in the Mountains of Ephraim, beyond the reach of the
king's soldiers. There he was joined by the remnant of the fiery
members of the Pious who had managed to escape from the
caves. Many other courageous youths followed the aged leader
to defend the fatherland and the Law. Mattathias urged his
followers: "Brave men, disregard your own lives. The war we
have been forced to wage is by no means light and easy. You
must prepare yourselves for a very long and severe struggle.
But let us have confidence in our Father in Heaven, because it
is for the sake of His great name that we are ready to give
our lives."

Inspired by the firm belief and confidence of the aged priest,
the pious men of peace, hitherto accustomed only to the study
of the Law, now became brave warriors. This handful of men,
hiding in hollows and caves, were prepared to give their lives
in defense of their country, although they were weaponless and
inexperienced in the art of war.

Mattathias took care to avoid an open battle with the Syrians
and the Greeks. He was aware that the enemy, in addition to
being well armed and well trained, greatly outnumbered his
handful of men. He therefore decided to wage a guerrilla warfare. Being thoroughly acquainted with every nook and corner
of the country, he and his men would swoop down on towns
and villages, destroy the altars erected to the Greek idols, and
vanish into the mountains. If he came across a small Greek or
Syrian band, Mattathias would attack and destroy it. But when
a strong force of the king's soldiers came in pursuit, the Jews

would quickly scatter in the mountains, and could nowhere be found.

In the year 167 B. C. E., when Mattathias knew that the end of his life was near—he had passed his hundredth birthday—he summoned his brave sons and followers to his bedside and charged them: "Brave warriors, I appoint my eldest son Simeon as your adviser, and my younger son Judah as your commander. Neither flinch nor waver. Be ready to give your lives for the religion of your fathers, and bravely fight the battle of the Lord in defense of your Holy Land. Throughout the ages no one that put his trust in God was disappointed." And after blessing them, he died. The words of the dying priest left a lasting impression upon his brave band of followers.

10. *Judah Maccabee*

Under the leadership of Judah Maccabee, the resistance to Antiochus became stronger. A very brave warrior himself, Judah inspired with courage all who came in contact with him. When not fighting, he was gentle and kind-hearted and simple, but in the hour of battle he possessed the ferocity of an enraged lion. And he was always guided by the wise counsel of his older brother Simeon.

At first Judah followed the tactics of his father. Secretly, or in the dark of night, he would attack small bodies of Greek troops and destroy them. But when the number of his followers increased, Judah ventured an open battle with the enemy. In the first open battle which he fought, in the year 166 B. C. E., Judah and his men were victorious. Apollonius, the commander of the Syrian army, was killed; most of his men fell dead or wounded on the battlefield, and the rest fled. The Jews took their victory as a sign that God had not forsaken His people, but had at last come to their rescue. They got as spoils the weapons they so sorely needed, and Judah took possession of Apollonius' sword, which he carried in all succeeding battles.

Guided by some treacherous Hellenists, Heron, a Syrian commander, led a large army into the mountain stronghold of Judah and his men to avenge the death of Apollonius. When the Jewish warriors first beheld the large numbers of the enemy, they lost courage. But their commander Judah reminded them that they were fighting in defense of their lives, of the lives of their wives and children, and of the Law of God. After the Jewish warriors had fasted and fervently prayed to God, Judah led them to battle. He stationed his army near the pass of Beth-Horon to await the enemy. Falling suddenly upon Heron's men, they routed them completely. The Syrians left eight hundred dead on the battlefield, the rest having fled westward towards the land of the Philistines. Their victory over a superior force inspired the Jewish warriors with even greater confidence. The neighboring nations were filled with fear and awe at the skill and heroism of the Maccabees and the courage of the Jewish people.

At first, king Antiochus paid little attention to the uprising of the Jews. But when he learned of the defeat of his troops and the bravery of Judah Maccabee, he realized that he had underestimated the power of the Jews, and he determined to wipe them out once and for all.

The half-crazy Antiochus managed to obtain enough money to hire soldiers for a year Half of these hired troops he led in person against the rebellious countries on the other side of the Euphrates. The other half he placed under the command of Lysias, a man of royal blood, whom he instructed to wage war against the Jews until every trace of the Jews and Jerusalem was destroyed. Even the unfaithful Jews, the Hellenists, who had been continually flattering the Greeks, were not to be spared. Antiochus intended to settle foreigners upon the soil of Judah.

The king's plan spread terror and despair among the Jews. Would the small band of troops at the disposal of the Maccabeean leaders be able to withstand the attack of a mighty, well-organized army, provided with elephants? In every village and city where the command of the king became known, the Jews clothed themselves in sackcloth and ashes, and there was weeping and fasting. Now that Antiochus planned to destroy the entire people, even those Jews who had formerly been indifferent, having no other choice, joined the Maccabeean forces. Thus the number of the defenders of Judah greatly increased.

11. *The Battle of Emmaus and Beth-Zur*

Lysias entrusted his lieutenant Gorgias with the conduct of the war against the Jews. Gorgias led his army of forty thousand men, including cavalry, along the plain of the Mediterranean Sea into the heart of Judah. Samaritans and Philistines, the enemies of the Jews, joined the vast army of the Syrians and Greeks. Gorgias was so sure of victory that he invited slave dealers to accompany his army and to be prepared with money and chains to take possession of the captive Jews.

In the meantime, the Jewish warriors, whose number had grown to six thousand, gathered about Judah. Before leading them into battle, their commander called a solemn assembly in the mountain city of Mizpah. A multitude of people from the neighboring towns assembled to participate in the solemn day of prayer. In the garb of mourning, the people fasted the entire day, and offered prayers to God for help and mercy. Judah, in accordance with the Scriptural law, announced to his army that whosoever had been newly married, or had built a new house, or had planted a vineyard, or who lacked courage, was at liberty to withdraw from the army. He then divided his army into four divisions, each under the command of one of his brothers, and proceeded to meet the enemy at Emmaus, a few hours' journey from Mizpah.

Gorgias planned to surprise the Jews in a night attack, but Judah outwitted him. Under cover of darkness, Judah broke camp, turned westward through familiar bypaths, and placed himself in the rear of the enemy. Gorgias led his men at night toward the Jewish camp, but found it empty. He took it for granted that Judah and his men feared to meet him in open battle and had withdrawn into the mountains. Immediately he started in pursuit. This had been the object of Judah's strategy. He followed in the rear of the enemy, reached their camp and set fire to it. Then he continued in the track of the troops. At the break of day, Gorgias realized that the enemy he was seeking in the mountains was really behind him. But all his divisions were scattered, and there was not enough time to concentrate them. He could master but one division which he ordered to throw itself into the path of the pursuing Jews.

Judah Maccabee had, meanwhile, arranged his forces in order of battle, and fired them with zeal for the approaching fight. With the battle-cry, "Salvation is the Lord's," the Jews threw themselves upon the Syrians with such fierceness that the enemy fled in all directions.

Judah warned his men: "Fall not upon the booty of the enemy, but keep yourselves in readiness to meet the other divisions of Gorgias' army." These brave warriors prepared to give them battle, but the battle was never fought. As soon as the Syrians and the Greeks saw the smoke ascending from their camp, they lost heart and fled southward to Philistia.

The victory won by the Jews at Emmaus, in the year 166 B. C. E., crippled the enemy, and inspired the Jews with new confidence. The fleeing army left behind a large supply of weapons which the Jews sorely needed. The Jews captured considerable booty—gold, silver, and the purses of the many slave merchants who had followed the enemy. With these Judah obtained the means necessary for the further pursuit of the struggle. With songs of thanksgiving and praise, ending in the refrain: "O give thanks to the Lord, for He is good, for His mercy endureth for ever," the victorious Jewish warriors returned to Modin.

Judah Maccabee realized that Lysias would make every effort to avenge the defeat of his general Gorgias. He therefore ordered his soldiers to remain in camp ready for new battles.

Meanwhile the Jewish army was constantly increasing, until it now numbered ten thousand men.

In the autumn of the following year, 165 B. C. E., Lysias himself led a large army against Judah. He pitched his camp at Beth-Zur, about fifteen miles south of Jerusalem. Judah and his ten thousand men went out to meet him. A pitched battle followed; and the violent attack of the Jews once again outweighed the skill and the greater number of the Syrian hired troops. Lysias retired defeated. The land of Judah was thus completely cleared of the enemy. Only in Acra, a fortress near the Temple in Jerusalem, some traitorous Hellenic Jews, with a small band of Syrian soldiers, still held out.

12. *Hanukkah*

After the two victories at Emmaus and Beth-Zur, quiet was restored in the land. Judah Maccabee and his followers knew that at least for some time the Jews would not be molested by the enemy. They took this favorable opportunity to enter Jerusalem. The sight of the Holy City had a crushing effect upon her faithful sons who had fought so bravely in her defense. The city was a wilderness, the Temple was deserted, its gates were burned, and its halls ruined. Altars to Greek idols stood everywhere, and on the sacred altar in the Temple stood the image of Zeus and the statue of the hated Antiochus.

The brave warriors, however, had no time to weep over the ruined Temple. They rapidly began the work of repairing and purifying it. They destroyed the images of Zeus and Antiochus, and put aside the defiled altar. A new altar was erected, new gates built, and new vessels provided for the Temple. All these preparations were completed within three weeks. Early in the morning of the twenty-fifth day of the month of Kislev (November, 165 B. C. E.), the Temple was re-dedicated to the worship of the God of Israel with sacrifices and prayer. The terror of the preceding three and a half years now gave way to feelings of joy and hope.

In connection with this, a remarkable story is told by the Jewish sages: "When the priests led by Judah Maccabee were about to kindle the *menorah* (candelabra) which were to burn in the Temple continually, they met with deep disappointment. The Jews were permitted to use in the candelabra only oil specially prepared for that purpose according to a certain formula prescribed by the Law of Moses. Jugs containing this holy oil were always sealed with the seal of the high priest to insure its genuineness. The priests searched everywhere for the oil, but none could be found. Finally they found a small jug sealed with the seal of the high priest, but it held only enough oil to keep the candelabra burning for one night. To the great delight of the victorious worshipers, however, a miracle occurred: the small amount of oil poured into the candelabra lasted eight full days, during which the Jews celebrated the dedication of the Temple."

The great victory of the Maccabees, and the dedication of the Temple marked the triumph of right over might, of Judaism over the idol-worship of the Greeks. The people from all the cities of Judah participated in the celebration. The inhabitants of Jerusalem illuminated their homes during the entire eight days of the celebration.

The Maccabees and the members of the Great Assembly decreed that the eight days following the twenty-fifth day of the month of Kislev be kept forever as a joyous festival in memory of the dedication of the Temple. Since that time, for more than two thousand years, these days are celebrated in every Jewish home as "Days of Dedication," *Hanukkah*, by the lighting of tiny candles or oil lamps.

13. *Death of Antiochus*

But the struggle against the tyrannical rule of the Syrian kings was not yet ended. Many new struggles awaited the Jews before they might secure real freedom and independence. Judah Maccabee therefore provided for the protection of the

Temple and the country. He surrounded the Temple with high walls, fortified it with strong, high towers, and stationed a garrison there to guard it against attack. He fortified Beth-Zur, the city from which Lysias had intended to penetrate the land of Judah.

In the meantime important news reached the Jews from Asia. The governor of Armenia had rebelled against Antiochus, and the king himself had led an army against him and had defeated him. Antiochus had then proceeded to conquer Parthia, but was there defeated and compelled to return empty-handed. Being hard pressed for money, he made an attempt to rob the temple of the goddess Anaitis in the city of Susa, in Elymais. This outraged the worshipers, who savagely attacked the king and forced him to withdraw. He was taken seriously ill, and in December, 164 B. C. E., he died in a state of insanity. The Rabbis have preserved the following interesting account of the death of this monster:

"Antiochus decided to crush the rebellion of Judah and utterly to destroy all the Jews. He gathered a very large army, and he himself proceeded at the head of the warriors. On the way to Judah he was stricken with leprosy. Though racked with pain, the wicked king would not give up his evil intention of destroying the whole land of Judah.

" 'O Sire,' pleaded the king's officers and councillors, 'return now to your land, and when you have been cured of your sickness, you will muster an army again to crush the rebels.'

"The king was enraged at their words, and angrily retorted: 'I have no cause to fear anything. I possess the oceans and the seas and the land, and who can prevent me from accomplishing my purpose? Proceed by forced marches to Jerusalem, and let me have the pleasure of exterminating the enemy.'

"The king had hardly finished his arrogant words, when his chariot happened to pass by one of the elephants which were to be used in the war against the Jews. The elephant suddenly became frightened and uttered a loud roar. Startled by the

trumpeting of the elephant, the king's horses upset the chariot
on the top of the king's afflicted body. The fall fractured some
of his bones, and he could no longer remain seated in his
chariot. His bodyguard had to carry him on their shoulders,
but the king's crushed, leprous body gave forth a terrible stench,
and the bodyguard, unable to endure the awful odor, deposited
the body of the king on the ground and fled.

"The king, writhing in terrible agony and pain, prayed: 'If
the God of the Jews will heal me from my illness, I will visit
His city Jerusalem, and will fill it with silver and gold. I will
open my treasure-stores and consecrate them to the Temple of
God. I will go among all the nations of the world and declare:
"There is none like the God of Israel.'

"But his prayers remained unanswered. His bones and flesh
rotted on him while he was still alive. Thus did the wicked
Antiochus die a horrible death in a strange land."

14. *War with Lysias; Death of Eleazar*

On his deathbed, Antiochus appointed his friend Philippus
guardian of his young son Antiochus Eupator who was to succeed him to the throne of Syria. On account of the death of
Antiochus, Lysias remained inactive toward the Jews for some
time.

For the time being, at least, Judah was then in no immediate
danger of an attack from the enemy without. There was, however, a dangerous enemy lurking within Jerusalem. The traitorous Jews, the Hellenists, under the leadership of Menelaus, still
occupied the fortress Acra, and caused great trouble to the loyal
Jews. Judah therefore laid siege to Acra, built ramparts, and
erected catapults to hurl heavy stones against its walls. A few
Hellenists, meanwhile, succeeded in escaping from the fortress,
and hastened to the young king Antiochus Eupator, laying
their grievances before him and pleading for help. They pointed
out to Eupator that should Acra fall into the hands of the

Maccabees, the rebels would become invincible. The Syrian court decided to take energetic measures against the Jews.

In the spring of the year 162 B. C. E., Lysias, accompanied by the youthful king Eupator, proceeded against Judah from the south with a large army and with many elephants. Judah Maccabee had only a few thousand soldiers available to defend the country against the attack. The garrison of Beth-Zur tried to hold the enemy back as long as possible. They fought very bravely until shortage of food forced them to surrender, on the condition, however, that they would be allowed to withdraw from the fortress in safety. The Syrians then moved upon Jerusalem. But now they were checked by Judah and his men. In the battle that followed, the Jewish warriors performed great feats of valor. Eleazar, one of Judah's brothers, crawled under the body of an elephant, upon which he thought king Eupator was riding, and attacked it, knowing full well that he would himself be crushed to death by the falling animal. Thus did the first of the five Maccabean brothers fall in battle. And though the Jews fought very bravely against odds, they could not withstand the superior numbers of the enemy.

Judah was forced to retreat to Jerusalem, where he intrenched himself in the fortress of the Temple and offered stout resistance. As the siege continued, however, the food supply of the Jews gave out. Many of the Jewish warriors left the Temple by subterranean passages and scattered throughout the country. Judah, his three brothers and a handful of followers alone remained. The Temple, the last refuge of Jerusalem, seemed about to fall for lack of food.

Suddenly Lysias received word that Philippus, who had been appointed by the dying Antiochus as the guardian of his son Antiochus Eupator, had gathered a large army in Media and Persia and was marching upon Antioch to displace Lysias. Lysias was compelled to raise the siege against the Temple in order to lead his army against Philippus, and he persuaded king Eupator to make peace with the Jews. A treaty of peace was concluded, by which the Jews were granted unlimited religious liberty and the fortress of the Temple was spared.

The many struggles of the Maccabees were thus rewarded with success. Religious liberty was guaranteed. Jews were no longer to offer sacrifices to Zeus. The Syrian court no longer protected the traitorous Hellenists, who were now compelled to leave the fortress Acra, and whose leader Menelaus was killed by the order of Lysias. This traitor who had disgraced his own people for ten years, now died at the hand of those whom he had sought to flatter and whose customs he had slavishly imitated.

15. *The Defeat of Nicanor*

There was peace again in the land of Judah, and the Jews were now able to resume their normal occupations. The hero, Judah Maccabee, was appointed high priest. But there were still some Hellenists who hated Judah Maccabee and his followers, and they waited for an opportunity to begin the struggle again.

Important changes took place at that time in the royal court of Syria. Prince Demetrius, who had been robbed of the throne by Antiochus Epiphanes, had been held in Rome as hostage. Now he left Rome and returned to Syria, where he succeeded in removing king Eupator and Lysias, and placed himself on the throne.

Another Jewish traitor, Alcimus, decided to profit by this succession. He and his friends went to Demetrius with rich gifts and complained to him: "O Sire, Judah Maccabee and his followers the pious Jews are the cause of the recent rebellions and disturbances. While Judah Maccabee lives, there can be no peace in the land of Judah." The new king welcomed these complaints, and decided to show the Jews that he was the master of their land. He appointed Alcimus high priest in the place of Judah, and he ordered the stern commander Bacchides to proceed to Jerusalem with an army of soldiers to crush Judah and his followers.

Both Bacchides and Alcimus arrived at Jerusalem with the assurance that they wanted nothing but peace, but Judah and his followers were not deceived by their promises. They knew that the new high priest and the Syrian commander intended to take their lives. But most of the pious Jews suspected nothing, and welcoming Bacchides and Alcimus, they willingly surrendered the Temple and the city to them. Alcimus took a solemn oath that he would restore peace and prosperity in the land. But as soon as he took possession of the city and the Temple, he ordered Bacchides to kill in one day sixty of the most prominent pious men who had gone over to his side.

This outrage saddened the hearts of the Jews throughout the country. They now realized that Alcimus was not sincere in his promises, for he had violated the oath of peace he had taken in the presence of all the people in the Temple. Men and youths who loved freedom and their country again gathered about Judah Maccabee at Modin. And in the year 161 B. C. E., the flames of civil war blazed forth anew. Judah continually attacked Alcimus and his men, spreading such terror in their ranks that they dared not remain any longer in the villages, but withdrew to Jerusalem. Alcimus hastened to Antioch to put new complaints before king Demetrius.

Thereupon the new king ordered Nicanor, the commander of the elephant troops, to proceed without quarter against the rebellious Jews. Wishing to gain time until the arrival of his troops, Nicanor thought it wise to appear friendly at first and to postpone the attack. In the meantime, however, Nicanor learned of Judah's valor and bravery, and, becoming an admirer of the great Maccabee, he desired to make peace between Judah and the king. He sent an emissary to Judah and proposed peace terms agreeable to the Maccabees. A personal interview between the two commanders took place, and Nicanor wa greatly impressed by Judah's personality.

Alcimus immediately complained to king Demetrius: "O Sire, your general Nicanor is acting against the order given him. He is talking words of peace to Judah Maccabee, and he is even favoring the Maccabees. General Nicanor intends to appoint Judah high priest against the wish of the king." Demetrius thereupon sent strict orders to Nicanor: "Break off all negotiations with the rebellious Judah Maccabee, and send him in chains to Antioch."

Fortunately Judah was warned in time that he could no longer depend upon the friendship of Nicanor, and he withdrew to the mountains. Nicanor and his troops followed. A battle took place between the two forces in which Nicanor was defeated and was forced to retire to the fortress Acra. Nicanor, embittered by this defeat, decided to renew the war with energy. He went to the Temple Mount and demanded that Judah Maccabee be delivered to him. Thereupon the priests and the members of the Great Assembly said:"Commander, we are loyal to the king and Syria. But we are unable to comply with your request, for Judah is not in our midst, nor are we aware of his whereabouts." In reply, Nicanor raised a threatening hand against the Temple and declared: "I swear by the gods of Greece and Syria, that I will reduce the Temple to ashes, if Judah Maccabee is not delivered to me."

Nicanor, at the head of a mighty army, pursued Judah and pitched his camp in the mountains. Judah, with only three thousand men, took his stand four miles from Nicanor's camp, and urged his warriors to fight bravely and courageously. A legend tells that, to encourage his men, Judah related to them a dream he had dreamt the preceding night: "The figure of Onias, the just and upright high priest, appeared before me last night, with his hands raised in prayer to the Almighty for his people Israel. There appeared another man on the scene, gray-haired and of wonderfully charming countenance and glorious majesty. Thereupon Onias turned to me and said: 'This venerable man is the prophet Jeremiah, who in his great

love for his people always prays for the safety of the Holy
City.' Whereupon the holy prophet of God, stretching forth
his right hand, gave me a golden sword, and said: 'Take this
golden sword, a gift from the Almighty, and with it you shall
smite your enemies.' "

Cheered by the words of Judah, the small Jewish army attacked Nicanor's host, and Jewish valor was again victorious
over the superior numbers of the Syrians. Nicanor lost his life
at the very beginning of the battle, and his army fled in all
directions. The inhabitants of the towns and villages, through
which the Syrians fled, joined in the pursuit and annihilated
the enemy, so that not one escaped. The day of this victory,
the thirteenth day of the month of Adar, 160 B. C. E., was
thereafter observed as a festival, under the name "Nicanor's
Day." Nicanor's head and the arm he had raised in threat
against Jerusalem were hung by the victorious troops on the
walls of Jerusalem as a trophy.

This is the story told by the tiny candles of Hanukkah.

Asarah Betebet

FAST DAY (TEBET 10)

The tenth day of the month of Tebet is observed as a fast day by the Jews. On this day they neither eat nor drink until the stars become visible in the evening. The Jews mourn on the tenth day of Tebet because on that day, in the year 586 B. C. E., Nebuchadnezzar, King of Babylon, at the head of a mighty army, approached the City of Jerusalem and laid siege to it. This sad event marked the beginning of the fall of the Kingdom of Judah and the destruction of the First Temple that had been built by King Solomon.

If the tenth day of Tebet occurs on a Saturday, when no fasting is permitted, the fast is postponed to Sunday.

For a full description of this historical event, read pages 237-241, below. See also page 228, for the significance of fasting among the Jews.

Hamishah Asar Bishebat

THE JEWISH ARBOR DAY (SHEBAT 15)

THE NEW YEAR OF TREES. *Hamishah Asar Bishebat*, the fifteenth day of the month of *Shebat*, is called in the Talmud
rosh hashanah leilanot, the New Year of Trees. In Israel the
day marks the beginning of the season of the budding of trees.
Outside Israel, it is generally celebrated by partaking of a va-

riety of sweet fruits, especially Palestinian fruits, such as grapes, raisins, almonds, dates, and figs. A special fruit for the day is the carob seed, or St. John's bread.

Among Jews residing outside of Israel, *Hamishah Asar Bishebat* is celebrated as Palestine Day. In Hebrew schools, the festival is observed with special parties, assemblies, and entertainments for parents. The plays, games, movies, recitations, and songs all deal with Palestine, its geography and its products. Similar celebrations are held by some community centers and synagogues. Children and grown-ups buy Jewish National Fund tree certificates. The money is used for planting trees in Israel.

IN ISRAEL. Trees play an important role in the rebuilding of Israel. They beautify the country; they bear fruit; they provide shade and shelter to man, beast, and bird; they afford protection from winds and storms; they prevent soil erosion; they provide lumber for building homes and making furniture; and, most important of all, they help drain the malaria-breeding swamps.

During the many centuries that Jews were away from Palestine, the country was denuded of trees and shrubs. Today, when Israel is a sovereign state, and hundreds of thousands of Jews are being settled in the land, the trees of Palestine are no longer things to be remembered. They are living things to be planted by sturdy Jewish pioneers.

In Israel, therefore, the festival of *Hamishah Asar Bishebat* has assumed a character of great importance; it has become the Jewish Arbor Day. Since traditionally this has been called a children's holiday, the youngsters in Israel are given the privilege of planting new trees, amidst a most impressive celebration. The Israeli Government has recently adopted a program of planting hundreds of thousands of trees in the *Negeb,* where hundreds of settlements are being built in the vast stretches of desert lands.

Fast of Esther

(ADAR 13)

The day before Purim—the thirteenth day of the month of Adar—is a day of fasting for the Jew. He neither eats nor drinks until after the evening reading of the Scroll of Esther, one of the books of the Bible. This day is known as *Taanit Ester* (Fast of Esther), because Queen Esther, before going to King Ahasuerus to plead for her people, begged Mordecai to have all the Jews of Shushan fast for three days. Therefore, all the Jews, in the days of Mordecai and Esther, established one of these three days, the thirteenth of Adar, as a public fast day for all generations to come. To this day, the Jew, faithful to the ordinances of his sages, fasts on this day, and prays for deliverance from the modern Hamans.

If Purim falls on a Sunday, the fast of Esther is observed on the preceding Thursday, the eleventh of Adar, because on Saturday no fasting is allowed, and to fast on Friday would interfere with the preparations for the Sabbath. If, however, some one mistakenly neglects to fast on Thursday, he must then do so on Friday, the twelfth of Adar.

For a full explanation of this fast, see the story of Purim that follows.

Purim

(ADAR 14)

I. CELEBRATION OF PURIM

ON PURIM THE JEW LAUGHS. *Purim* is the Jew's day of laughter. It is his day of dancing, merrymaking, feasting, and drinking.

On *Purim* the Jew displays the greatness of his soul, his unswerving faith in his God and his people. Haman, the hater of the Jews, and Mordecai, the Jew, who insists on worshiping God in his own way, are not mere figures in history. Hamans are to be found in every land where there are Mordecais, Jews determined to observe their traditions of life and thought.

The Jew laughs; he does not lose courage. He resists the Hamans who seek to destroy him. He knows that right and not might will eventually triumph. He is convinced that in the end the determined Mordecais will overcome the heartless Hamans as of old. Therefore, the Jew celebrates Purim with all his heart.

WHAT IS PURIM? The holiday takes its name from the word *purim,* meaning *lots.* Long ago, when the Persians gained dominion over the land of Judah, a wilful king, Ahasuerus, swayed by his wicked prime minister, Haman, agreed to destroy all the Jews in his vast domain. Having been warned that all enemies of the Jews had in the past met with failure, Haman, being superstitious, decided to cast lots to determine the most favorable day for the slaughter. The lots indicated that day to be the thirteenth day of the twelfth month, Adar.

Haman, of course, could not have foreseen that these lots would furnish a name for his intended victims' most joyous festival. He could not have known that his plot had been doomed to failure by the Almighty, who had prepared the remedy for the blow long before the blow could be struck.

It happened that before Haman was appointed prime minister, King Ahasuerus had executed his first queen, Vashti, for disobedience, and had then chosen, in her place the charming Jewish maiden Esther. When the king, yielding to Haman's wish decreed death for all Jews, Mordecai, Queen Esther's cousin, induced her to intercede for her people. By her plea to the king the Jews were saved.

Accordingly, the Jews ordained that, "They and their children should keep two days of *Purim* every year, throughout every generation, every family in every province and in every town; that the days of *Purim* should not be blotted out from the memory of the Jews." Ever since then, Jews all over the world have celebrated *Purim* each year on the fourteenth and on the fifteenth day of Adar with feasting and gladness. On a leap year, *Purim* is observed in the second Adar.

PREPARATION FOR PURIM. During the fast of Esther, Jewish housewives busy themselves with preparing the *Purim* feast. A special kind of baking has been adopted for this occasion. Some of the dishes have names symbolic of the historical events to be commemorated. There will be the three-cornered loaves or cakes filled with poppy-seeds or with chopped prunes and raisins. These have become known as *Hamantaschen,* after the triangular cap which Haman is believed to have worn. In some localities it is the custom to bake *kreplach* for Purim. This is a three-cornered fritter, filled with minced meat, and boiled either in soup or separately, and served with soup.

READING THE MEGILLAH. *Megillah,* scroll, is the name given to one of the Biblical works, the Book of Esther, in which the story of *Purim* is told. Many years ago, the Great Sanhedrin, of which Mordecai is said to have been a member, ordained that the *megillah* be read on *Purim,* both on the evening of the thirteenth day of the month of Adar, and again on the morning of the following day. Everyone, man, woman, and child, is obliged to hear the *megillah* read.

Towards evening, the Jews assemble in the synagogue to hear the story of Haman's downfall and Mordecai's victory. They bring along their children, that they may be trained from early youth to hear the *megillah* read. Those unable to go to the synagogue hear the *megillah* read at home.

After the stars become visible to the naked eye, the reader unrolls the whole *megillah,* and then folds it up, to give it the appearance of a letter, *iggeret,* as the *megillah* is called in the Bible. The reader then recites three benedictions, each of which is answered by all present with a hearty *Amen.* Then slowly, in a measured tone and to the traditional melody, the reader chants the contents of the *megillah.* Everyone listens attentively to each and every word, for should one miss a single word, one's obligation to hear the *megillah* read has not been fulfilled.

The Jew reveres the synagogue in which he worships his God, and he permits nothing to be done or said there which might imply contempt for the holy place. But on *Purim,* when he makes sport of the Hamans of the past and present, the Jew allows and sometimes even encourages conduct which on other days would be impermissible in the synagogue.

Coming to the synagogue, the children are given toy pistols and rattles of all kinds, commonly known as *gragers.* At the mention of the name of Haman, the children begin shaking their rattles and shooting their pistols, while the adults hiss, stamp, and shout, until the place is alive with noise.

MERRYMAKING ON PURIM. The Jew, as a rule, celebrates his festivals with merriment, but at the same time with a certain degree of reserve and solemnity, in accordance with his religious principles and traditions. Frivolity and intoxication he does not tolerate.

Purim, however, is a special occasion. *Purimspielers,* Purim players, men and youngsters dressed in funny clothes, go about in the streets singing *Purim* songs, dancing, joking, and performing clowning tricks for which they receive a few coins. Some stage *Purim* plays on subjects having a direct bearing upon the *Purim* festival. The characters are the well-known *Purim* heroes: King Ahasuerus is modeled after the town official; Haman resembles the town drunkard; Queen Vashti looks like a fat woman; Esther is a shy young maiden; and Mordecai is a fellow with a long beard and a big hunch on his back. Others dramatize the story of David and Goliath or the story of Joseph and his brethren.

Boys and girls walk from house to house in grotesque masks and indulge in all kinds of fun. They are often given a few coins for singing comic songs, one of the most popular of which is: *"Heint is Purim, morgen is oys, git mir a penny, un warft mich aroys."* (Today is Purim, tomorrow it is over; give me a penny, and throw me out.)

SHALOAH-MANOT. Mordecai commanded the Jews to "make *Purim* days as days of feasting and gladness, and of sending portions to one another, and gifts to the poor."

Faith and charity are therefore essentials in the celebration of *Purim*. On every festival the poor are remembered, and surely they are never neglected on *Purim*. Towards evening, before *Purim* has set in and before the reading of the *megillah*, the Jew begins to provide means for taking care of the poor. It is customary for every Jew to give half the monetary unit current in the country, to commemorate the half-shekel the Jews were accustomed to give for the buying of the public sacrifices during the existence of the Temple in Jerusalem. These contributions are known as *mahatzit ha-shekel*, half a shekel. The general practice is for every person to give three half-shekels according to the number of persons in the family. The money is then distributed among the poor.

On *Purim* even the poorest Jew who is himself dependent upon charitable contributions, is obliged to give at least two gifts to two persons, one gift to each. Whoever is willing to accept charity, Jew or non-Jew, must be allowed to participate. If one lives in a community where there are no people willing to accept charity, one must either send the *Purim* money to a charitable institution, or keep it in his possession until he meets some poor person who will accept it. Women, too, must contribute charity on this day.

On *Purim* the Jew also complies with the law of "sending portions to one another (*shaloah manot*)." Everybody sends at least two gifts to one of his friends, no matter whether this friend be rich or poor. Strictly speaking, these gifts should be made of food which may be eaten without further preparation, such as boiled meats, confectionery, fruits, and wines. One may not give raw foods or other articles. But custom now permits gifts such as books, wearing apparel, and other useful things.

THE PURIM SEUDAH. Purim is celebrated mostly by feasting; and so every Jewish family must enjoy at least one festival meal, to be begun towards the evening of the fourteenth of Adar. This meal is known as *Seudat Purim*, Purim feast.

The Purim *seudah* is a happy family dinner. Food and drink are of the best. The *Hamantaschen* (triangular-shaped loaves), and the *kreplach* (three-cornered fritters), prepared the day before, are now served. Turkey is a popular dish. Whole peas and broad beans, known as *bubb,* boiled in salt water, is a favorite dish. In some localities the *Purim* gifts are distributed to the members of the family at the *seudah.*

SHUSHAN PURIM. Because the Jews who lived in Shushan, capital city of Persia, were permitted by King Ahasuerus, at Queen Esther's request, to defend themselves against their enemies on the fifteenth day of Adar, this day was named *Shushan Purim,* the *Purim* of Shushan. Even today the Jewish people are accustomed to feasting and rejoicing on *Shushan Purim,* which is the second day of *Purim* mentioned in the Book of Esther.

To discover the real reason for the Jew's laughter on Purim, read the following story of *Purim,* embellished with all the wonderful tales and legends which have been handed down by the sages of old.

II. THE STORY OF PURIM

1. *An Unfortunate Queen*

This came to pass in the days of the Persian king Ahasuerus, who reigned over a hundred and twenty-seven provinces from India to Ethiopia. In the third year of his reign, the king made

a royal feast for all the grandees and the princes of the provinces, which lasted one hundred and eighty days. The guests
were seated on couches of pure silver and gold, and they were
even allowed to inspect the king's glittering treasures of silver
and gold and precious stones. All marvelled at the glory of
Ahasuerus' kingdom.

When this great feast was over, King Ahasuerus made another feast which lasted seven days for all the people of Shushan, the capital city. It was held in the royal gardens which
had been richly decorated. Food and drink were served lavishly
by the mighty king in vessels of pure gold.

Queen Vashti, too, prepared a feast for the women of Shushan and for the wives of the grandees and nobles. Her banquet equaled in splendor that given by her royal husband, and
was held in the halls of the palace.

On the seventh and last day of the feast, when the king and
the nobles were merry with wine, they began to converse about
women. The Persian nobles boasted: "The charm of the Persian woman surpasses that of all other women in the world."

The nobles of Media contended: "In this wide world, there
is no woman superior to the Median woman."

"Silence," shouted the king, who was deep in his cups; "all
of you are wrong. My first queen, Vashti, is neither a Persian
nor a Mede, but a Babylonian, yet she is by far the fairest of
all women."

"Indeed," shouted back the assembly, who were no more
sober than the king; "let queen Vashti be brought hither that
we may judge for ourselves."

The king thereupon commanded seven of his chamberlains
to bring Vashti to his presence. But Vashti was a proud queen,
and refused to come at the bidding of the king.

The seven chamberlains returned, and falling upon their
knees before the king, reported the refusal of the queen.

The king was greatly angered by Vashti's refusal. He immediately summoned the seven princes of Persia and Media,

who sat in the first rank of the kingdom, and he inquired of them: "What shall we do to the queen Vashti, according to law, because she has not done the bidding of king Ahasuerus?"

Said Memuchan, one of the seven princes: "Sire, Vashti the queen has not done wrong to the king alone, but even to all the princes, and to all the people of all the provinces of king Ahasuerus. For when this deed of the queen shall become known to all women, they will despise their husbands, saying: 'King Ahasuerus commanded Vashti the queen to be brought before him, but she disobeyed him and came not.' All women in the realm will follow the queen's example. If it please the king, therefore, let there be issued a royal order and let it be written among the laws of the Persians and the Medes, that Vashti come no more before the king Ahasuerus; and let her royal dignity be given to another better than she. And when the king's decree shall be published throughout all his kingdom, all wives shall give honor to their husbands."

The speech of Memuchan pleased the king and the princes. And Ahasuerus ordered that Queen Vashti be put to death for her disobedience. He then sent letters to all his provinces, to each province according to its own language and script, that every man should be the sole ruler in his own house, and all his commands be obeyed.

2. *Esther Is Chosen Queen*

In time, the fury of King Ahasuerus was appeased, and he remembered with regret Vashti and the decree that brought her death. Then said the king's servants that ministered to him: "Let the king appoint officers in all the provinces of his kingdom, that they gather together the fairest maidens and bring them to Shushan the capital, to the house of the women, under the custody of Hegai, the king's chamberlain, keeper of the women; and the maiden that pleases the king be queen in place of Vashti." The advice pleased the king, and at his command the most beautiful maidens of the realm were invited to the city.

There was a certain Jew in Shushan, whose name was Mordecai, of the tribe of Benjamin, and a descendant of Saul, first king of the Israelites. With the king of Judah, he had been carried into exile from Jerusalem by Nebuchadnezzar, the king of Babylon. He had brought up Hadassah—Esther—the daughter of his uncle; for she had neither father nor mother, and Mordecai had adopted her as his own daughter.

She was called Hadassah, which in Hebrew means "myrtle"; and people said that she was rightfully named Hadassah, because the fame of her good virtues and her charm and beauty spread far and wide, just as the fragrance of the myrtle pervades the air in the place where it grows. She was also known as Esther, the Hebrew word for Venus, the morning star, because of her modesty and dazzling beauty. For, like the morning star, she was at first a hidden light, and suddenly shone in all her brilliance upon Israel in time of darkness and despair.

When the maidens had been gathered together in Shushan the capital, in the custody of Hegai, Esther too was among them. And Hegai, seeing her, found her pleasing, and he gave her seven maidens to attend to her needs, and provided her with the best comforts in the house of women.

At last, when Esther was for the first time brought before the king, he marvelled at her beauty, her poise, and her grace, and without hesitation he decided that it was she who should wear the royal crown and be queen in place of Vashti. He summoned Hegai to the palace and ordered him to guard her well, and to deny her nothing that her heart desired. So content was the king with his choice that he at once removed the portrait of his late Queen Vashti, and replaced it with that of Esther.

The exalted station in which Esther suddenly found herself did not affect her simple ways and manners. She remained modest and as silent as before, observing the laws of her faith as in the house of Mordecai. Hegai, the chief keeper of the women, was by no means pleased with Esther's modesty. One day he said to her: "Noble lady, you make no effort to preserve your beauty, and you even refuse to partake of any food but vegetables, bread, and water. When the king becomes aware of it, he will blame me for neglecting my duty, and he may send me to the gallows."

"Don't be afraid, good Hegai," replied Esther; "I know I shall keep my good health with the diet I have chosen." And indeed Esther was right, for she grew more and more beautiful as the days passed. Hegai, at once pleased and astonished, loaded Esther down with the costliest jewels in the king's treasury.

Mordecai, mindful of the perils to which Esther was exposed, walked every day before the court of the house of the women to ascertain her well-being and what would become of her. One day Mordecai said to Esther: "I know that you will soon be chosen queen of the realm. Pray keep your descent and your faith a secret, and do not disclose it to any living being."

"Dear protector, why do you make this request of me?" asked Esther in great bewilderment.

"You well know the nature of the king," replied Mordecai; "that he is erratic and whimsical, and that in his mad fury he caused the death of his beloved queen. I fear that should the king ever become angry with you, he will appease his wrath not only by taking your life but also by destroying all the Jews in his realm."

"I understand, I understand," replied Esther thoughtfully, and she promised to keep her descent a secret.

It was the custom that, when a maiden reached her turn to go before the king, whatsoever she desired to enhance her beauty was given her. But when the time had come for Esther to appear before the king, she asked nothing but what Hegai, the keeper of women, appointed. And yet Esther found favor in the sight of all those that looked upon her.

The king loved Esther above all the women, and she seemed

lovelier in his sight than all the other maidens; and he set the royal crown upon her head and made her the first queen of all the land. This took place in the seventh year of the reign of King Ahasuerus.

Now Ahasuerus made every effort to learn from Esther the secret of her descent. He bestowed many honors upon her to induce her to divulge the secret. He tendered a great feast to all his princes and his grandees, which he called the "feast of Esther"; in her honor, he exempted the provinces from taxation; and he gave her many kingly gifts. But Esther guarded her secret very carefully.

Then the king earnestly pleaded with Esther to reveal her nationality: "You see that for your sake I have done certain things which no other king has ever done before me, and you still refuse to disclose your secret to me. Pray tell me to what nation you belong."

To this Esther replied: "I know neither my family nor my people, for I lost my parents in early infancy. I am an orphan, and God, the Father of the orphans, in His mercy, has brought me up."

3. *Mordecai Saves the King's Life*

Bigthan and Teresh, two of the king's chamberlains, were angry with the king because they were reduced from the position of councilors to that of butlers, and they plotted vengeance against their sovereign.

One day, while Mordecai sat in the king's gate, he overheard the following conversation between Bigthan and Teresh: "It is impossible to use violence against the king without being detected, for he is constantly surrounded by numerous courtiers and attendants. It would be easier to poison him. Let us drop poison into his cup of wine before handing it to him. As his butlers, we can easily carry out our plan when we are ready."

The two conspirators saw Mordecai sitting near them, but

they took it for granted that he would not understand them, since they were using their native tongue, the Tarsian. They did not know that Mordecai had been a member of the Sanhedrin, the highest Jewish court, and that, therefore, he knew all the seventy languages of the world.

Thus it was that the plot became known to Mordecai, and he told it to Esther the queen; and Esther reported it to the king in the name of Mordecai. And at the command of the king, it was recorded in the book of the chronicles of the Medes and the Persians how the faithful Mordecai had saved the life of the king.

4. *Mordecai's Pride*

In those days, King Ahasuerus honored Haman, the son of Hammedatha the Agagite, and advanced him, and set his seat above all the princes and grandees in the royal court. The king's servants, that were at the king's gate, bowed down and prostrated themselves before Haman; for it was the command of the king that all bow low before Haman and do him honor. But Mordecai bowed not down, nor prostrated himself before Haman.

Then the king's servants, that were at the king's gate, said to Mordecai: "Why do you transgress the king's command? Tell us, pray, wherein you are better and greater than we are, that we should prostrate ourselves before Haman and pay him homage, while you disobey the order of the king and refuse to bow to him?"

"Listen, O men without understanding," said the brave Mordecai; "hearken to my words and make a proper reply to them. How can I bow to one born of woman and whose life is but of a few days' duration? At man's birth, there is suffering and shedding of tears; in his youth pains and groans; all his days are full of trouble; and in the end he returns to dust. Shall I then prostrate myself before such a being? I bend the knee before God alone, the only living One in Heaven above."

"And who is the God before whom you bend the knee?" inquired the servants of the king.

Mordecai answered: "The God whom I fear and before whom I bend the knee is the ever-living One; He holds the earth in His arms; he stretches out the heavens in His might; He darkens the sun when it pleases Him; He illuminates the dark; He has set a bound to the waters of the seas, they rage and yet cannot pass their limit to overflow the land. With His word He created the heavens and the earth. The sun, the moon and the Pleiades run before Him; the stars and the planets are not idle for a single moment; they rest not; they speed before Him as His messengers, going in every direction, to do the bidding of Him who created them. To Him alone praise is due; Him alone must we worship, and before Him alone must we prostrate ourselves."

The pagan-minded officers of the king understood not the meaning of Mordecai's words. Daily they spoke to him, but he hearkened not to them. They reported Mordecai's statement to Haman, who was full of anger. But it seemed contemptible in the eyes of Haman to lay hands on Mordecai alone; for it had been made known to him who the people of Mordecai were; therefore he sought to destroy all the Jews, the people of Mordecai, in the entire kingdom of Ahasuerus.

5. *The Casting of Lots*

Haman had a trustworthy friend, Zaharan, to whom he made known his wicked design. And Zaharan, who was well acquainted with the history of the Jews, thereupon said with a smile: "You with your plot remind me of the story of a bird who grew angry at the sea, and undertook to make it dry."

"I would very much like to hear about this bird," said Haman.

And Zaharan began: "Once upon a time, a heron built its nest along the shore of the sea, and there it raised its little ones. Daily the mother bird would fly to distant parts to bring food for her little ones. One day, when the heron returned from her daily flight, she found no trace of her nest or of her little ones; the merciless billows of the sea had risen very high and had swept away her nest together with her young. The heron grew very angry at the outrage, and in her great anger she exclaimed: 'O you mischievous sea! I am going to take my revenge on you; I will dry up your proud billows.' And, true to her word, she immediately started out upon her great task. She took a mouthful of water and spilled it on the sand, and then she took a mouthful of sand and spilled it in the water. Ceaselessly she repeated the process, taking time neither to eat nor drink. 'I have a great task before me,' she said; 'I must not permit myself to rest or sleep until it is accomplished.'

"Another bird, noticing the heron at her labor, inquired: 'Pray tell me, what are you trying to do?'

"The heron replied sadly: 'This proud, haughty sea has destroyed my children; so I will not rest until I dry up its waters.'

"The bird laughed heartily, and said to the heron: 'Even if the creatures of the whole world should come to your aid, you would not be able to accomplish your task.' "

Haman was vexed at his friend's story. "You are talking nonsense," he said. "I am not a silly bird, and the Jews cannot be compared to the mighty billows of the sea."

Nevertheless, Haman, being superstitious, was affected by what Zaharan had told him, and he began to doubt whether he would succeed in destroying the Jews after all. In order to determine, therefore, the day and the month most favorable for his infamous undertaking, he resolved upon the casting of lots. In the first month, which is the month of Nisan, in the twelfth year of the reign of King Ahasuerus, they cast *pur,* that is, the lot, before Haman day after day, and month after month, until the lot pointed to the twelfth month, which is the month of Adar. "This is the month!" exclaimed Haman with great joy. "For it is during this month that their leader Moses died."

The angels in heaven saw Haman's cruel joy, and they said:

"O thou villain! In the month of Adar, Moses, the leader of Israel, was also born, and he shall plead Israel's cause."

6. *The Evil Decree*

Haman, the hated enemy of the Jews, went to the palace of the king and spoke to King Ahasuerus, saying: "O great king, permit me to relate to you some of my experiences, I think they will prove to be of great benefit to the crown."

"Speak," Ahasuerus commanded.

And Haman said: "O sire, through your great kindness and graciousness I have been raised to the highest office in the realm. To repay, at least in a small degree, the favors bestowed upon me, I have spared neither time nor money to investigate the various peoples subject to the crown, in order to determine which of them are loyal and which are disloyal to the king.

"Most of them, yea all of them, I have found to be loyal. They observe the customs of the land and obey the laws of the king. But there is a certain people scattered and dispersed among the peoples in the provinces of the kingdom; their laws are different from the laws of every other people, and their religion is different from the religion of every other land. They pay no heed to our laws and customs, and they do not execute the decrees of the king. Therefore it profits not for the king to suffer them. If it pleases the king, let it be written down that they be destroyed. And I will put ten thousand talents of silver into the king's treasury."

Ahasuerus took the signet ring from his hand, and gave it to Haman, the enemy of the Jews, saying: "The silver you can keep, and as for the people, do with them as it seems good to you."

On the thirteenth day of the first month of Nisan, in the twelfth year of the reign of Ahasuerus, all the scribes were called together, and they wrote letters, according to Haman's orders, addressed to the king's lieutenants, and to the governors, and to the princes of the peoples. In the name of King Aha-

suerus were they written, and they were sealed with the king's
ring. They were sent by runners into all the king's provinces,
bearing the command to destroy, to slay, and to bring death
to all Jews, young and old, women and children, in one day,
upon the thirteenth day of the twelfth month of Adar, and to
seize their property as spoil.

The runners went forth with all speed with the king's decree,
admonishing everyone to prepare for the fatal day. The decree
was proclaimed first in Shushan, the capital. The king and
Haman sat down to drink; but the people of Shushan were
troubled. Deep pain and sorrow overwhelmed the Jews who
appeared to be helpless in the face of doom. Many an honest
pagan was disturbed by the horrible fate that awaited hundreds
of thousands of innocent people.

Drunk as much with revenge as with wine, Haman departed
from the king's court well satisfied with his work. He boasted:
"My method is not like that of Esau, who desired to slay his
brother Jacob but to keep his children as slaves. It is not like
the plan of Pharaoh, who sought to destroy only the men of
Israel, but to spare the women. Neither is it like the policy of
Amalek, who pursued the Jews and smote the laggers and the
feeble, but left the strong and the brave. It is not like the
method of Sennacherib, who exiled the Jews and allowed them
to reside in a land as good as their own. Nor is it like the plan
of Nebuchadnezzar, who carried them away into exile, and
settled them near his palace. Because I have seen clearly the
folly of all these plans, I have resolved in one mighty blow to
destroy all Jews, old and young, strong and feeble, so that no
trace of their existence may remain upon the face of the earth."

7. *Mordecai Pleads with Esther*

When Mordecai became aware of Haman's evil design, he
rent his clothes; and putting on sackcloth and ashes, he went
out into the midst of the city, crying loudly and bitterly. He
came even before the king's gate where none might enter

clothed in sackcloth. In every province to which the king's decree came, there was great mourning among the Jews, and fasting and weeping, and wailing; and many covered themselves with sackcloth and ashes.

When Esther's maidens and her chamberlains told her that Mordecai was before the portals of the palace, clothed in sackcloth and ashes, Esther was exceedingly pained. She sent garments to clothe Mordecai that he might remove his sackcloth, but he would not accept them. "God forbid," said he, "that I should array myself in court attire, while my people are in danger." Then Esther sent her chamberlain Hathach to Mordecai, that he might learn the meaning of his words. And Mordecai told Hathach of all that had happened, and of the ten thousand talents of silver that Haman had offered for permission to destroy the Jews. And Mordecai gave him the copy of the king's decree, and bade him show it to Esther, and to charge her to go before the king to plead for her people.

Hathach delivered Mordecai's message to Esther, and he brought back from Esther to Mordecai the following reply:

"All the servants of the king and all the people of the king's provinces know that the punishment of death awaits that man or woman that dares enter the king's inner court without being called. Only that person to whom the king shall hold out the golden sceptre, may thus enter and live; but I have not been called to the king these thirty days."

And Mordecai replied through Hathach: "If you neglect this chance to save Israel, you will be obliged to give account to the Heavenly Court. Do not think that unlike all the Jews you shall escape in the king's house. For if you remain silent now, relief will come to the Jews from another source; but you and your father's house will perish. And who knows whether you have not come to royal dignity for such a time as this, to save Israel? Else, how should your miraculous history be explained?"

Moved by Mordecai's pleas and arguments, Esther bade Hathach return with this answer:

"Go, gather together all the Jews of Shushan, and fast you for me, and neither eat nor drink for three days, by night and by day; Moreover, I and my maidens will fast likewise; and I will go to the king, in spite of the law; and if I perish, I perish."

And hearing this, Mordecai went his way, and did as Esther had commanded him.

8. *Haman Builds Gallows for Mordecai*

Accompanied by her attendants, one on either side, and a third bearing her train heavily studded with precious stones, Esther went to the palace. Fearlessly she entered the inner court, and stood motionless before the startled and angry king. Under the wrathful eyes of Ahasuerus she shuddered and bowed her head.

A fervent prayer arose in the queen's heart:

"Father in heaven, do not forsake me, the most pitiable of orphans. O God, do not deliver us into the hands of Haman."

And the Father in heaven took pity on the helpless orphan, who, relying on Him, had risked her life for the sake of her people. He sent down angels to help her; they enveloped her face with threads of grace, and raised her head in pride. The king became enchanted by her charm and noble bearing, and he held out the golden sceptre that was in his hand. But Esther's knees had grown so weak that she was unable to reach the sceptre. Again the angels came to her aid, and helped her draw near and touch the top of the sceptre. And Esther knew that she was safe.

Then the king spoke to her in a voice soft with kindness, saying: "What do you desire, Queen Esther, for whatever you request, even to the half of the kingdom, it shall be given you."

And Esther answered: "Mighty king, if it seem good to you, I would that the king and Haman come this day to the banquet which I have prepared in the king's honor."

"Cause Haman," the king at once ordered, "to make haste, that it may be done as Esther has said."

That day the king and Haman came to the banquet that Esther had prepared.

And during the banquet the king said to Esther: "Whatever your petition, it shall be granted you; and whatever your request, even to half of the kingdom, it shall be performed."

"If," said Esther, "I have found favor in the sight of the king, and if it please the king to grant my petition, let the king and Haman come tomorrow to the banquet that I shall prepare for them; then, my lord, will I disclose the object of my desire."

Ahasuerus accepted the queen's invitation at once, and commanded Haman to be present again the following day at Esther's table.

Haman left Queen Esther's palace full of joy and glad of heart. As he went all paid him homage, and his heart swelled with pride. But when at the king's gate he saw Mordecai neither rise for him nor move, he was seized with an almost uncontrollable anger which he mastered only with the greatest difficulty. He sent for Zeresh, his wife, and his friends, and he recounted to them the glory of his riches, and how the king had promoted him, and how he had been advanced above all the princes and servants of the king. "My coffers are filled with costly and rare treasures," he said, "and I am chief of the nobles and grandees. Yea, Esther, the most charming queen, did let no man come in with the king to the banquet that she had prepared except myself; and tomorrow too I am invited by her together with the king." Suddenly the mild expression on his face changed to one of hatred, and he added: "Yet all this avails me not. What I eat and drink loses its savor, and all my honor and distinction are marred by the thought of Mordecai."

Then said Zeresh his wife and all his friends: "Let gallows be built fifty cubits high, and in the morning speak to the king, that Mordecai be hanged thereon· then may you go merrily with the king to the queen's banquet." Haman was pleased with the advice, and he at once engaged workmen to erect the gallows.

9. *A Night Without Sleep*

That night throughout all Persia and Media there was no sleep for the Jews, but only tears and lamentations for their sad plight. They had begun even to lose faith in Esther.

"Yes," they said, "we thought that Esther would plead with the king to save us from the hands of the wicked Haman. But instead, she has invited Haman to feast with Ahasuerus in her palace. Now we have none to rely upon but our God in heaven."

That night, after preparing the banquet for the following day, Esther could not sleep for worry and anxiety, fearing lest her plan to ensnare Haman in the presence of the king might fail.

Haman too did not sleep, but spent the night supervising the building of the gallows. He rushed back and forth among the workmen, spurring them on with promises of high wages if the work were speedily completed. At last the sound of the hammers ceased, and the fifty-cubit-high scaffold stood ready for Mordecai. Haman, his wicked eyes gleaming with delight, went up and measured the gallows by his own body, and said aloud: "Ah, it fits me perfectly: it will do very well for the hanging of that stubborn, proud Mordecai; he is about as tall as I am."

Suddenly a malicious thought occurred to him to surprise Mordecai that very night. Accordingly he went to the Jewish house of study, where he found Mordecai in sackcloth and ashes, surrounded by hundreds of hungry children, who had joined their elders in the three days' fast. From the children's eyes shone a heavenly light that glowed with faith in an unseen power, as if they had nothing to fear in this world.

Haman heard Mordecai speaking to the children. His voice was weak, but clear and unfaltering:

"Tonight we celebrate Passover. Our Father in heaven performed great miracles and wonders for our forefathers, and freed them from the cruel hand of the Egyptian ruler Pharaoh. Many years ago tonight he slew the first-born of the Egyptians. On this night Abraham slew the kings who had taken his nephew Lot into captivity; Jacob wrestled with an angel, yet did not meet defeat; the stars wandered completely from their course, when the Jews fought with Sisera. Now, you know, my beloved children, that with God there is no night. It was the promise of the Almighty that at some future time He would create a bright, joyous day that would never again be veiled in the darkness of night."

Haman was surprised by what he saw and heard; and his hatred increased against Mordecai and against the proud Jewish youngsters. Maddened with rage, he ordered that all the children be put in chains. "First," he cried, "I will hang all these, and then I will hang Mordecai."

Grief-stricken, the mothers ran to their children; and weeping, they brought them food, but the children laid their hands upon their books, and said: "By the life of our teacher Mordecai, we shall neither taste food nor drink; we are ready to perish by fasting."

All who were there—children, teachers, mothers and fathers—thereupon burst into loud lamentations. Their heartfelt cries pierced the heavens and reached the presence of the Almighty. The angels in heaven addressed the Almighty: "O Master of the universe, we hear the voice of suffering lambs and sheep."

The faithful shepherd Moses hurried into the presence of God, saying: "O merciful God, Thou knowest well that the voices are not lambs and sheep, but of the young of Israel, who for three days have been fasting, and are now languishing in fetters. Tomorrow these little ones will be slaughtered for the pleasure of the heartless Haman."

At this moment of crisis, God had compassion upon the Israelites for the sake of the innocent children.

Neither did King Ahasuerus sleep that night. Disturbing thoughts kept beating in his brain: "What secret reason has the queen for inviting Haman to the banquets? Perhaps they are lovers and are even now conspiring against me! Do they plan to take my life, that Haman may succeed me to the throne of Persia?" The restless king grappled with his thoughts. "Where are my friends? Would they not warn me if such a conspiracy existed? Is it possible, then, that I have no true friends after all? But why? Have I failed to reward them for their loyalty— those who have been true to me?"

He called to his servant, commanding him to bring the chronicles recording what had occurred in his kingdom. The records were read before the king, and it was found written how Mordecai had told of Bigthan and Teresh, who had sought to kill the king. Then Ahasuerus asked: "What honor and what dignity has been bestowed on Mordecai for this?" And the king's servants replied: "None."

10. *Haman Humiliated*

At that moment Haman had entered the outer court of the palace. He had come to seek permission from the king to hang Mordecai on the gallows that he had prepared for him. As Haman paced restlessly back and forth, the king noted his presence in the anteroom, and inquired: "Who is in the court?" The king's servants replied: "Behold, Haman is in the court." "Let him come in," said the king.

When Haman entered, the king said to him: "What shall be done to the man whom the king delights to honor?" Now Haman was a crafty man, and he thought: "Whom should the king delight to honor but myself? What shall I ask for? Wealth I possess, and hold the greatest and highest office in the realm." Suddenly a thought flashed through his mind, and he addressed the king: "For the man whom the king would honor, let the royal apparel be brought which he usually wears, and the horse that the king rides upon, and let the royal crown be set on his head; and let these things be delivered into the hand of the noblest of your princes, that he clothe therewith the man whom the king delights to honor, and cause him to ride on your horse through the streets of the city; and let your prince proclaim before him: 'Thus shall it be done to the man whom the king delights to honor.' "

The king addressed Haman, choosing his words with care: "Your advice pleases me. As you are the king's noblest prince, go, then, to our treasure chambers, and gather these things: a cover of fine purple; a garment of fine silk gemmed with diamonds and pearls and decked with golden bells; the golden crown brought from Macedonia for my coronation; the sword and coat of mail that were sent to me from Ethiopia; and the two veils embroidered with pearls which I had as gifts from Africa. From the royal stable, lead forth the black horse which I rode at my coronation. And with all these, seek out Mordecai, for he is the one whom I delight to honor."

Haman stood motionless with alarm and stupefaction. Then, in a trembling voice, "Honored king," he asked, "which Mordecai shall I seek? There are many men by that name in the realm of the king."

"Mordecai, the Jew," said the king.

"There are many Jews named Mordecai," ventured Haman.

"The Jew Mordecai who sits at the king's gate," said the king.

Haman's voice trembled even more as he said: "This man is my enemy and the enemy of my house; I would give him ten thousand talents of silver rather than do him this honor."

"Ten thousand talents of silver shall be given him," said the king severely, "but these honors, too, you will show him."

"O my lord and king," pleaded the grief-stricken Haman. "Mordecai is a common man and will not appreciate these honors. Appoint him ruler over a city, or even a district, but do not force me to do him these honors."

"I will appoint him ruler over cities and over districts," replied the king with vexation, "but these honors you will show him."

"O gracious lord and king," cried Haman, "pray be not angry with me. You appointed me chief of all the grandees and satraps of your provinces. Let Mordecai take from me that high office, but spare me the humiliation of doing him these honors."

The king, enraged by Haman's pleas, commanded in a stern voice: "The man who has saved the king's life deserves to be chief of my grandees, nobles and satraps, but these honors you shall show him. Go, without another word, and execute the will of the king." Ahasuerus then turned to Harbonah and Abzur, two of his trusted courtiers, saying: "Go with him and see that he carries out my wish to the letter."

Falteringly, and with a heavy heart, the abject Haman went to the king's treasure chambers and to the royal stables, and having gathered all the things which the king had commanded, he brought them to the synagogue where Mordecai the Jew was praying. He approached Mordecai and said: "Arise, pious son of Abraham, Isaac, and Jacob. Your sackcloth and ashes were worth more than my ten thousand talents of silver. My money was spurned by the king, but your prayers were accepted by your Father in heaven."

Mordecai looked up at Haman. "Wicked man," he said, "are you not satisfied with taking my life, that you come to mock me in my last moments upon earth?"

"I have not come to mock you," replied Haman dejectedly. "Here is the royal apparel in which the king ordered me to clothe you."

Mordecai was stunned. There before him stood the proud and haughty Haman, transformed into a humble messenger of the king.

Haman then dressed Mordecai in the king's robes, placed the

golden crown upon his head, and helped him mount the king's horse, which he led through the streets of the city, proclaiming: "Thus shall be done to the man whom the king delights to honor."

Despite the sudden change in his fortunes, Mordecai ended the day as he had begun it, in prayer and fasting. The procession over, he took off the royal garments, again covered himself with sackcloth and ashes, and returned to the king's gate. The king's command to destroy the Jews had not been revoked.

Haman went home, mourning and with his head covered, for the blow he had suffered was severe. He told his wife Zeresh and his friends all that had happened, and they said to him:

"If Mordecai, before whom you have begun to fall, be of the seed of the Jews, you shall not conquer him, but shall surely be defeated. Their God has compared them at times to the dust upon the ground, and at times to the stars in heaven. When they fall low, they fall as low as the dust of the ground, but when they rise, they rise as the stars in heaven. At first, when we saw Mordecai fall low, we thought he would fall still lower. Now that he is beginning to rise, he will continue to rise to the very heavens."

As they were speaking, the king's chamberlains came to summon Haman to the queen's banquet.

11. *Haman's Downfall*

There was foreboding in his now humble heart as Haman seated himself at Esther's table and heard the king repeat his words of the day before: "Whatever your petition, Queen Esther, it shall be granted you; and whatever your request, even to half of my kingdom, it shall be done."

With the courage of one prepared for death, Esther answered: "If I have found favor in your sight, O king, and if it please the king, spare my life at my petition, and the life of my people; for we are sold, I and my people, to be slain and to perish. Had we been sold as bondsmen and bondswomen, I had held my peace."

King Ahasuerus was puzzled, and he said to Esther: "Who is he, and where is he, that dared presume in his heart to do this to you and your people?"

Esther said: "One who is our enemy; even this wicked Haman."

At her words, Haman's eyes went wide with terror. Choking with anger, the king rose and paced across the room. His brain seemed to burn with fire, and he went out into the garden for a breath of cool air. Haman threw himself upon his knees before Esther the queen, pleading for mercy. When the king returned, he found Haman fallen upon the couch where Esther was reclining. Ahasuerus, blind with fury, thought that Haman was attempting to use violence against the queen, and he roared: "Will he even force the queen before my very eyes?"

He summoned the royal servants. They came at once and covered Haman's head as a sign—according to the Persian custom—that Haman had fallen into disfavor with the king.

Then said Harbonah, the king's chamberlain: "In Haman's house stands a gallows fifty cubits high, which Haman has prepared for Mordecai who saved the king's life."

Thereupon the king exclaimed: "Let Haman be hanged on the gallows he has prepared for Mordecai!"

12. *The King's Second Decree*

On that day, King Ahasuerus deeded the house of Haman, the enemy of the Jews, to Esther the queen. And when Esther told the king of her relationship to Mordecai, the king summoned Mordecai, and he gave him the ring which he had taken from Haman. Moreover Esther gave Mordecai command of the house of Haman.

Now Esther spoke once more to the king, kneeling, and beseeching him with tears to revoke the evil design of Haman against the Jews. She pleaded: "If it please the king, and if I have found favor in his sight, and it seem right before the king, let new letters be written to reverse that devised by Haman decreeing the destruction of the Jews."

To Esther and to Mordecai the king said: "Behold, I have given Esther the house of Haman, whom they have hanged on the gallows because he plotted to destroy the Jews. Write, then, concerning the Jews, as seems good in your sight, in the king's name, and seal it with the king's ring; for whatsoever is written in the king's name and sealed with the king's ring, no man may reverse."

The king's scribes were called in on the twenty-third day of the month of Sivan, and they wrote as Mordecai commanded, to the governors and princes in one hundred and twenty-seven provinces, from India to Ethiopia, to each in his native language. The letters, written in the name of King Ahasuerus and sealed with the king's ring, were carried by horsemen on the swift steeds of the king's service. They brought the message to the Jews, that on the thirteenth day of the month of Adar, in every city, they should gather their forces, to destroy and slay all who would assault them.

And in the name of the king there was sent a second edict, saying:

"King Ahasuerus sends this letter to all grandees, nobles, satraps, and to all his subjects on water and land: may your peace be great. Haman, the son of Hammedatha, who was close to the king and into whose hands the government was entrusted, did by his intrigues and falsehood, mislead the king, and wrote letters that all the Jews of the realm be killed on one day. In the belief that Haman had at heart the welfare of our empire, I consented to the issuance of that decree. I have since discovered that this man, who enjoyed our kindness, praise, and dignity, was a traitor to our person and our kingdom, which he hoped to seize for himself. For his own selfish motives, he persuaded me to decree that honest men be killed and innocent blood be shed. Therefore, I have ordered that the son of Hammedatha be hanged on the gallows which he had prepared for Mordecai, who once saved your king from death at the hands of conspirators. Now, Queen Esther, for whose sake I distributed many gifts and have granted many concessions to my subjects, is a cousin of the wise and honest Mordecai. I now rescind the edict decreeing the death of the Jews, and hereby desire my subjects to honor and befriend the children of Israel."

Mordecai was invested with Haman's office at court. He went forth from the presence of the king in royal apparel of white and blue, wearing a crown of gold and a robe of fine purple linen. The city of Shushan rejoiced; the Jews once more knew light and gladness, joy and honor. In every province and every city where the king's command was heard, there was happiness and feasting among the Jews. And throughout the land, many non-Jews turned to the faith of Mordecai.

13. *Purim*

On the thirteenth day of the twelfth month, Adar, the Jews met together in their cities in all the provinces and prepared to shatter the planned onslaught of their enemies. The attack came, but none could withstand the Jews, for the fear of them had gripped the people. The princes, the satraps, and the governors sided with the Jews because they feared Mordecai, who had become powerful in the king's house and whose fame had spread throughout the realm. Defending themselves, the Jews smote their enemies with the sword. In Shushan alone, the Jews slew five hundred men, among them the ten sons of Haman, whose bodies the king ordered to be hanged upon gallows. But the Jews took no spoils.

There still remained many friends of Haman in the capital who threatened the lives of the Jews. Queen Esther begged King Ahasuerus to permit the Jews of Shushan another day to rout their enemies. And so, on the fourteenth day of Adar, the battle continued, and three hundred of the Jews' enemies were killed on that day. Again the Jewish victors took no spoils.

Similar battles were fought throughout all the land, and the Jews with the help of the king's officers killed seventy-five thousand of their enemies; but of the spoils they took nothing. On the fourteenth day of Adar—in Shushan on the fifteenth day—the Jews rested, spending the day in feasting and gladness.

Mordecai then ordered all of the Jews of the realm to observe every year the fourteenth and the fifteenth days of the month of Adar, the days of sorrow which had been transformed into gladness; and he commanded that they spend these two days in joyous feasting, in exchanging gifts with one another, and in giving to the poor. These two days they called *Purim,* signifying the lots which Haman had cast for their destruction.

And the Jews took it upon themselves and upon their children to keep these two days every year, throughout every generation, in every family, in every city, and in every province, that the memory of these two days of Purim might never perish from the face of the earth.

Passover (Pesah)

THE FESTIVAL OF FREEDOM
(NISAN 15-22)

I. CELEBRATION OF PASSOVER

WHAT IS PASSOVER? When our forefathers, in olden times, were held as slaves in Egypt, God sent two messengers, Moses and his brother Aaron, with a plea to the Egyptian King, known among his subjects as Pharaoh, to let His people go out of Pharaoh's land as freemen. Pharaoh refused to listen to the word of God, and for this he and the Egyptian people were punished with ten plagues. The last of these plagues was the slaying of the firstborn sons of the Egyptians. At midnight, the Angel of Death visited the homes of the Egyptians, killing their firstborn sons; but he *passed over* the houses of the Israelites and spared their firstborn. This Festival is therefore called *Passover,* or in Hebrew, *Pesah.*

THE FESTIVAL OF FREEDOM. Passover is the Jewish festival of freedom, *zeman herutenu,* literally, the season of our freedom. It commemorates the birth of a free nation, and the Almighty's deliverance of our forefathers from slavery in Egypt through His servant Moses.

Just after midnight, on the fourteenth day of the Jewish month of Nisan, when the tenth plague fell upon the Egyptians, Pharaoh drove the Jews from the land. The Jewish women had no time to bake the bread for which they had prepared the dough. They had not even time to allow the dough to be leavened. It is written in the Holy Bible: "And the Egyptians were urgent upon the people to send them out in haste: for they said: 'We are all dead men.' The Jewish people took their dough before it was leavened, and they carried their kneading-troughs bound up in their clothes upon their shoulders."

AN AGRICULTURAL FESTIVAL. The festival of Passover not only commemorated the departure of the Israelites from the land of Egypt; it was celebrated also as an agricultural festival in the land of Israel during the existence of the first and second Temples.

Like all peoples who live by the soil, the Jews when in Palestine joyfully celebrated the harvest seasons. Palestine, a semi-tropical country, had several harvests. The grain harvest lasted seven weeks, and was observed by the Jews as a season of gladness and joy. This festive season began with the harvest of barley on the second day of Passover, the sixteenth day of the month of Nisan.

No one had been permitted to eat of the new crop of grain until the second day of Passover, when a thanksgiving offering

was brought to the Almighty in gratitude for the products of
the soil which He had caused to grow. The offering — called
omer (sheaf) in Hebrew—was a sheaf of the new barley, the
first of the cereals to ripen. The grain harvest ended with the
harvesting of wheat on the fiftieth day after the bringing of the
omer, and this occasion was celebrated by the Festival of *Shabuot,* Pentecost.

THE OMER. The amount of grain specified for this thanksgiving offering was three *seahs,* an ancient Palestinian measure.
This had to be reaped either on the day it was to be brought
into the Temple, or during the preceding night. The grain
was taken preferably from a field in the neighborhood of
Jerusalem if the grain growing there was ripe enough; otherwise it was gathered elsewhere.

This grain was to be reaped by three persons, each with his
own sickle and basket. On the day before Passover, messengers
were sent by the Jerusalem court to a designated field to bind
the heads of the barley-stalks in sheaves. This served to lighten
the work of the reapers. At nightfall of the first day of Passover, each of the three reapers, in the presence of a vast crowd,
asked the court messengers for permission to reap, by repeating
each of the following questions three times: "Has the sun set?
Is this the sickle? Is this the basket? Shall I reap?" To each of
the first three questions, the messengers answered, "Yes"; to
the last question they replied, "Reap."

The grain having been gathered, it was brought to the hall
of the Temple, where it was first threshed and then parched.
It was afterwards ground into coarse meal, one-tenth of which
was set aside and sifted through thirteen sieves to make it
very fine. The flour was then presented to the priest, who prepared it as a meal-offering by pouring oil and frankincense over
it, "waved" it, and then burned a handful of it on the altar.
The remainder was eaten by the priests. The "waving" was
done in this manner: The offering was placed on the extended
hands of the priest. The priest first moved his hands backward

and forward to acknowledge God's sovereignty over nature, and then upward and downward to acknowledge His sovereignty over heaven and earth; and in the name of the people he offered thanks to Him for the products of the soil. After the *omer* offering the people were permitted to make use of the new crop.

A PILGRIM FESTIVAL. Passover was the first of the three great pilgrim feasts, when the people of Palestine, from far and near, travelled in gala procession with their families and servants to Jerusalem, the Holy City. The Jews began their pilgrimage before Passover so that they might eat of the paschal lamb, the Passover offering, in Jerusalem, near the Temple of God. For the Lord commanded them: "Three times a year shall your males appear before the Lord your God in the place which He shall choose: on the feast of unleavened bread, on the feast of weeks, and on the feast of tabernacles."

THE TIME OF THE FEAST. According to the Law of God, Passover was to be celebrated for seven days, extending from the fifteenth to the twenty-first day of the month of Nisan. However, the sages decreed that, in countries outside the land of Israel, Passover should be observed for eight days, including the twenty-second day of Nisan, and that we must abstain from doing manual work on the first and second days as well as on the seventh and eighth.[1]

This decree of the sages did not apply to the land of Israel. Therefore the Jews residing in Israel observe Passover for only seven days, in accordance with the Law of God.

While the month of Tishri is the beginning of the Jewish civil year (pages 20-22 above), the month of Nisan is the beginning of the Jewish ecclesiastical, or religious, year. Therefore, when dealing with religious matters, Nisan is always designated as the first month, while in reality it is the seventh month in the civil year. For such was the command of the Almighty (Exodus XII, 2): "This month shall be unto you the

---

1 See pages 45-46 above.

beginning of months; it shall be the first month of the year to you."

LEAVENED FOOD IS FORBIDDEN. It is forbidden to eat *hametz,* leavened food, during the eight days of Passover. Even pots, pans, china, and silverware used throughout the year are considered as *hametz,* and may not be used during Passover. Jewish housewives thoroughly cleanse such utensils before Passover and put them away where they cannot be easily reached, in order to preclude the possibility of their being used through error during the Passover Festival. As a rule, they keep in readiness, from year to year, a complete set of tableware and kitchen utensils for use on the Passover.

THE SEARCH FOR LEAVEN. The Lord God commanded through Moses that the Jew abstain from eating *hametz* (leaven) during the Passover week, and that he also remove all manner of leavened food from his domain, so that during the Passover week, "No leaven shall be found in your houses," (Exodus XIII:19); and (Exodus XIII:7): "No leavened bread shall be seen with you, in all your borders."

Before the approach of Passover, preparations are begun for the removal of leaven to comply with the Law of God. The Jewish housewife sees to it that her home is thoroughly cleansed from cellar to garret, so that on the thirteenth day of Nisan no trace of leavened food remains. Rooms and storehouses, where leaven might have been brought in throughout the year, are carefully swept and cleaned on that day.

A formal search for leaven, known as *bedikat hametz,* was instituted by our sages many centuries back. This search must take place on the thirteenth day of Nisan, on the evening before the Passover, immediately after nightfall. If the first day of Passover occurs on a Sunday, the formal search is made after nightfall on Thursday evening, the twelfth day of Nisan.

The search for leaven is carried out in the following manner: The father of the household, or another in his absence, puts away in a safe place all the *hametz* that has been left for food or for sale, and covers it up. He then deposits a few crumbs of bread in some noticeable place, generally on one of the window-sills in each room, takes a wooden spoon and a small brush, or a few whole feathers, and then lights a wax-taper or candle. The searcher, accompanied by another member of the household, and with the lit taper or candle in his hand, makes a complete round of the house, searching every nook and corner, to be sure that no leaven is left there. While making the rounds, he gathers up all the leaven he can find. Coming to the window-sills where the crumbs of bread have been deposited, he carefully sweeps the crumbs with the brush or with the feathers into the wooden spoon, leaving no crumbs on the sill.

When gathering up the crumbs from the first window-sill, the searcher pronounces the following benediction: "Blessed be Thou, O Lord our God, King of the universe, who hast sanctified us by Thy commandments, and hast commanded us concerning the precept of cleaning away the leaven." The crumbs have been deposited on the window-sills before the formal search is made, precisely to make certain that the searcher will be able to clean away some leaven, so that he can pronounce the above benediction; for, otherwise, he would not be permitted to pronounce the benediction, as the law is that no benediction may be pronounced unless the act mentioned in it is actually performed immediately after its utterance.

Completing the search for leaven, the searcher nullifies whatever *hametz* remains in his possession, by resolving to consider it as non-existent, entirely valueless and comparable to dust, and as something for which he has no use. He performs that resolution by reciting the special formula prescribed by the sages: "All manner of leaven that remains in my domain, which I have not seen or removed, shall be considered null and void, and accounted as the dust of the earth." If the searcher does not understand the formula in the language in which it is written (the Aramaic), he should recite it in the language he understands best.

The searcher takes whatever leaven he has found, together with the spoon and brush or feathers, and carefully ties them together. He puts it away where it may easily be seen by him on the following morning.

BURNING HAMETZ. On the fourteenth day of Nisan, the day preceding the Passover, before eleven o'clock in the morning, the master of the household burns the leaven he has put away the evening before, together with the spoon and brush or feathers. If the first day of Passover occurs on a Sunday, the burning of the *hametz* takes place on Friday, the thirteenth day of Nisan.

After burning the leaven, he recites the following formula as ordained by the sages: "All manner of leaven remaining in my domain, whether it be visible to me or invisible, whether I have removed it or have failed to remove it, shall be considered null and void, and accounted as the dust of the earth."

SELLING HAMETZ. Any manner of leavened food, remaining after eleven o'clock in the morning of the day before Passover, the time limit set for the burning of *hametz,* can neither be eaten nor sold to a non-Jew at any time; and at no time may anyone derive benefit from it. If therefore a person has leavened food in his possession which he does not wish to destroy or burn, and he wants to derive benefit from it after Passover, he must sell it to a non-Jew, before eleven o'clock, the morning of the day before Passover. As not everybody is familiar with the law regulating such sale and therefore is not in a position to comply with the legal requirements, it is the custom to sell the leaven to the Rabbi of the community, who, as agent, sells it in turn to a non-Jew.

MATZAH AND LEAVEN BEFORE PASSOVER. On the day before Passover, all Jews abstain from eating leavened food after one-third of the day has passed; that is, one-third of the time between dawn and the appearance of the stars, usually about ten o'clock in the morning. They likewise abstain from eating *matzah* during the entire day before Passover, so that the *mat-*

zah may be eaten with relish at night when everybody is duty bound to eat it and pronounce a benediction over it.

FAST OF THE FIRSTBORN. Because the Almighty spared the firstborn of the Jews when slaying all the firstborn of the Egyptians, there developed a custom for the firstborn among the Jews to fast on the day before Passover. If the first day of Passover occurs on a Sunday, the fast of the firstborn takes place on Thursday, the twelfth of Nisan.

However, if the firstborn are invited to a feast in celebration of a religious duty, such as circumcision or redemption of the firstborn, they need not then observe the fast, but may partake of food to celebrate the occasion. It is therefore the custom for a student of the Law to complete the study of one of the Tractates of the Talmud the day before Passover, so that he may celebrate the occasion by feasting. Such celebration is known as a *siyum,* or commencement, and is considered a feast in honor of performing a religious duty. The firstborn of the community are invited by the student to celebrate the *siyum* with him. By this invitation, they become exempt from fasting, and donate instead a certain sum of money to charity.

MATZAH. The *matzah* (unleavened bread) which the Jews eat during the Passover week, is known in Jewish literature as *lehem oni* (the bread of affliction), because it is reminiscent of the hardships of our forefathers in Egypt. *Matzah* has no special flavor, as it contains neither salt nor yeast. The dough for baking *matzah* must not be allowed to become leavened. For this reason, while kneading the dough, special precautions are taken against fermentation. It must be kneaded quickly, rolled into shape, and then perforated to keep the *matzah* from rising and swelling.

Matzah is also symbolic of the haste with which our forefathers departed from the land of Egypt, the land of their woe, that midnight when Pharaoh drove them without bread from the land, forcing them to carry their unbaked bread with them wrapped in bundles.

WHEN MATZAH MUST BE EATEN. While one is forbidden to eat leavened food, the eating of *matzah* is not compulsory during the entire eight days of Passover. One may eat any other food that one prefers, provided it is not classed as leavened. On the first two nights of Passover, however, the eating of *matzah* is compulsory. Everyone must eat some *matzah* during the evening meal (*seder*); for this was commanded by God through Moses: "In the first month, on the fourteenth day of the month in the evening, ye shall eat unleavened bread."

Before eating the *matzah* on these two nights, the following two benedictions are spoken: "Blessed art Thou, O Lord our God, King of the universe, who bringest forth bread from the earth." And: "Blessed art Thou, O Lord our God, King of the Universe, who hast sanctified us with Thy commandments and hast commanded us concerning the precept of eating unleavened bread."

THE MATZAH FUND. At the approach of any Festival, the first duty of every Jew is to give thought to persons in need, to those less fortunate than himself. He must help provide the orphan and widow with food and other necessities. In every Jewish community, therefore, there has been handed down, from time immemorial, the beautiful custom of every Jew donating, according to his means, toward a *matzah* fund, known as *maot hittim*, money for wheat. The object of this fund is to provide every poor Jew with *matzah* and with all other things necessary for the enjoyment of the Festival. It was called "money for wheat," because in former years the head of every Jewish family used to purchase for himself a supply of wheat suitable for Passover; he would bring the wheat to a mill, which had been cleansed and prepared for Passover use, where it would be ground into flour. He would then bring the flour to a bakery specially fitted out for the baking of *matzah*.

THE PASCHAL LAMB. Before inflicting the tenth plague upon the Egyptians, God told Moses that every Jewish family should prepare a lamb and bring it as an offering to Him, at sunset.

on the fourteenth day of the month of Nisan. He commanded them to sprinkle some of the blood of the lamb on the doorposts of their homes, saying that when the Angel of Death would descend to slay the firstborn sons of the Egyptians, he would pass over the houses of the Jews wherever the blood was sprinkled, and he would spare their firstborn.

The Almighty then commanded the Jews through Moses, that in later years, when the Jews would build the Holy Temple in the promised land, they should sacrifice the paschal lamb as a Passover-offering at that holy place. With the loss of the Temple, all sacrifices ceased, and with them also the sacrifice of the paschal lamb. There are, however, to this day some people who still go through the ceremony of roasting a lamb for the Passover. The Samaritans, for instance, who remained in Palestine throughout the years of exile, still observe this practice.

THE SEDER NIGHTS. On the first two nights of Passover, the *seder* is celebrated. *Seder* is the special order or program designated for these two nights. No other ceremony among the Jews is performed with such pomp and gladness of heart as the *seder*. This interesting ceremony was originally designated to stimulate the interest of the Jewish child in the glorious past of his people, and to inspire him with the hope for the future. When the child asks, upon seeing the special order of things on *seder* night, "what is the meaning of all this?" he is told in explanation the story of his people's deliverance from the Egyptian bondage. And, by reciting the *haggadah,* the special book adopted for the *seder* night, the entire family, man, woman, and child, are imbued with a spirit of loyalty to their God and their people. They are encouraged by an unswerving faith in their God to face the trials of life. As their fathers, they say, were helped in time of darkness and persecution, so they too will survive their tormentors, until at last the true Messiah will bring an era of freedom, justice and good-will to men.

THE FOUR CUPS OF WINE. In the afternoon of the fourteenth day of Nisan, the Jewish housewife, assisted by all members of the family, begins setting the table for the *seder,* spreading it with the best linen in her possession, and decorating it with the family's best china and silverware, especially kept from year to year for the Passover. One goblet or wineglass is placed on the table for each and everyone who is to participate in the *seder* service. Every participant, whether male or female, must, during the course of the *seder* service, drink exactly four cups of wine, mead, or grape juice, as a symbol of the four Biblical expressions used by the Almighty in promising the Jews redemption from the Egyptian bondage (Exodus VI: 6-7): "*Vehotzeti,* and I will bring you out; *vehitzalti,* and I will deliver you; *vegaalti,* and I will redeem you; *velakahti,* and I will take you out to Me for a people."

THE CUP OF ELIJAH. There is, however, a fifth divine promise in the Bible, which follows the above four, and that is (Exodus VI: 8): "*Vehebeti,* and I will bring you to the promised land." Some Jewish legal authorities would, therefore, have it that a fifth cup of wine is required in the *seder,* because there are five divine promises. Talmudic authorities left the decision of all mooted questions of law to the prophet Elijah, who, in time to come, will decide them, and the question of the fifth cup, too, was left to the same judge. There developed therefore the custom of placing an extra large brimming cup of wine in the center of the table for the prophet Elijah.

Moreover, this prophet, who was taken up to heaven alive in a fiery chariot drawn by fiery horses (II Kings II: 11), is believed to have become immortal and to have become the heavenly guardian angel of the Jewish people. Elijah is the great champion of righteousness and of pure worship of God, who at times brings good fortune to poor, pious people. It is he who is present at the celebration of every circumcision; and it is he who will appear, in the end of days, to announce the arrival of the Messiah. At that time, this messenger of God will announce to the dwellers of the earth, the good tidings of peace and salvation, of comfort to the sorrowing, of the resurrection of the dead, and of the establishment of the Divine Kingdom upon the earth.

On Passover night, at the celebration of the Feast of Freedom, the Jews invite Elijah to their homes, thereby indicating their implicit faith that some day the Almighty will send down this immortal prophet to announce their deliverance from the hands of the modern Pharaohs. This also gave rise to the custom of opening the door during some stage of the *seder* service, in order that the long-expected messenger, proclaiming the final redemption of mankind from oppression, might enter the house as a most welcome guest.

THE SEDER PLATTER. There is placed before the person conducting the *seder* ceremony, a large platter on which are to be found the following *seder* symbols: three whole *matzot,* each wrapped separately in a special cover or napkin, to represent the three divisions of Israel—priests, levites and laymen; a roasted shank bone, placed on the right, symbolizing the paschal lamb which was offered when the Temple was in existence; on the left, a roasted egg, which represents the freewill offering, *haggigah,* which was presented on each day of the Feast during the existence of the Temple in Jerusalem; in the center, bitter herbs (horse-radish), symbolic of the bitterness of the Egyptian bondage; underneath the shank bone, a dish of *haroset,* a paste-like mixture of nuts, apples, cinnamon, and raisins, finely chopped and mixed with wine, which in appearance resembles mortar, symbolic of the hard construction labor of the Jews in Egypt; and parsley or watercress placed underneath the egg. In addition, parsley, watercress, lettuce, or boiled potatoes and a dish of salt water are set upon the table for the whole company.

A POSITION OF FREEDOM. An improvised couch, generally consisting of a few cushions placed on the left side of an armchair, is provided for the person conducting the *seder* ceremony.

According to the Oriental custom, the position assumed by freemen is one of reclining on the left side while eating. As a sign of freedom from the Egyptian bondage, it is customary for the person conducting the ceremonies to follow this precedent of the Orient.

SANCTIFICATION (KIDDUSH). All these preparations having been made, the men depart for the synagogue for the *maarib* (evening) service. On the first two nights of Passover, the *kiddush* is not chanted by the *hazan* (cantor) during the evening service, because persons who have no families must be given the opportunity to participate in the *seder* ceremonies. At the conclusion of the services, greetings are exchanged either in Yiddish, *gut yom tov* (happy holiday), and the response is, *gut yom tov, gut yohr* (happy holiday, happy year); or in Hebrew, *hag sameah* (happy holiday). The mistress of the house, remaining home, symbolizes the joy which the Festival brings into the Jewish home, by lighting the Festival candles and pronouncing the necessary benedictions.

The men, on their return from the synagogue, greet the members of the house with a cheerful *gut yom tov,* or *hag sameah.* All goblets or wineglasses are then filled with wine— always a token of festivity among the Jews—and the master of the house recites over his wine the *kiddush,* the sanctification of the Festival. All participants then drink, but before doing so, they recite the benediction: "Blessed be Thou, O Lord our God, King of the universe, Creator of the fruit of the vine." Mead, unfermented raisin wine, or grape juice may be used instead of wine by the women, children, and all those who abstain from drinking fermented wine, after reciting the appropriate benediction.

PARSLEY DIPPED IN SALT WATER. The person conducting the ceremony, usually the master of the house, as priest of the occasion, washes his hands without saying the benediction generally recited upon hand-washing. All present then dip a piece of parsley, watercress, lettuce, or boiled potato in salt water to make it palatable, but before eating it, they say the benediction: "Blessed are Thou, O Lord our God, King of the universe, Creator of the fruit of the earth." This is a token of gratitude to God for the products of the soil.

THE APHIKOMAN. During the existence of the Temple in Jerusalem, the paschal lamb—the Passover sacrifice—was eaten at the close of the meal. After having partaken of the sacrificial meat, no other food might be eaten. When the offering of sacrifices ceased with the destruction of the Temple, a piece of *matzah* was eaten instead at the close of the meal. This piece of *matzah* was known as the *aphikoman,* the Greek word for *dessert.*

The master of the house takes the middle *matzah,* of the three wrapped in the folds of the cover, breaks it into two unequal parts, replaces the smaller part in the fold of the napkin, and hides the larger part to be distributed by him among the participants at the end of the meal as the *aphikoman.* For, no *seder* meal can be properly carried out, unless it is concluded with the eating of the *aphikoman.*

As the *seder* ceremonies are intended primarily to arouse the curiosity of the children, a charming custom developed, according to which the children steal the *aphikoman,* while the head of the family feigns not to notice the theft. When the time comes to distribute the *aphikoman,* the master of the house, not finding it in its place, offers a reward for its surrender, so that the *seder* meal may be properly ended. After some negotiations with the children's spokesman, he finally agrees to redeem the *aphikoman* by some gift; whereupon the children, happy with their victory, return the stolen *aphikoman.*

THE HAGGADAH. After breaking the middle *matzah,* all begin reciting the special services composed for the *seder* nights, contained in a book known as the *haggadah.* This little book opens with a very remarkable passage: "Let all who are hungry come and eat. Let all who are in want come and celebrate the Passover with us." This invitation to the hungry and the needy, offered at a time when the Jew feels free and full of hope, in the midst of his happy family, at a table full of good food and wine, again reflects the charitable character of the Jew.

THE FOUR QUESTIONS. The cups are refilled with wine, and the youngest person among the participants asks the four questions, as recorded in the *haggadah,* as to why and how the *seder* nights differ from all other nights of the year. The questions are directed to the master of the house, who responds to the four questions with words beginning: "Because we were Pharaoh's bondsmen in Egypt," and continuing with the narrative of Israel's deliverance from the Egyptian bondage. Then the services and the festive meal proceed as the *haggadah* provides.

FIRST TWO DAYS. On the first two days of Passover, no manual labor may be performed, and all Jews enjoy rest, peace, and happiness. Even cattle belonging to Jews must be allowed to rest on a Festival. Only food needed for human beings may be prepared and cooked. (See *Erub Tabshilin* page 40 above.)

At the *musaf* (additional) service at the synagogue, on the first day of Passover, we include a prayer for dew, called simply *tal* (dew). Jews in every part of the world pray that there be plenty of dew in Israel during the summer months, when there is no rain at all.

During the *maarib* service of the second day of Passover, we begin to count the *omer* (see *Omer,* page 130, and Sephirah Days, page 188), pronouncing the necessary benediction over it. If one neglected to count the *omer* at the synagogue, he may do so during the *seder* service at home.

The *seder* service in its entirety is repeated on the second night of Passover.

HOL HAMOED. The first two days of strict holiday are followed by four days of *hol hamoed,* semi-holidays, during which work may be performed.

It is customary to read the Song of Songs (*Shir hashirim,* one of the Biblical poetic books) in the synagogue, when one of the days of *hol hamoed* occurs on the Sabbath (if not, on the seventh day of Passover), before reading the portion of the Torah.

THE LAST TWO DAYS. On the seventh day, after the departure of the Jews from Egypt, Pharaoh gathered a mighty army with many horses and chariots, and pursued the Jews who were at the Red Sea. The Almighty then performed for the Jews the great miracle of dividing the Red Sea, through which they passed as if on dry land while the Egyptians and their horses and chariots were drowned in the Red Sea.

Therefore did the Almighty command that the Jews observe the seventh day of Passover as holy, and as a time at which no manner of work is to be performed. This rest day was extended to include the eighth day of Passover. (See page 45 above.)

On the eighth day of Passover, during the morning services at the synagogue, Memorial Services (*yizkor*) are held for the departed. If one is unable to attend the synagogue services, one may recite the Memorial Services at home.

In lands outside Israel, it is not permitted to partake of leavened food on the eighth day of Passover before the appearance of the stars.

II THE STORY OF PASSOVER

1. *The Egyptian Bondage*

When Jacob, the father of the twelve tribes, migrated from Canaan into Egypt, the whole Hebrew family numbered seventy souls, including Joseph and his family who had already been in Egypt. These Hebrews styled themselves "Sons of Israel," or "Israelites." This was to distinguish them from other kindred Hebrew tribes, who likewise were either the descendants of Abraham or of Isaac.

Egypt was then a great military power; its rule extended over a great part of Africa, and even reached Western Asia. It was the earliest civilized country that we know of. It was full of palaces, temples, and pyramids, the latter having been used as burial places for the kings. They had been built long before the Israelites came into Egypt, and they are still in existence today. There were also obelisks—tall columns, on which the Egyptians used to write their histories. The wise men of Egypt were familiar with many arts. But in spite of all this, their religion was chiefly the worship of animals, dead kings, and various images.

The Israelites settled in Goshen, a province of northern Egypt, which is irrigated and made fertile by a tributary of the Nile. There they lived the life of simple shepherds, observing the customs and speaking the language they had brought with them from Canaan. They remembered the teachings of their ancestors, and believed in one Supreme Being, the Creator of heaven and earth.

As the years passed, the children of Israel grew in numbers and became very powerful. Pharaoh, the king of Egypt, began to fear these foreigners and looked with suspicion upon them.

Pharaoh, therefore, said to his people: "Behold, the people of the children of Israel are too many and too mighty for us; come, let us deal wisely with them, lest, when any war befall us, they join our enemy, fight against us, and depart from our land. Let us crush the proud spirit of the Israelites by reducing them to slavery. We must fortify the cities of Pithom and Rameses (Tanis and Heliopolis), and make them strong enough to withstand the attack of the foe. Let a royal decree therefore go forth throughout the lands of Egypt and Goshen that all inhabitants, Egyptians as well as Israelites, must help build fortifications. Let them be forced to do hard labor for the benefit of the state, digging ditches, building store-cities and erecting giant obelisks, pyramids, and royal palaces. Let taskmasters be appointed at once to carry out the royal decree and see to it that the proud Israelites perform their daily tasks."

The councilors agreed with Pharaoh, and the royal decree immediately went forth that all able-bodied men be enlisted for work. Pharaoh himself set an example to his people. He took trowel and basket in hand, put a golden brick-mould on his neck, and went about among the people at work. The overseers, who had been appointed by Pharaoh to supervise the work, now urged the people to follow the king's example. "You see the king himself at work," they said. "Will you not follow his example?"

The Israelites went to work, and laid the moulds upon their necks, little suspecting the guile that was in the heart of Pharaoh and his councilors. During the day, the Israelites made a large number of bricks. At the close of the day, Pharaoh said to the overseers: "The number of bricks the Israelites have made this day must henceforth be their daily task. On no day shall they dare make less."

For a month the Egyptians worked together with the Israelites, and the Israelites were paid their regular wages. Then, little by little, the Egyptians were withdrawn until finally only the Israelites remained. But now they received no wages at all, and were reduced to slavery. The Israelites were also sent as slaves to plough the fields, prune the fruit trees and do menial labor in the homes of the Egyptians.

Harsh and cruel men were appointed as their overseers. An Israelite daring to ask for wages, or fainting under his heavy burden, was either severely beaten by the overseers or put in the stocks. The Israelites were kept at work without rest from early dawn till late at night. At the end of the day, they were not even permitted to go home to their wives and children, but were forced to sleep in the open fields, upon the bare ground.

But the more the Egyptians tried to crush the spirit of the Israelites and to diminish their numbers, the more they multiplied, and the more they were sustained by faith in their God, the God of Abraham, Isaac and Jacob. A voice descended from heaven saying: "I promised their father Abraham that I would make his children as numerous as the stars in heaven, and you, O wicked Pharaoh, contrive to prevent them from multiplying, by reducing them to slavery. We shall see whose words shall stand, Mine or yours."

While the men of Israel lay exhausted in the fields after their day's work, their faithful wives made every effort to relieve and strengthen them. Daily they would hasten to the spring to bring cold water for their men to drink, and, by the grace of the All-merciful, each time they would draw up their pitchers from the spring, they would find them filled, half with water and half with fish. The women would then prepare the fish, and whatever other food they could find, and bring it to their husbands in the field. They would go there in the dark of night so as not to be seen by the Egyptian overseers, and would encourage the men with cheerful words of consolation, soothing their weary hearts, and giving them fresh hope and energy to carry on.

2. *The Pious Midwives*

In the many years that the children of Israel spent in slavery, in spite of their hardships, their numbers and their might increased. The Egyptian councilors, seeing that their plot was doomed to failure, complained to Pharaoh. "Sire," they asked, "what advice can you give us concerning them?" He replied: "I can think of no new tortures for the Israelites; let us hear what you, wise men, would have me do."

Balaam, the son of Beor, one of the king's councilors, then spoke to Pharaoh: "It is well, indeed, that the king has put heavy tasks upon the Israelites and reduced them to slavery; but that alone is not enough. It is necessary that their number be lessened, that they may not overwhelm us by the sheer weight of number and drive us from the land. Therefore let the king give orders to the Hebrew midwives to kill every male child that shall be born to the Hebrews, sparing only the lives of the female children."

Balaam's advice pleased the king well. He summoned at once the Hebrew midwives, Jochebed and her daughter Miriam, and commanded them to slay all the male children being born to the Hebrews, but to allow their daughters to live.

Miriam was then but a mere child; nevertheless she was of great assistance to her mother in caring for the women and their babies. Mother and daughter showed the utmost kindness to the newborn babies; they would wash them, say pretty things to them, and strengthen the weakened mothers with cordials and tonics. As a result of the patient care taken by these kind nurses, no child came into the world lame or blind or with any other bodily defect. The Jewish people named the mother *Shiphrah* (soother or beautifier), and the daughter *Puah* (the helper).

When the brave little Miriam now heard Pharaoh's wicked decree, she exclaimed: "Woe to him! for God will punish him for his cruelty." Pharaoh grew angry, and he ordered the executioner to behead her at once; but the mother fell on her knees and implored the king's pardon, saying: "O sire, pray forgive her; she is only a foolish little girl."

The heart of the stern ruler was softened, and, assuming a gentler tone, he explained to the midwives that the female children were to be spared, and that male children were to be quietly put to death, without the knowledge of the mothers. "Now," continued the king, "you hear my command; if you fail to obey my wishes, you shall be cast into a furnace of fire."

But the pious midwives feared God, and disobeying Pharaoh's command, they let the male children live. The king sent for them, and demanded: "Why have you acted against my will?" The midwives said to Pharaoh: "Sire, the Hebrew women are not like the Egyptian women; for they give birth before the midwife comes to them."

For their bravery and kindness, God dealt well with the

midwives. To Jochebed the great leader Moses was born,
and from Miriam's union with Caleb sprang forth the royal
house of David.

3. *A Bad Dream*

Five years had passed since Pharaoh had issued his last
decree to the Jewish midwives, when one night Pharaoh dreamt
that, as he sat on his lofty throne, a godly old man stood
before him, holding a pair of scales in his hand. The old man
bound together all the nobles, elders, and great men of Egypt,
and put them on one scale of the balance. On the other scale
he put a suckling child, and the child outweighed them all.

Pharaoh, startled by the strange dream, awoke early in the
morning, and at once summoned his three favorite councilors,
Jethro, Job, and Balaam. "Hearken to my dream," said the
king to them, "and tell me its meaning."

Thereupon Balaam said: "O king, may you live forever. The
dream signifies that a child will be born among the Hebrews,
who shall bring destruction to our people and to our land. He
will lead the Hebrews with a strong hand out of the land of
Egypt, and before him all nations will tremble. Take heed therefore, most powerful king, for grave danger threatens you and
all your people."

"What can be done?" exclaimed Pharaoh in dismay. "All
that we have devised against this people has failed. How then
can we weaken them and reduce their numbers?"

"Let the king suffer me to give counsel," said Jethro.

"Speak, you have my permission," Pharaoh replied.

"May the king's days be multiplied," began Jethro. "This
is my counsel: The people you plot against are a great people.
God chose them in the days of old from amongst all nations
of the earth, and He is their protector and shield. All who
resist them are doomed to destruction; all who favor them,
prosper. Therefore, O king, hearken to my words, lighten their
task, and extend to them your favor."

The haughty Egyptian ruler was enraged at Jethro, and ordered that he be driven from the land. Thereupon Jethro fled from Egypt and settled in the land of Midian.

The king turned to Job and said: "Job of Uz, give us your counsel and opinion."

"O mighty ruler," pleaded Job, "I am unable to give counsel in this matter; I am at a loss and know not what to say."

Then Balaam rose again and spoke: "Great king, all your attempts against the Hebrews have failed, and the Hebrews continue to thrive. My advice therefore is that all their new-born sons be drowned in the Nile, so that the leader who threatens your safety and the safety of the land may be done away with at birth."

"This pleases me well," said Pharaoh, and he at once appointed Egyptian nurses to take care of the Hebrew women. He threatened with death any who dared disobey his decree. He charged, too, all his people, saying: "Every son that is born to the Hebrews shall you cast into the river."

The Hebrew women thereupon ceased calling for the nurses, and concealed their newborn children. Pharaoh sent officers in the land of Goshen, where the Hebrews dwelt, to search out the hidden babies to drown them.

Fearing the king's officers, the Hebrew women, who were about to give birth, would go out into the field, and sit down under the shade of an apple tree. God in His mercy would then cause a deep sleep to fall upon the suffering woman, during which she gave birth. On awakening, the unhappy mother, dreading the king's penalty, would abandon the child —if it were a son—in the field and return home, exclaiming: "O most Merciful One! into your hands I have committed my child." God would then send down His angels, who washed and dressed the babe, smeared his body with ointments, and stretched his limbs. Then they put two smooth pebbles into his little hands, from one of which he sucked milk, and from the other honey. God also caused the hair of the babes to grow long, down to their knees, and this served as clothes to protect them from heat and cold.

When, at last, the Egyptian officers became aware of these things, they prepared to slay all the children who were in the fields. "Open thy mouth," said the Almighty to the earth, "and protect my innocent children." Immediately the earth opened and received the babies into a large cave where they were sheltered until they grew up. They were fed butter and honey by angel hands, and they grew strong and healthy.

The Egyptians brought oxen and ploughed the fields, in the hope of destroying the vanished infants, but their efforts were in vain; they were unable to harm them. When the babies grew up, the earth would open its mouth and vomit forth the children, who thus sprang forth from the soil like beautiful flowers, and were guided home in safety, unseen by the Egyptians.

4. A Great Leader Is Born

A man from the tribe of Levi, named Amram, took to him as wife a maiden named Jochebed, a daughter of Levi. The woman bore a daughter who was named Miriam, which in Hebrew means "bitterness," for it was at the time of her birth that the Egyptians began to embitter the lives of the Hebrews. These were the same mother and daughter, the pious midwives, who risked their lives to save the Hebrew children. Five years later, Jochebed bore Amram a son whom he named Aaron.

One day the spirit of prophecy came upon little Miriam, and she announced: "My father and mother will soon have another son, who shall deliver Israel from the hands of the Egyptians." And after six months, Jochebed gave birth to another son. At his birth the house was filled with light like the brightness of sunshine. Amram kissed his daughter Miriam on the forehead and said: "Daughter, I know now your prophecy was true."

The mother's anxiety for her newborn son increased daily

as she noted his beauty, for he was like an angel of God in size and noble appearance. She hid the baby for three months, but longer than that she could not, for she knew that the Egyptian officers were watching her, and that should the child be discovered, she and her husband would lose their lives. She fashioned a basket of bulrushes, coated it with pitch, and lined it with clay, that the smell of the pitch might not irritate her little one whom she then placed in the basket. She put the basket in the flags by the river's br'nk. Amram, forced to expose the child to danger, struck Miriam a blow upon the head, saying bitterly: "Now, daughter, where is your prophecy?"

Miriam stood at a distance and with her eyes anxiously followed the basket as it floated in and out among the reeds; and she wondered whether her prophecy would come true.

At that moment the angels surrounded the throne of the Divine Justice and complained: "Lord of the world, shall this wonderful child perish this day by water?"

"You know that I behold all things," replied the Almighty. "This child shall not perish by water, for he is destined, at the head of My people, to chant the great song of deliverance from water. They that seek to find salvation in their own evil ways, shall find destruction, but they that trust in Me shall never be confounded. The history of this child shall be witness to My almighty power."

The king of Egypt had an only daughter whom he dearly loved, the beautiful princess Thermutis. Although she had been married for some time, she was childless, a fact that troubled the princess and her royal father, for they desired a son who might succeed the king to the throne of Egypt.

At the time the wonder-baby was abandoned by his parents, the Almighty caused the weather to become unbearably hot, and among those who suffered from its effects was Princess Thermutis, who went to seek relief by bathing in the water of the Nile. On reaching the bathing place, she noticed the little basket floating among the bulrushes on the surface of the

water, and sent one of her maids to swim out and bring it to
her. But the princess, in her great anxiety to know what the
little basket contained, could not wait until the maid delivered
it into her hands, but reached forth and opened it. She was
astonished to behold the face of a child that shone with a
splendor like that of the sun. She gazed at the babe with wonder
and admired its beauty.

The maids, noticing that the princess took a liking to the
baby, protested and said: "Beloved princess, this is one of the
Hebrew children who were cast into the river according to the
command of your royal father. It happens at times that a king's
decree goes unheeded; yet it should be observed at least by his
own children and members of the family. Surely it behooves
not the princess to oppose the order of her father and to act
against his will."

The maidens had scarcely spoken these words when they
vanished from the face of the earth. The angel Gabriel had
come down from heaven and had caused them all to sink into
the bowels of the earth, save her who swam for the basket.
Just as the princess was about to return the baby to the water
to abandon it to its fate, Gabriel gently struck the child on the
ear, and it began to weep; and the princess, touched by the
weeping of the helpless infant, decided to save it from death.

The princess sent at once for an Egyptian nurse, but the infant would not suckle at her breast. She called for other
Egyptian women, but still the child would not drink. For the
Almighty said: "Let the good mother who took tender care of
so many little children, be now rewarded and have her own
child restored to her."

Then Miriam, the babe's sister, came to the princess and
said: "Noble lady, vain are all your attempts to give the child
the breast from one of a different people. If you would have
a Hebrew woman, then let me fetch one, and the child will
suck at once."

Miriam's advice pleased the princess. "Go," she said, "and seek me a Hebrew mother to nurse the child."

With winged steps Miriam hastened home and brought her own mother to the princess. The baby readily took nourishment from Jochebed and ceased to cry. Princess Thermutis said to her: "Take this child away, and nurse it for me, and I will pay your wages."

5. *Moses Becomes "Heavy of Speech"*

For two years the child remained with its happy parents, and after that Jochebed weaned him, and brought him to the king's daughter. Charmed with the child's great beauty and unusual intelligence, Princess Thermutis adopted him as her son. She called him Moses, because she *drew him out of the water*. Thereupon a voice from heaven was heard crying: "Daughter of Pharaoh! because you have had compassion on this little child and have called him your son, therefore do I call you *Bithia* (the daughter of God). The foundling whom you cherish shall be called by the name you gave him—Moses —and by no other name shall he be known, withersoever his fame shall spread under the whole heaven."

When Moses was three years old, Bithia led him into the palace of her royal father Pharaoh. The queen sat by the king, and Balaam, the son of Beor, with his two sons, and all the princes of the realm were sitting at the table in the king's presence. The princess presented the child to the king, and said: "Oh, father! this child of noble appearance is not really my son; he was given to me in wondrous fashion by the divine river Nile; therefore have I brought him up as my son, and destined him to succeed you on your throne since no child of my own has been granted to me." With these words Bithia laid the child in the king's arms. The king, impressed with the child's beauty, pressed him to his heart and kissed him.

But the joy of the royal family was soon disturbed. The infant took the crown from off the head of the king and playfully placed it on his own head. All present were terrified. They thought that this act was an omen that evil would come to the king through this strange child that was before him.

Balaam, the son of Beor, now spoke: "My lord and king! you well remember the dream of the old man holding the scale, and the interpretation given by your servant. This child is of Hebrew extraction, and is wiser and more cunning than befits his age. Let not the king think that, being a mere child, he took the crown unknowingly. His act is a sign that when he grows older he will take the crown from your head and put it on his own. He will take from you your kingdom, and will either destroy or enslave your people. My advice therefore, O king, is that you kill him before he grows up to become a menace to you and your country."

"We will take other counsel," said Pharaoh, "before we decide the fate of this child."

The king at once called for all the wise men of the land, and the angel Gabriel, in the form of an old man, appeared with the councillors. Some advised that the child be burnt with fire, and others that he be slain with the sword. Then Gabriel spoke up and said: "Let no innocent blood be shed. The child is too young to know what he is doing. O king, let his understanding be tested in this wise, before you put him to death: Let a bowl of live coal and a bowl of glittering precious stones be placed before him. If he takes the stones, then he has understanding and discerns between good and evil; but if he stretches his hand toward the burning coal, then we shall know that he is innocent and that he took the crown without any purpose or design."

The king was well pleased with the advice, and he ordered his servants to do as the old man suggested. When the bowls were placed before Moses, he was about to thrust his hand out towards the glittering jewels. But the angel Gabriel, who had now made himself invisible, caught his hand and directed it toward the red hot coals. The live coal which he snatched burned his fingers and he touched his mouth with it, thus burning part of his lips and part of his tongue; and this explains why Moses said, in after days: "I am slow of lips and slow of tongue."

Pharaoh and his councillors were now convinced of the innocence of the child, and Princess Bithia was permitted to take him from the king's presence, and bring him up in her own palace.

6. *The Flight of Moses*

Although Moses was acknowledged as the grandson of Pharaoh, and as heir to the crown, he cared little for his greatness. He visited Jochebed very often, and from her he learned who were his true people, and who were his real parents. He visited his brethren in Goshen almost daily. He saw their terrible oppression, and heard them groan under their heavy burdens. But the young prince was helpless, and he cried out: "Alas! I had rather die than continue to behold the cruel oppression of my brothers."

Moses sought to ease their lot by shouldering part of their burden and toil. He took the excessive loads from the women and the old men, and gave them to the young and the strong to carry. By doing this, Moses not only gave relief to the weak, but he gained favor with Pharaoh, who thought he was merely trying to get work done more efficiently. Moses also lightened the suffering of the people by speaking to them encouraging words: "Be of good cheer, relief is not so far off as you think— calm follows the storm, blue skies succeed black clouds, sunshine comes after rain."

And a heavenly voice was then heard, saying: "Moses, because you have dismissed all thought of high position at the king's court, and have cast your lot with the suffering children of Israel, whom you treat as your brethren, therefore will I, too, lay aside all heavenly and earthly affairs and converse with you only."

One day Moses said to Pharaoh: "Sire, I have a petition to lay before you."

"Speak on, my son," Pharaoh replied.

Then Moses spoke: "It is known that if a slave is not given rest at least one day a week, he will soon die from overwork. Now the children of Israel are given no day of rest. Their work therefore is slow and unsatisfactory, and in time to come they will all perish from overwork. Give them rest one day in the week to renew their strength, and you shall have better work done and save the lives of the much-needed slaves."

Pharaoh was impressed by the argument of Moses, and he asked: "Which day shall be given them?"

"Suffer them to rest on the seventh day of the week," said Moses.

The king consented, and a royal decree was published throughout Egypt and Goshen: "To the sons of Israel! Thus says the king: 'Do your work in six days, but on the seventh day of each week you shall rest; on this day you shall do no labor. Thus shall you do at all times, according to the command of the king and of Moses, the son of Princess Thermutis.'"

Then there was great rejoicing in the land of Goshen. The day appointed by Moses as the day of rest was Saturday, later ordained by God to the Israelites as the Sabbath day.

One day Moses saw an Egyptian overseer smite a Hebrew. He looked about him, and seeing no one, he slew the Egyptian, and buried him in the sand. Moses had used no deadly weapon; he had simply pronounced the Name of God, and the Egyptian had fallen dead.

The next day he beheld two Hebrews fighting one another. They were Dathan and Abiram of the tribe of Benjamin. When Moses saw Dathan raise his hand to smite Abiram, he stayed his hand and said: "Wicked man, why do you strike your comrade? It is evil for men to lay violent hands on one another."

"Beardless young man," said Dathan boldly, "who has ap-

pointed you ruler and judge over us? We know well that you
are the son of Jochebed, although people call you the son of
Princess Bithia. Will you slay us as you slew the Egyptian yesterday, by pronouncing the Name of God?"

Dathan and Abiram then went before Pharaoh and told him
that Moses had slain an Egyptian taskmaster. The king grew
furious, and exclaimed: "Enough evil has been prophesied of
him, and I did not heed it, and now he lifts his hand against
my servants!" And Pharaoh ordered the arrest of Moses, and he
was condemned to death by the sword.

Now Moses was brought forth to be executed. He ascended
the scaffold, and the executioner stood over him with the sword.

The angels then presented themselves before God, and said:
"Master of the universe! Moses is in peril."

"I will take up his cause," God replied.

"But," the angels urged, "his death sentence has been pronounced; nay, they have led him to the place of execution, and
the executioner is now standing over him with his sword."

"I will take up his cause," was again God's reply.

When Pharaoh gave the word, the executioner mightily
smote Moses' outstretched neck with his sharp sword. But the
Lord made his neck as hard as ivory. Ten times did the executioner smite, and each time the sword proved harmless.

Thereupon the angel Michael, in the guise of the executioner,
grasped the sword in his hand. He instantly gave the executioner the appearance of Moses and cut his head off. Meanwhile Moses fled unobserved, and went to the land of Midian.

7. *The Wonderful Rod*

Upon arriving in Midian, Moses sat down beside a well, to
which the seven daughters of Reuel the priest of Midian, came
to draw water and fill the troughs to water their father's flock.

Reuel, the priest of Midian, was no other than Jethro, who,
after taking flight from Egypt, had settled in Midian. There
the people advanced him to the position of priest and prince

over the whole tribe. But as time passed, Jethro grew more and more convinced that the idols he and his people worshipped were vain and useless, and he began to believe in one true God in heaven.

One day he called together the people of his tribe, and said to them: "Lo, I have grown old and am unable to perform the duties of a priest before your gods. Choose therefore whomever you will to succeed me."

After some time the Midianites learned the truth, that Jethro had given up the priesthood because he despised their gods, and they placed him under a ban, that none might give him food or drink, or perform any service for him. Thus it came about that all Jethro's shepherds and servants had forsaken him, and he was unable to obtain even the slightest help from the sons of the tribe. His seven daughters were therefore compelled to pasture and water the flock themselves.

The seven maidens had on that day gone early to the well, for they knew that the shepherds would molest them on account of the ban, and would even deny them water from the well. Finding no shepherds there, they lowered their pitchers one by one, and with much trouble filled the troughs. Suddenly the shepherds came up, drove the maidens away, and led their own sheep to the troughs the maidens had filled.

Moses rebuked the shepherds for their injustice, and saved the maidens from their hands. He lowered his own pitcher, and the water from within the well leaped up and overflowed. He first let the maidens' flocks drink, and then he watered the flocks of all the shepherds, lest more ill-feeling should arise among them.

It was the same well at which Jacob had met Rachel, the well that God had created at the beginning of the world, the opening of which He made in the twilight of the first Sabbath-eve.

The seven maidens went home, and Moses secretly followed them until they reached their destination, so that no mischief might befall them at the hands of the shepherds, and then he returned to the well.

When the maidens came to Jethro their father, he said: "How is it that you are come so soon today?" And they said: "An Egyptian delivered us from the shepherds, and moreover he drew water for us, and watered the flock." Jethro said "Where is he? Why is it that you have left the man? Call him that he may eat bread."

Moses was content to stay with Jethro. Zipporah, one of Jethro's seven daughters, was as beautiful as the morning star. Brave princes from many lands had come to Jethro to ask for her hand.

In Jethro's garden there grew a wonderful rod—the rod which the Holy One, praised be He, created in the twilight of the first Sabbath eve, and which he gave to Adam. Adam had given it to Enoch; from him it descended to Noah, then to Shem, then to Abraham, then to Isaac, and finally to Jacob, who brought it to Egypt and gave it to his son Joseph. Upon the death of Joseph, his house was pillaged by the Egyptians, and the rod was taken with other loot into the palace of Pharaoh. At that time Jethro was at the head of Pharaoh's sacred castes, and as such he had an opportunity to see the rod on which were engraved the Ineffable Name, and the ten plagues which God would one day visit upon the Egyptians. Jethro stole the rod, and for many years it remained in his house. One day, as he was walking in his garden carrying the rod, he stuck it into the ground. When he tried to remove it, he found that it had sprouted and put forth blossoms; and he was unable to pull it from the ground. "Now," said Jethro to those who came to ask for the hand of his daughter Zipporah, "he who can pluck this staff from the ground, shall take my daughter as his wife."

The valiant chiefs of Edom and Moab came and tried, but failed; they could not budge the staff.

One day Moses, on passing through the garden, noticed the wonderful rod in the ground. He walked over and drew it from the earth. When Jethro returned to the garden, he found Moses holding the staff in his hand, whereupon Jethro cried out: "This is the man called by God to be prince and a great man among the Hebrews, who is to become famous throughout the world." And he gave him his daughter Zipporah for a wife. She bore him a son whom he called Gershom; for he said: "I have been a stranger in a strange land."

8. *Pharaoh's End*

And it came to pass that God punished the wicked Pharaoh for his cruelty and visited him with a leprosy that covered his entire body, from the crown of his head to the soles of his feet. The king summoned all his magicians and wise men of the land, and commanded them: "Advise me how I may be cured of this terrible malady."

"You can regain your health, O king," said his advisers, "only by bathing in human blood."

Pharaoh accordingly had his officers snatch Hebrew babes from their mothers, and slaughtered them, and in their blood he bathed himself. Every day, during the ten years that the king suffered from leprosy, an Israelitish child was killed. But it was in vain. At the end of ten years his leprosy changed to boils, and he suffered more than ever.

Now, two of the king's officers came and reported to the king: "The children of Israel are idle in their labor, and do not carry out the king's orders." The report angered the king greatly, and he exclaimed: "Now that I am ill they disregard my orders. Harness my chariot and lead me to Goshen, and I will punish these base slaves for their disobedience."

The king was put upon a chariot, and he set out for Goshen, accompanied by many chariots and horsemen. When he and his men reached the border of Goshen, the king's steed entered a narrow passage where it suddenly took fright, slipped, and fell. The chariot overturned and fell upon Pharaoh, and the horse, too, fell upon him. The king's sore flesh was torn and bruised, and he cried out in agony. His servants put him on their shoulders and carried him back to Egypt.

For three years the cruel king suffered horribly, dying at last in shame and disgrace. But his successor, the new ruler, surpassed him in cruelty and wickedness. If, for some reason, an Israelite was unable to make the required amount of bricks, his house was entered by the overseers, his children were taken from their mother by force and mortared into the building in place of the missing bricks. At times they would even force fathers to put their own babies into the walls. The father would place his own child on the rising wall and cover him with mortar and bricks. The father's tears would run down upon the child, while the child, being buried alive, would weep and cry bitterly, but there was no one to heed his cries.

The groans and the sighs of the unfortunate parents, and the bitter cries of the dying children reached heaven, "and God heard their groaning, and He remembered His covenant with Abraham, with Isaac, and with Jacob."

9. *The Mission of Moses*

Moses tended the flock of Jethro his father-in-law with great care, choosing always an open meadow as his pasturing place, to prevent the sheep from grazing in private fields and from doing harm to the property of others.

One day, while Moses was tending his flock in a dry field, he saw that one of the lambs had left the flock and was trying to escape. Moses pursued it, but the lamb ran so much the faster, and fled through valley and over hill, till it reached a mountain stream; then it halted and drank.

Moses now came up to it, looked at it with troubled countenance, and said: "My dear little friend! Then it was thirst that made you run so far and seem to flee from me; and I knew it not! Poor little creature, how tired you must be!"

When the little lamb was through drinking, Moses took it up, placed it upon his shoulder, and carried it back to the flock.

While Moses was carrying the lamb, there came a voice from heaven: "You, who have shown such great love, such great patience toward sheep, are surely worthy to be called upon to shepherd My people, the children of Israel."

Another day Moses led the flock to the farthest end of the wilderness, and came to the mountain of God, to Horeb. The angel of the Lord appeared to him in a flame of fire out of the midst of a bush. Moses looked, and, behold, the bush burned with fire, and yet the bush was not consumed. Moses said: "I will turn aside now, and see this great sight, why the bush is not burnt." As Moses approached, the Lord called to him out of the midst of the bush, saying: "Moses, Moses," and Moses answered: "Here I am." And He said: "Draw not nigh hither; put off your shoes from your feet, for the place whereon you stand is holy ground." The voice continued: "I am the God of your father, the God of Abraham, the God of Isaac, and the God of Jacob." Moses hid his face, for he was afraid to look upon the Divine Apparition. And God said: "Moses, because you are humble and think you are not worthy to look upon the Divine Apparition, therefore shall you stay with Me in heaven forty days and forty nights; you shall behold the Divine Presence, and your face shall send forth beams resembling the rays of the sun, so that people shall fear to approach you."

And God spoke again: "I have surely seen the affliction of My people that are in Egypt, and have heard their cry by reason of their taskmasters; for I know their pain; and I am come down to deliver them out of the hand of the Egyptians, and to bring them up out of that land to a good and large land, to a land flowing with milk and honey, to the place of the Canaanite, the Hittite, the Amorite, the Perizzite, the Hivite and the Jebusite. Now, behold, the cry of the children of Israel is come to Me; moreover I have seen the oppression wherewith the Egyptians oppress them. Come now therefore, and I will send you to Pharaoh, that you may bring forth My people the children of Israel out of Egypt."

Moses asked: "Who am I, that I should go to Pharaoh, and that I should bring forth the children of Israel out of Egypt? And were it possible for me to bring the children of Israel out of Egypt, how can I provide this great people with food and drink in the wilderness? How shall I be able to provide the sick, the children, and the babies with their needs?"

And God answered: "Certainly I will be with you; and this shall be a token to you that I have sent you: when you have brought forth the people out of Egypt, you shall serve God upon this Mountain."

"Behold," said Moses, "when I come to the children of Israel, and shall say to them: 'The God of your fathers has sent me to you'; and they shall say to me: 'What is His name?' what shall I say to them?"

"I am that I am," said the Lord. "I am known by My acts; when I judge My creatures, I am called Elohim, 'Judge'; when I rise to battle against the sinners, I am Lord Zebaot, 'the Lord of Hosts'; when I wield My might and power, My name is El Shaddai, 'Almighty God'; and when I bestow My mercy upon the world, I am Adonai, 'Lord.' But to the children of Israel shall you say: 'I am He that was, that is, and that ever shall be; I am He that is with them in their present bondage, and He that shall be with them in their future bondage.' "

"But the life of Israel is now full of suffering and sorrow," protested Moses; "why bring them tidings of future sufferings?"

God said: "Thus shall you say to the children of Israel: 'I AM sent me to you.' I am the One that redeems them from their present bondage. And tell them further that at My will an angel can stretch out his wings from heaven and touch the earth, and at My will three angels can find room under one tree; at times My majesty can fill the whole world, and at others, when I will it otherwise, I speak from a bush."

10. *Moses Punished*

Moses hesitated to accept God's mission, and he began to argue in a new vein, saying: "The people will not believe me, nor hearken to my voice; for they will say: "The Lord has not appeared to you."

The Lord said to him: "What is in your hand?"

Moses replied: "A rod."

The Lord said: "Cast it on the ground."

Moses did as the Lord bade him, and the rod became a serpent; and he fled before it.

The Lord said to Moses: "Put forth your hand, and take it by the tail." Moses put forth his hand, and laid hold of it, and it became a rod in his hand.

This was the Almighty's way of showing Moses that he deserved punishment for having doubted the faith of His children, and that he had followed the example of the slanderous serpent that had persuaded Eve to eat the fruit of the tree of knowledge.

The Lord then said to Moses: "Put now your hand into your bosom." Moses put his hand into his bosom; and when he took it out, behold, his hand was leprous, as white as snow. The Lord said: "Put your hand back into your bosom." He put his hand back into his bosom; and when he took it out, behold, it was once again his natural flesh. And God said: "If they will not believe you, nor hearken to the voice of the first sign, they will believe the voice of the latter sign." Leprosy is the punishment for slander, and because Moses slandered the children of Israel, God caused his hand to become leprous.

Moses, however, was still unwilling to accept the mission and he began to plead his unfitness for the task. "O Lord, I am not a man of words; for I am slow of speech, and of slow tongue." And the Lord said to him: "Who has made man's mouth? Or who makes a man dumb, or deaf, or seeing, or blind? Is it not I the Lord? Now therefore go, and I will be with your mouth, and I will teach you what you shall speak."

Moses argued: "A grandchild is closer to a man than his nephew. Nevertheless when Lot was to be rescued from Sodom, you sent angels to his aid because he was Abraham's nephew.

But now, when the life of sixty myriads of Abraham's grand-children is at stake, you choose to send me, a mortal, and not the angels. When the Egyptian bondwoman Hagar was in distress, you sent five angels to stand by her, and to redeem sixty myriads of the grandchildren of Sarah you send me, one born of woman. O Lord, deliver them, I pray you, by the hand of him, the prophet whom you will send in days to come."

"Not to Israel, but to Pharaoh, do I send you," said God. "Him whom you mentioned I will send to Israel at the end of days; Elijah will appear to them before the great and terrible day."

Moses was not satisfied and he argued: "O Lord of the world, but my brother Aaron is older than I am, and he is accustomed to prophesy to Israel in your name and comfort the people in their distress. How then can I ignore the good work of my older brother and take upon myself to be the redeemer of Israel?"

God said: "Behold, Aaron your brother the Levite comes forth to meet you; and when he sees you he will be glad in his heart. You shall speak to him, and put the word in his mouth; and I will teach you what you shall do. He shall be the spokesman to the people, and you shall be to him in God's stead. And you shall take in your hand the rod, wherewith you shall perform the signs. And because you have hesitated to accept My mission, you will lose the priesthood; for it was ordained by Me that you should be the priest and Aaron the Levite. But because you have refused to execute My will, you shall be the Levite and Aaron your brother shall be the priest."

11. Moses Meets Aaron

Moses now yielded and said: "O merciful God, I am ready to accept your mission. However, I cannot return to Egypt unless I first obtain the permission of my father-in-law Jethro, for he has been kind to me, and he has provided me with food and shelter."

God was pleased with this request, and He told Moses that he should first go to Midian and ask for permission to go to Egypt.

So Moses went to Jethro his father-in-law, and said to him: "Let me go, I pray you, and return to my brethren that are in Egypt, and see whether they are yet alive." And Jethro said to Moses: "Go in peace."

As Moses prepared to leave, the Lord said to him: "Have no fear to return into Egypt, for all the men are dead that sought your life." Moses took his wife and his sons, mounted them upon an ass, and holding the rod of God in his hand he set out for the land of Egypt.

And the Lord having said to Aaron who was in Egypt: "Go into the wilderness to meet Moses," Aaron went and met Moses in the mountain of God, and kissed him. Aaron then asked: "My brother, where have you spent all these years since you have left us?"

"In Midian," replied Moses.

"And who are these people with you?" asked Aaron.

"They are my wife and sons," said Moses.

"Where are you going with them?"

"To Egypt," replied Moses.

"What!" cried Aaron; "have we not sorrows enough on account of those already in Egypt, that you desire to take more into the land?"

Moses knew that Aaron was right, and he sent his wife and sons back to Jethro in Midian.

Moses now told Aaron all that the Lord had said to him, and all the signs with which he had charged him. And Moses and Aaron went and brought together all the elders of the children of Israel. And Aaron repeated to them all the words which the Lord had spoken to Moses, and performed the signs in the sight of the people.

At first the elders paid little heed. They knew that Jacob, before his death, had confided to Joseph the secret mark by

which the people would know him whom God had chosen as
their redeemer. Joseph had confided the secret to the brothers
who survived him, and Asher, the last of the twelve brothers
to die, had confided it to his daughter Serah, who was still
alive.

The elders betook themselves to Serah and said: "Mysterious
woman, a man named Moses has appeared, claiming to be the
one whom God has delegated to redeem His people from bondage. You are the only mortal alive possessing the secret mark
handed over by our father Jacob." Then they told her the exact
words of Moses. When she heard from them that Moses had
said in the name of God: "I have surely visited you, and seen
that which was done to you in Egypt," she exclaimed with great
joy: "Yes, this is the true redeemer; for these are the very words
by which the true redeemer was to announce the redemption
in the name of God."

Then the people believed; and when they heard that the Lord
had remembered the children of Israel, and that He had seen
their affliction, they bowed their heads and prayed.

Moses then invited the elders to go with him to Pharaoh.
But they lacked the courage to appear before the king. All had
started out together with Moses, but one by one they dropped
off stealthily on the way, until in the presence of Pharaoh
Moses and Aaron stood alone, deserted by all. This greatly displeased the Almighty, and He said: "When My beloved servant Moses shall ascend the Holy Mountain to receive the commandments, the elders shall not be permitted to ascend with
him. They shall accompany him on the way to Me only as far
as they have accompanied him on the way to Pharaoh, and they
shall have to wait for him until he descends."

12. *In Pharaoh's Palace*

It happened that the day that Moses and Aaron appeared
before the gates of Pharaoh's palace was the king's birthday.
Many kings from near and far had come to do him homage,

and to present him with costly crowns. When the attendants told the king that there were two old men at the gate of the palace seeking admission, the king asked: "Have these old men brought me crowns?"

"They have brought nought with them," was the reply.

"Then let them not be admitted," said the king.

The king's palace was surrounded by thousands of soldiers; seeing them, Moses and Aaron became frightened; but the angel Gabriel appeared and led them unobserved into the palace.

"Who admitted these men without my permission?" cried the king in great fury, and he ordered the guards to be punished, some by death and others by torture. Angrily he dismissed the two intruders. New guards were posted at the entrances, and, at each gate, two lions were chained that no man might enter the palace without the express permission of the king.

But the next day Moses and Aaron again entered the palace in spite of the guards and the lions. Moses merely raised his rod, and the lions leaped towards him joyfully, and followed him, barking like dogs.

"Who are you? and what is your wish?" asked the puzzled Pharaoh.

Moses and Aaron replied: "The Lord, the God of Israel says, 'Let My people go, that they may hold a feast to Me in the wilderness.' "

"What is the name of your God? Why did he not send me a crown on my birthday? Who is your God that I should hearken to his voice and let Israel go? I know not the Lord, and moreover I will not let Israel go."

As Pharaoh looked angrily at the messengers of God, he was suddenly stricken with awe; for before him he saw two men, tall as the cedars of Lebanon, their faces radiant like the sun, the pupils of their eyes shining like the morning star. His voice softened at once. "Wait until I fetch the books of chronicles in my archives, in which are recorded the names of the gods of all nations, and I will see whether or not the God of the Hebrews you speak of is recorded there."

The books were brought before the king, and the scribe read the long list of gods: the gods of Egypt, Midian, Ethiopia, Ziddon, Canaan, and so on until the list was exhausted. Pharaoh turned with scorn to Moses and Aaron: "Now, you see, there is no mention of your God in the chronicles."

"O king," said Moses, "you seek the living in the graves of the dead. Your chronicles contain the names of the gods that have no life, but our God is the God of life, the King of eternal life."

"Can you describe to me the God of whom you speak?" asked Pharaoh. "Is he young or old? How many countries has He under His dominion? How many battles has He fought? How many lands has He conquered? How many warriors does He lead forth to war?"

"The strength of our God and His power fills the whole world," replied Moses; "His voice calls forth flames of fire; His words shatter mountains. Heaven is His throne, and the earth His footstool; His arrows are flames, His spears torches, His shield clouds, and His word the lightning-flash. He has created the mountains and the valleys. He has brought forth spirits and souls; He suspended the earth by a word; He covers the heavens with clouds; at His word the rain and the dew descend; He causes plants to grow from the ground; He nourishes and sustains the whole world; he removes kings from power or causes them to ascend the throne."

"I have no need of your God," answered Pharaoh haughtily; "I have created myself and the river Nile, and there is no other god besides me in the land of Egypt." He then turned impatiently to them, saying: "Wherefore do you, Moses and Aaron, cause the people to break loose from their work? Get you under your burdens."

13. *Moses Complains*

The same day Pharaoh commanded the taskmasters of the people: "You shall no longer give the people straw to make bricks. Let them go and gather straw for themselves. And you shall diminish nothing from the amount of bricks, which they have made heretofore. Because they are idle, therefore they cry, saying, 'Let us go and sacrifice to our God.' Let heavier work be laid upon the men, and let them not heed lying words."

The taskmasters did as they were commanded, and the people were scattered throughout all the land of Egypt to gather straw. And the Israelite foremen, whom Pharaoh's taskmasters had set over the workmen, were beaten. "Why," they were asked, "have you not fulfilled your appointed task in making bricks both yesterday and today as heretofore?" Then the foremen came and cried to Pharaoh, saying: "Why deal you thus with your servants? They give us no straw, yet they say to us: 'Make bricks'; and, behold your servants are beaten, but the fault is in your own people and not in us." "You are idle," said Pharaoh, "you are idle; therefore you say: 'Let us go and sacrifice to the Lord.' Go therefore now and work; for though there shall be no straw given you, yet you shall diminish nought from your daily task."

So the children of Israel had to continue going out into the fields to pick straw, and when they failed to produce the required number of bricks, the Egyptian taskmasters ordered the elders of Israel to give them the names of those who were delinquent. Because the elders refused to give the names, they were severely beaten by the taskmasters. Then God spoke to the elders: "Because you were gentle and kind to My suffering children, therefore a day will come when will I cause My holy spirit to rest upon you, and you shall be honored and revered by all the people." This frightful period of Israel's agony lasted six months. Meanwhile Moses had gone to Midian, leaving

Aaron in Egypt, and when he returned he again went with
Aaron to Pharaoh.

The officers of the children of Israel met Moses and Aaron
as they came forth from Pharaoh's palace, and they said to
them: "The Lord look upon you, and judge; because you have
put a sword in the hand of Pharaoh and his servants to slay
us." Moses thereupon prayed: "Lord, why have you dealt ill
with this people? Why have you sent me? For since I came to
Pharaoh to speak in your name, he has dealt ill with this people; neither have you delivered your people.

"O Master of the world! The punishments meted out by you
to the generation of the Flood, to the generation of the Confusion of Tongues, and to the inhabitants of Sodom, were just.
But what have the children of Israel done, that they are oppressed more than any other people on the face of the earth? Is it
because Abraham said: 'Whereby shall I know that I shall in-
herit it,' for which you did rebuke him, saying: 'Know of a
surety that your seed shall be a stranger in a land that is not
theirs'? Why, then, are not the descendants of Esau and Ishmael
held in bondage, too? Are they not likewise the seed of Abraham? But if you will say: 'What concern is it of yours?' then
I ask you: 'Why have you sent me to Egypt as your messenger?'
For, behold, O Lord, Pharaoh dealt wickedly with the children
of Israel, and their redemption has not yet come."

The angel Shaftiel then went before the Almighty and said:
"Master of the world! Does it behoove your prophet to speak
thus? Does he not know that you are able to accomplish whatever seems good in your eyes? Certainly he deserves punishment
for having spoken thus."

"But he spoke thus to Me not on his own behalf," replied
the Almighty, "but out of compassion for the children of Israel:
therefore his unbecoming words shall be forgiven."

And the Lord said to Moses: "Now shall you see what I will
do to Pharaoh; for by a strong hand shall he let them go, and
by a strong hand shall he drive them out of the land."

14. *"The Strong Hand of God"*

God spoke to Moses: "I appeared to Abraham, to Isaac, and to Jacob, and I have established My covenant with them to give them the land of Canaan. Moreover I have heard the groaning of the children of Israel, whom the Egyptians keep in bondage; and I have remembered My covenant. Therefore go and say to the children of Israel: 'I will bring you out from under the burdens of the Egyptians, I will deliver you from their bondage, and I will redeem you with an outstretched arm and with great judgments. I will take you to Me for a people, and I will be a God to you. I will bring you into the land which I promised to give to Abraham, to Isaac, and to Jacob; and I will give it to you for a heritage; I am the Lord.' "

And Moses spoke to the children of Israel; but because of their cruel oppressors, they hearkened not to him.

The Lord then said to Moses: "Pharaoh's heart is stubborn; he refuses to let My people go. Go to Pharaoh in the morning, as he goes out to the water, and you shall stand by the river's brink to meet him. You shall say to him: 'The Lord, the God of the Hebrews, has sent me to you, saying: "Let My people go, that they may serve Me in the wilderness," and hitherto you have not hearkened. Behold, I will smite with the rod that is in my hand upon the waters of the river, and they shall be turned into blood. The fish in the river shall die, and the river shall become foul; and the Egyptians shall be loath to drink water from the river.' "

And the Lord said also to Moses: "Say unto Aaron: 'Take the rod, and stretch out your hand over the waters of Egypt, over their rivers, over their streams, over their pools, and over their ponds of water, that they may become blood, and there shall be blood throughout the land of Egypt, both in vessels of wood and in vessels of stone.' "

For three weeks Moses repeated God's warning of the plague of blood to Pharaoh and to the Egyptians, but they would not heed it. Then Moses gave his staff to Aaron who smote the waters of the river, in the sight of Pharaoh, and in the sight of his servants; and the river was turned to blood. The fish that were in it died; and it became foul, so that the Egyptians could not drink its water; and the blood flowed over the land of Egypt. The Egyptians dug around the river's banks for water to drink; but the new wells, too, contained nothing but blood.

The Egyptians then visited the land of Goshen where the Hebrews had plenty of good water to drink, but as soon as the Egyptians took the water into their cups, it turned to blood. They begged the children of Israel to take handfuls of water and allow them to drink from their hands, but no sooner did the water touch the lips of the Egyptians than it turned to blood. They asked the Hebrews to drink with them from the same bowl, but it was of no avail, for the water turned to blood in their mouths.

After seven days the Lord spoke again to Moses: "Go to Pharaoh, and say to him: 'If you refuse to let My people go, I will smite all your border with frogs. The river shall swarm with frogs, which shall go up and come into your house, and into your bed-chamber, and upon your bed, and into the houses of your servants, and upon your people, and into your ovens, and into your kneading-troughs.' "

But when Pharaoh paid no heed to Moses' warning, the Lord said to Moses: "Say to Aaron: 'Stretch forth your hand with your rod over the rivers, over the canals, and over the pools, and cause frogs to come upon the land of Egypt.' " Aaron stretched forth his hand over the waters of Egypt; and the frogs came and covered the land of Egypt. Then Pharaoh called for Moses and Aaron, and said: "Entreat the Lord, that He take away the frogs from me, and from my people; and I will let the people go, that they may sacrifice to the Lord." And Moses said: "When shall I entreat for you?" And he said: "Tomorrow." And Moses said: "Be it as you said; that you may know there is none like the Lord our God." Then Moses appealed to the Lord; the frogs vanished from the houses, the courts, and the fields. Pharaoh, seeing that there was relief, hardened his heart, and hearkened no longer to the Israelites.

The Lord said to Moses: "Tell Aaron to stretch out his hand, and smite the dust of the earth, that it may become gnats throughout all the land of Egypt." And Aaron obeyed the Lord, and there were gnats upon man and beast; for the dust of the earth had become gnats in the land of Egypt. The Egyptian magicians with their secret arts tried to bring forth gnats, but they could not. Then the magicians said to Pharaoh: "This is the finger of God." But Pharaoh's heart was hardened, and he would not heed them.

The Lord said to Moses: "Arise early in the morning, and stand before Pharaoh, as he comes forth to the Nile; and say to him: "Thus says the Lord: 'Let My people go, that they may serve Me. Else, I will send swarms of flies upon you, upon your people, and into your houses; the houses of the Egyptians shall be filled with swarms of flies, and also the ground whereon they live. But I will set apart the land of Goshen, in which My people dwell, that no swarms of flies be there; to the end that you may know that I am the Lord in the midst of the earth.' " The haughty Pharaoh ignored God's warning, and grievous swarms of flies entered the houses of Pharaoh and his servants; and the land of Egypt was ruined by them. Pharaoh sent for Moses and Aaron, and said: "I will let you go, that you may sacrifice to the Lord your God in the wilderness, provided that you go not far away. Entreat for me." Moses said: "Tomorrow I will entreat the Lord that the swarms of flies may depart from Pharaoh, from his servants, and from his people; but let not Pharaoh deal deceitfully with me again." Moses prayed to the Lord, and the Lord removed the swarms of flies, so that none remained. But Pharaoh hardened his heart again, and did not let the people go.

The Lord then said to Moses: "Go to Pharaoh, and tell him: 'Thus says the Lord, the God of the Hebrews: Let My people go that they may serve Me. For if you refuse to let them go, and will yet hold them, lo, the hand of the Lord is upon your cattle which are in the field, upon the horses, upon the asses, upon the camels, upon the herds, and upon the flock; there shall be a very grievous murrain. And the Lord shall make a division between the cattle of Israel and the cattle of Egypt; and there shall nothing die of all that belongs to the children of Israel.' " And the Lord appointed a set time, saying: "Tomorrow the Lord shall do this in the land." And so it came to pass, and all the cattle of the Egyptians died, but not that of the children of Israel. Nevertheless the heart of Pharaoh was stubborn, and he did not let the people go.

The Lord said to Moses and to Aaron: "Take handfuls of furnace soot, and let Moses throw them heavenward in the sight of Pharaoh. And it shall become small dust over all the land of Egypt, and boils with blains shall break forth upon man and upon beast, throughout the land of Egypt." And Moses and Aaron did as they were told. Boils with blains appeared upon every man and beast among the Egyptians. The magicians could not stand before Moses because of the boils. But the heart of Pharaoh was hardened, and he hearkened not.

The Lord said to Moses: "Rise up early in the morning, and stand before Pharaoh, and say to him: 'Thus says the Lord, the God of the Hebrews: Let my people go that they may serve Me. Surely now I had put forth My hand, and smitten you and your people with pestilence, and you had been cut off from the earth. But for this cause have I made you to live, to show you My power, and that My name may be declared throughout all the earth. Still you exalt yourself against My people, and will not let them go. Behold, tomorrow near this time I will cause a most grievous hail to fall, such as has not been in Egypt since the day it was founded. Now, therefore, gather, hasten in your cattle and all that you have in the field; for every man and beast that shall be found in the field, and shall not be brought home shall die by the hail that will come down upon them.' " Some feared the word of the Lord and brought their servants and their cattle into the house; others heeded not the word of the Lord and left both servants and cattle in the field.

The Lord said to Moses: "Stretch forth your hand toward heaven, that there may be hail in all the land of Egypt." And Moses stretched forth his hand toward heaven; and the Lord sent thunder and hail; and fire ran down the earth.

The hail smote man and beast and herb, and broke every tree of the field—everywhere but in the land of Goshen, where the children of Israel were. Pharaoh sent for Moses and Aaron, saying: "This time I have sinned; the Lord is righteous, and I and my people are wicked. Entreat the Lord, and let there be an end to these mighty thunderings and hail; and I will let you go, and you shall stay no longer." Moses said to him: "As soon as I am gone out of the city, I will spread forth my hand to the Lord; the thunders shall cease, neither shall there be any more hail; that you may know that the earth is the Lord's. But as for you and your servants, I know that you will not yet fear the Lord God." Moses went out of the city, and spread forth his hands to the Lord; and the thunder and hail ceased so suddenly that the hail that was already in the air remained suspended in space. Many years later part of the suspended hail fell upon the Amorites when Joshua engaged them in battle. When Pharaoh saw the rain, hail, and thunder cease, he hardened his heart once more, and he did not let the children of Israel go.

Now Moses and Aaron again addressed Pharaoh, repeating the words of the Lord: "Thus says the Lord, the God of the Hebrews: 'How long will you refuse to humble yourself before Me? Let My people go, that they may serve Me. Else, if you refuse to let My people go, behold, tomorrow will I bring locusts within your borders; and they shall cover the face of the earth, that one shall not be able to see the earth; and they shall eat every tree which grows for you out of the field; and your houses shall be filled with them, and the houses of all your servants, and the houses of all the Egyptians; such as neither your fathers nor your fathers' fathers have seen, since the day that they were upon the earth to this day.' " And they turned, and went out from Pharaoh.

Pharaoh's servants implored him: "Let them go, that they may serve the Lord their God; know you not yet that Egpyt is destroyed?"

And Pharaoh recalled Moses and Aaron, and he said to them: "Go, serve the Lord your God; but who are they that shall go?" And Moses answered: "We will go with our young and with our old, and with our sons and with our daughters, with our flocks and with our herds; for we must hold a feast unto our Lord." Angrily Pharaoh withdrew his consent and drove Moses and Aaron from the palace.

Then the Lord said to Moses: "Stretch out your hand over the land of Egypt that the locusts may come." Moses put forth his hand, and an east wind arose which swept across the land all that day and night; and the following morning, the east wind brought the locusts. The locusts covered the whole land, eating every herb and fruit which had not been destroyed by the hail; no green thing remained, neither tree nor herb, throughout all Egypt. Then Pharaoh called for Moses and Aaron, and he said: "I have sinned against the Lord your God, and against you. Now therefore I pray you forgive my sin only this once, and entreat the Lord your God to take away this death from me." Moses did as Pharaoh asked. And the Lord sent a strong west wind which carried the locusts into the Red Sea, so that not one remained in all Egypt. But Pharaoh's heart was hardened, and he did not let the children of Israel go.

The Lord said to Moses: "Stretch out your hand toward heaven, that there may be darkness over the land of Egypt, even darkness which may be felt." The plague of darkness was intended by the Almighty to punish not only the Egyptians, but also certain unworthy Israelites who had scorned God's message of redemption. These Israelites had said: "Here in the land of Egypt we have grown rich, and have plenty to eat and drink. Then why go in search of another land?" God therefore decided to punish those proud Israelites by not letting them leave the land of Egypt. But had He killed them in Egypt before the departure, the Egyptians would have said: "The Israelites, too, are visited with a plague; then it is not the God of the Hebrews that has punished us." For this reason God said: "Because you were well satisfied with your wealth and cared not for the suffering of your brethren, you shall die and be buried in Egypt, unperceived by the Egyptians, during the three days of darkness."

Moses stretched forth his hand toward heaven; and darkness pervaded the land of Egypt for three days. The Egyptians could not see one another; neither did any rise from his place for three days; but all the children of Israel had light in their dwellings. Pharaoh called to Moses and said: "Go you, serve the Lord; only let your flock and your herds remain; let your little ones also go with you." Moses said: "You must also give us sacrifices and burnt-offerings, that we may sacrifice to the Lord our God. Our cattle also shall go with us; not a hoof shall be left behind." But the heart of Pharaoh was hardened, and he would not let them go. Pharaoh said to Moses: "Get you from me, take heed to yourself, see my face no more; for in the day you see my face you shall die." Moses said: "You have spoken well; I shall never see your face again."

15.   *Freedom at Last*

The Lord said to Moses: "Yet one plague more will I bring upon Pharaoh and upon Egypt; afterward he will let you go. Speak now to the people, and let every man ask of his Egyptian neighbor, and every woman of her neighbor, jewels of silver and jewels of gold."

The Lord spoke again to Moses and Aaron, saying: "This month shall be to you the beginning of months; it shall be the first month of the year to you. Speak to the children of Israel, saying: In the tenth day of this month every man shall take a lamb, a lamb for a household; and if the household be too little for a lamb, then shall he and his neighbor next to his house take one according to the number of the souls. The lamb shall be without blemish, a male of the first year; you shall take it from the sheep, or from the goat; you shall keep it until the fourteenth day of the same month; and the whole assembly of the congregation of Israel shall kill it at dusk. They shall take the blood, and sprinkle it on the two side doorposts and on the lintel of the houses wherein they shall eat it. That night they shall eat the flesh, roasted with fire; with unleavened bread and bitter herbs they shall eat it. Eat not of it raw, nor sodden at all with water, but roasted with fire. You shall let nothing of it remain until the morning; but that which remains of it until the morning you shall burn with fire. And thus shall you eat it; with loins girded, your shoes on your feet, and your staff in your hand; and you shall eat it in haste. For I will go through the land of Egypt in that night, and I will smite all the firstborn, both man and beast. And the blood shall be to you for a token upon the houses where you are; and when I see the blood I will pass over you, and there shall no plague be upon you to destroy you, when I smite the land of Egypt. This day shall be unto you for a memorial, and you shall keep it a feast to the Lord, throughout your generations for ever. Seven days shall you eat unleavened bread; for whosoever eats leavened bread from the first day until the seventh day, shall be cut off from Israel. The first day and the seventh day shall be a holy day to you, no manner of work shall be done in them, save that which every man must eat; that alone may be done by you."

Moses summoned all the elders of Israel, and said to them: "Take you lambs according to your families, and kill the passover lamb. You shall take a bunch of hyssop, and dip it in the blood that is in the basin, and strike the lintel and the two side doorposts with the blood that is in the basin; and none of you shall go out of the door of his house until the morning. For the Lord will pass through to smite the Egyptians; and when He sees the blood upon the lintel and on the two side doorposts,

He will pass over the door, and will not suffer the destroyer to come into your houses to smite you." And the children of Israel did as the Lord had commanded Moses and Aaron.

It came to pass at midnight, that the Lord smote all the firstborn in the land of Egypt, from the firstborn of Pharaoh that sat on his throne to the firstborn of the captive that was in the dungeon; and all the firstborn of the cattle. Pharaoh and all his servants, and all the Egyptians rose up that night; and there was a great cry in Egypt; for there was not a house where there was not one dead. Pharaoh at once called for Moses and Aaron, and Princess Bithia, the foster-mother of Moses thus spoke to the ambassador of God: "Why have you brought all this evil upon my people and me?"

"Ten plagues did the Lord bring upon Egypt; did any of these plagues afflict you?" inquired Moses.

"None did any harm to me," replied the Princess; "but when I see the sad plight of my father and my people, I cannot rejoice at my own safety."

"They have not hearkened to the voice of the Lord," said Moses, "therefore did all this evil come upon them. Let your father proclaim that the children of Israel are his slaves no longer, but the servants of the Lord our God, and you shall be saved from death."

Now said Pharaoh: "Rise up, get you forth from among my people, both you and the children of Israel; and go, serve the Lord, as you have said. Take your flocks and your herds, as you have said, and be gone; and bless me also." And the Egyptians were impatient for the Israelites to be out of the land, for they said: "We are all dead men." In their haste the Israelites took their dough with them before it was leavened, and carried their kneading-troughs bound in their clothes upon their shoulders. The children of Israel asked the Egyptians for jewels of silver, and jewels of gold and raiment. The Lord gave the people favor in the sight of the Egyptians, so that they let them have what they asked.

While all the Israelites were busy acquiring riches, Moses thought of Joseph's coffin. He knew that the children of Israel could not leave Egypt without it; for Joseph before his death had adjured the children of Israel, saying: "God will surely remember you; and you shall carry my bones away hence with you." For three days and three nights, Moses hunted up and down through the land of Egypt in search of the coffin. But his search was in vain; the coffin was nowhere to be found.

Finally Serah, the daughter of Asher, the son of Jacob, met Moses who was tired and exhausted, and she asked in amazement: "Why this weariness? Wherefore this sad look?"

Moses replied: "For three days and three nights I have made a fruitless search for Joseph's coffin. Perhaps you, being the only survivor of the house of Jacob, know where his coffin is to be found."

Silently Serah led Moses to the Nile, and pointing her finger, said: "In this spot rests the coffin of Joseph. At his death, the Egyptians, knowing the Israelites could not depart from Egypt without the bones of Joseph, made a leaden coffin for him, sealed it securely on all sides and sank it in the Nile. The magicians with their secret arts sank it in such a way that it could not be removed."

Thereupon Moses took Joseph's cup, and from it cut four flat plates. On the first he engraved a lion, on the second an eagle, a bull on the third, and a human being on the fourth. He threw the first plate, with the lion on it, into the river, and said: "Joseph, Joseph, the hour for the redemption of Israel has arrived, the Divine Presence lingers here only for your sake, and the clouds of glory wait your coming. If you will show yourself, well and good; if not, then we are released from our oath." But the coffin remained in the depths of the Nile.

Then Moses threw into the river the second plate bearing the figure of the eagle, and repeated the same words; but the coffin remained at the bottom of the Nile. He cast into the water the

third plate with the engraving of the bull, and for the third
time called upon Joseph to appear, but without avail. Finally
he threw into the river the fourth plate, which bore the figure
of a human being, and he requested that Joseph come forth.
This time there was a sudden stir upon the water; and the coffin
rose to the surface. Moses hurriedly put the coffin on his
shoulder, and with great joy carried it away.

16.   *The Miracle at the Red Sea*

It came to pass, when Pharaoh had let the people go, that
God led them not by the way of the land of the Philistines, although that was near; for God said: "Lest the people change
their mind when they see war, and return to Egypt." But God
led the people by the way of the wilderness beside the Red Sea;
and they went up armed from the land of Egypt. They took up
their journey from Succoth, and encamped in Etham, at the
edge of the wilderness. The Lord went before them by day
in a pillar of cloud, to show them the way; and by night in a
pillar of fire to give them light; the pillar of cloud by day,
and the pillar of fire by night, never departed from before
the people.

The Lord then spoke to Moses, saying: "Speak to the children
of Israel, that they may turn back and encamp before Pi-Hahi-
roth, between Migdol and the sea, before Baal-zephon, the
Egyptian god of the desert. And Pharaoh will say of the child
ren of Israel: 'They are entangled in the land, the wilderness
has shut them in.' When he will follow after them, I will get
Me honor upon Pharaoh and upon all his host, and the Egyptians shall know that I am the Lord."

Pharaoh first sent an army headed by his officers with orders
to bring the Israelites back. Upon reaching the camp of Israel,
the officers found the people feasting and celebrating. The commander spoke to Moses: "By the command of the great, mighty
king of Egypt, whose slaves you have hitherto been, I bid you
return to Egypt."

"The Lord our God, who has brought us forth from the land of Egypt," answered Moses, "has commanded us not to return to Egypt, but to go to a land flowing with milk and honey."

The officers of the king ordered their men to attack the Hebrews. In the encounter that followed, most of the king's men were slain. Those who were left went back to Egypt and reported to their king.

Pharaoh's anger rose, and he addressed his people: "We were smitten by plagues; we were forced to let our slaves depart from us; and now we have to sit by and see them escape with our riches. In this war I will not remain behind, seeking safety, as heretofore, but I will ride at the head of my army; I will take no greater share of the booty than any one of you, and I will waive the royal privilege of choosing and taking whatever I desire; furthermore all my treasuries will be opened, and all the silver, gold, and precious stones they contain will be divided equally among you."

Pharaoh made ready his chariot, and he took his people with him. He took six hundred chosen chariots, and all the chariots of Egypt, and captains over all of them, and he pursued the children of Israel. He overtook them at their encampment by the sea. The Israelites beheld the Egyptians, and they were afraid and cried out to the Lord. They said to Moses: "Because there were no graves in Egypt, have you taken us away to die in the wilderness? Wherefore have you dealt thus with us, to bring us forth out of Egypt? Is not this the word we spoke to you in Egypt, saying: 'Let us alone, that we may serve the Egyptians?' For it were better for us to serve the Egyptians, than that we should die in the wilderness." Moses said to the people: "Fear you not, stand still, and see the salvation of the Lord, which He will work for you today; for the Egyptians you have seen today, you shall see again no more for ever. The Lord will fight for you, and you shall hold your peace."

Moses began to implore God for the children of Israel, and the Lord said to Moses: "Wherefore do you cry to Me? Speak to the children of Israel, that they may go forward. Lift up your rod, stretch out your hand over the sea, and divide it; and the children of Israel shall go into the midst of the sea on dry ground. The Egyptians shall go in after them; and I will get Me honor upon Pharaoh, and upon all his host, upon his chariots and upon his horsemen. And the Egyptians shall know that I am the Lord." The angel of God, who always went before the camp of Israel, now went behind them; and the pillar of cloud stood no longer before them, but between them and the Egyptians, who therefore could not approach the camp of Israel that night. At daybreak Moses went to the shore of the sea, and said: "I am the messenger sent by the Creator of the world. Uncover your paths, O sea, for His children, that they may go through your midst on dry ground."

"I will not do your bidding," answered the proud sea, "for you are only a man born of woman; and, besides, I am three days older than you, O mortal of flesh and blood, since I was created on the third day of the Creation, whereas you were created on the sixth."

"O Lord," exclaimed Moses in anxiety, "the sea refuses to do your will."

"What does a master do with his disobedient servant?" inquired the Almighty.

"He beats him with a rod," said Moses.

"Do thus!" ordered the Almighty. "Lift up your rod, stretch out your hand over the sea and divide it."

Moses raised his rod, and stretched his hand over the sea, but the sea remained obstinate. Upon beholding the glory of God at the right hand of Moses, the sea lost its pride, and it thus spoke to the earth: "Come to my aid; make hollow places for me, that I may hide therein before the Lord of all created beings, blessed be He." The earth obeyed. The water of the sea went back and divided into twelve paths, one for each tribe of Israel to pass. A strong east wind that blew all night made the paths of the sea dry. The children of Israel went into the midst of the sea upon the dry ground; and the waters were a wall to them on their right hand and on their left.

17. *The Egyptians Are Found Guilty*

The Egyptians pursued; all Pharaoh's horses, chariots, and horsemen followed the Israelites into the midst of the sea. The Almighty in His glory appeared over the water, for He had come to drown the Egyptians. Uzza, the angel of the Egyptians, drew near and argued: "Lord of the world! You are called just and upright; why then do you desire to cause my children to perish in the sea? Have my children drowned or slain a single one of your children? If it be on account of the rigorous slavery that my children imposed upon yours, then consider that your children have received their reward for it, by taking silver and golden vessels from them."

The Almighty, blessed be His name, summoned all the angels, and said: "Judge you between Me and yonder Uzza, the angel of the Egyptians. In bygone days I brought famine upon his people, and My beloved Joseph, through his wisdom, saved them from destruction, and by reason of that they became his slaves. But when My children came into their land as strangers, they were in turn enslaved by the Egyptians. My children groaned under their heavy yoke, and I sent Moses and Aaron, My faithful messengers, to Pharaoh, to free them. When they spoke to him in My name, he refused to heed them. I punished him, but he remained obstinate and he made the yoke of the children of Israel still heavier and their lives more bitter. Now when I have redeemed My children from their heavy yoke, he seeks to destroy them."

The heavenly tribunal thereupon called out: "O Lord, you are just in all your ways; Pharaoh and his host deserve the punishment you desire to mete out to them."

Uzza heard their verdict, and pleaded for mercy: "O Lord of the world! My people deserve the punishment, but pray be merciful and have pity upon the works of your hand."

In an instant, the angel Michael flew to Egypt, fetched a part of a wall in which the body of a Hebrew child had been put in place of bricks, and standing with it in the presence of the Almighty, said: "O merciful God! Will you have pity upon this people, who killed innocent children so cruelly?" This silenced Uzza, and the Lord said to Moses: "Stretch your hand over the sea, that the waters may come upon the Egyptians, upon their chariots, and upon their horsemen." Moses stretched forth his hand over the sea, and when morning appeared the sea returned to its strength; and its waters covered the chariots and the horsemen, and of all the host of Pharaoh, not one remained. Thus did the Lord save Israel that day from the hand of the Egyptians.

The drowning of the Egyptians occurred at that hour of the morning when the hosts of heaven sing praises to the Almighty. They now gathered in great multitudes and were about to sing His praises, when the Lord silenced them, saying: "The works of My hand are drowning in the sea, and you desire to sing praises to Me!"

When the Israelites saw the dead bodies of the Egyptians upon the shore, they feared the Lord, and they believed in Him, and in His servant Moses.

Moses and Israel then wished to sing praises to the Lord, as did the angels in heaven, too. But God bade the angels wait, saying: "Let My children sing first."

All the children of Israel raised their eyes heavenward and sang praises to the Almighty. Infants, not yet able to speak, joined in the song; even babes stopped suckling at their mother's breasts to join in the melody. And there was not one soul in Israel who did not offer praise to God for the great deliverance. All in the camp of Israel were permitted to behold the glory of God; in fact, even the female slaves in Israel were allowed to see the presence of God at the dividing of the Red Sea.

The sea cast up many jewels, precious stones, and other treasures which had ornamented the Egyptian warriors and their horses, and the Israelites thus acquired great wealth. When Moses told them that it was time to march forward and begin their journey to the promised land, the Israelites were loath to leave the spot. Moses rebuked them: "Think you the sea will forever continue to yield you jewels and pearls?" Thereupon the Israelites, without complaint or murmur, followed their great leader into the wilderness.

Lag Baomer

SCHOLARS' FESTIVAL (IYYAR 18)

I. CELEBRATION OF LAG BAOMER

SEPHIRAH DAYS. The forty-nine days intervening between the second day of Passover and Shabuot (see page 206, below) are called *sephirah* (counting) days, after God's command that the Jews count them day by day. Religious Jews all over the world still count these forty-nine days. Every evening, after the stars have become visible to the naked eye, every Jew in the synagogue rises to his feet and recites the benediction: "Blessed be Thou, O Lord our God, King of the universe, who hast sanctified us by Thy commandments, and hast commanded us concerning the counting of the *omer*." After that he says: "Today is the (mentioning the proper day) of the *omer*."

In the course of time, the Jews met with persecution and hatred because of their religion, and many gave up their lives for the sake of their people and their Law. Some of these unfortunate events—one in particular which occurred during the Jews' last unsuccessful attempt under the leadership of Bar Kokhba to regain their independence from Rome—took place during the *sephirah* days. These days were therefore devoted to the remembrance of those martyrs, and are observed by the Jews not as a joyous season, but as days of mourning. During the *sephirah* days, therefore, no hair may be cut; no marriages may take place; no concerts and no dances may be held.

THE MEANING OF LAG BAOMER. *Lag* is a word composed of two Hebrew letters, *lamed and gimel*. Considered as numerals, these letters signify thirty-three, and denote the thirty-third day in the counting of the *omer*, corresponding to the eighteenth day of the Jewish month of *Iyyar*.

Lag Baomer is observed as a semi-holiday. All rules of mourning are dispensed with on this day. The observance of this semi-holiday has its source in incidents that took place after the Bar Kokhba revolution against Rome.

The Rabbis have recorded that, during the last revolution against the Romans, a dreadful plague broke out among the disciples of the great teacher Rabbi Akiba, who was an ardent supporter of the revolution. This happened during *sephirah* days; and because of the Jews' great respect for this celebrated scholar, these days were declared as days of mourning. On *Lag Baomer* the epidemic suddenly stopped, and therefore the sages ordered that day to be observed as a semi-holiday. For this reason, *Lag Baomer* has become known among the Jews as "Scholars' Festival," an occasion celebrated by Talmudic students with merrymaking.

According to another tradition, this semi-holiday is linked with the great scholar Rabbi Simeon ben Yohai. After the Roman victory over Bar Kokhba, the Roman Emperor Hadrian issued cruel decrees against the Jews, aimed at destroying the Jewish religion and culture. Circumcision, observance of the Sabbath, and the study of the Law were forbidden under the penalty of death. Rabbi Akiba and many other scholars who defied the Roman edict were tortured to death. Rabbi Simeon ben Yohai, who in defiance of the Roman edict, continued to instruct his students in the Law of God, managed to escape.

For twelve long years Simeon ben Yohai lived with his son Rabbi Eleazar in a cave in the mountains of Galilee. Fearing the numerous Roman spies in Palestine, Simeon and his son dared not leave their hideout even to obtain food. A carob-tree and a spring of water miraculously appeared in the cavern. During all the days of their hiding, they ate of the fruit of the carob-tree and drank from the water of the spring. In order to preserve their garments, they sat naked in the sand and their skin became covered with scabs.

At last the Prophet Elijah announced to them the death of the Roman Emperor and the consequent annulment of the death sentence against them. Then they left their cave. Simeon observed people engaged in farming and other pursuits, but neglecting the study of the Law. His anger was aroused by what he saw, and he struck the people with his furious glances. A voice then descended from Heaven ordering father and son to return to the cave, where they remained twelve months longer, until a heavenly voice bade them come forth. The great teacher then settled in Meron, a village near Safed in Palestine. It is a tradition among some pious Jews that Rabbi Simeon ben Yohai died on *Lag Baomer,* and that before his death he revealed to his pupils the deep secrets which were later incorporated in the mystic book called *Zohar.*

Lag Baomer has been set aside as a special holiday for schoolchildren. Carrying bows and arrows, they go with their teachers to nearby woods, and spend the day picnicking and playing all sorts of games, especially archery. The bow and arrow remind the Jewish youth of Rabbi Simeon ben Yohai because, according to tradition, the rainbow never appeared in the skies during his lifetime. They are also reminiscent of the great Jewish heroes of the past, and at the same time they arouse hope of the future redemption of the Jewish people through the Messiah. For, it is stated in the *Zohar*, that a bow of many colors will appear in the sky immediately before the coming of the Messiah.

The following pages tell the story of *Lag Baomer*, and of Bar Kokhba, one of the great heroes of our history, who made a last effort to free the Jews from the tyranny of Rome.

II THE STORY OF LAG BAOMER

1. *The Emperor Hadrian Deceives the Jews.*

In August, 117 C. E., Hadrian became emperor of Rome. He seemed at first to be a much milder man than his predecessors. He disliked long wars, and therefore adopted a more lenient colonial policy.

The Jews consequently benefited by Hadrian's leniency. The Jewish leaders demanded from Rome, as a condition of peace, permission to rebuild the city of Jerusalem and the Temple. Hadrian, fearing war, granted the request.

The Jews immediately prepared for the reconstruction. They organized a great campaign to raise the necessary funds. From Jews in all lands came generous contributions. Jews came in great numbers from foreign lands to help rebuild their homeland. And the Jews regarded the Emperor Hadrian as a friend.

The great expectations of the Jews, however, were doomed to disappointment. The Christians and the Samaritans—the ancient enemies of the Jews—bitterly opposed the rebuilding of Jerusalem and the Temple. Both sects did everything in their power to hinder the work. The Samaritans convinced Hadrian that the rebuilding of Jerusalem would encourage Jews to revolt against Rome. Not daring to revoke his promise, however, Hadrian sought to evade it. The Temple might be rebuilt, he declared, but not on its former site; Jerusalem might be restored, but only as a heathen city.

The Jews of course were embittered. A vast multitude assembled in the valley of Jesreel, and threatened war against Rome. But there were many Jewish leaders who realized that a rebellion against Rome would be hopeless. They called upon the great sage Rabbi Joshua, known as an advocate of peace, to calm the people. Rabbi Joshua then recounted this fable to the people: "Once upon a time, a lion, after devouring his prey, was greatly troubled by a bone which had stuck in his throat. In his pain, the lion promised a reward to anyone who would remove the bone. A crane with a long beak removed the bone from the lion's throat, and demanded his reward. But the lion answered mockingly: 'Is it not sufficient reward for you, ungrateful one, that you have escaped with a whole skin out of the lion's jaws?' In like manner," continued the sage, "let us be glad that we have until now escaped destruction at the hand of the Romans."

Rabbi Joshua's eloquence calmed the people for a time, but from then on the Jews hated the Roman Emperor. Hadrian, however, did not notice the changed attitude of the Jews. In the last decade of his reign he visited Judah, and on his return he reported to the Romans the friendly reception given him by the Jews. The Senate thereupon struck coins to commemorate Hadrian's presence in Judah. The coin pictured Hadrian and a female figure denoting Judah; they stood opposite one another near an altar on which both were about to offer a sacrifice; two

or three children, symbolizing the districts of Judah, stood nearby presenting palms to the emperor as a symbol of peace.

Hadrian had been seriously mistaken; for at that very moment the Jews were actually preparing for war. The weapons
forged for the Romans by the Jewish smiths were deliberately
made weak and almost useless; the Jews knew that these weapons might soon be turned against themselves. The conspirators
secretly built underground passages in the numerous caves of
the mountains of Judah to be used as storehouses for weapons
and provisions, and also as places of ambush for sudden attacks upon the enemy.

2. Bar Kokhba

At that time, Rabbi Akiba, the illustrious teacher, became the
religious head of the Jewish community. He took an active part
in the war preparations. He made many journeys to the Jewish
communities of Parthia and Asia Minor for the purpose of obtaining assistance in the restoration of the Jewish commonwealth.

Not until the rebellion was about to break forth in full force
did Hadrian become aware of it. But by now the Jews had
everything in readiness—weapons, means of communications,
warriors, and even a powerful leader capable of inspiring the
people with courage.

This great hero of the rebellion was Bar Kokhba. Nothing is
known of his descent and early life. Like many great revolutionary heroes, he emerged suddenly and spread terror among
the enemy. His real name was Bar Koziba, because his home
was at a place called Kazib. Bar Kokhba was the name given
him by Rabbi Akiba. When the great Rabbi first saw him, he
was so deeply impressed by his appearance that he exclaimed:
"This is the Messianic king." At that time he applied to him
the Biblical verse: "And a star (Hebrew, *kokhab*) has arisen
in Jacob." Rabbi Akiba believed that the hero would defeat
Rome and restore the glory of Israel.

There were, of course, some men who did not share Rabbi Akiba's belief. Rabbi Johanan ben Torto once said to Rabbi Akiba: "Grass will grow on your chin, Akiba, before the real Messiah makes his appearance."

Rabbi Akiba's recognition of Bar Kokhba as the Messiah had a great effect upon the masses. Jewish warriors from all countries flocked to the standard of the Messianic king. Even Samaritans and heathens joined in the revolt against Rome. The brave warriors numbered more than 400,000. The revolutionary leader was confident of victory. His own physical strength, and the prowess of his great army, caused him to utter words of blasphemy. "O Lord," he said, "if Thou refuse to help us, at least abstain from helping our enemy, and victory will be ours."

The governor of Judah at that time was the cruel and wicked Roman, Tinnius Rufus. The Jews called him Tyrannus (the tyrant) Rufus. With but a small number of troops at his disposal, Tinnius Rufus was powerless against the attack of Bar Kokhba, and was compelled constantly to retreat. Within a year, fifty strongholds and many cities, until then occupied by the Romans, had fallen into the hands of the Jews.

At first, Hadrian did not regard the Jewish revolution as serious. But on hearing reports of one Roman defeat after another, he at once sent reinforcements under the command of his ablest generals. Legions from Phoenicia, Egypt, Arabia, and distant provinces were dispatched to Judah. Two of Rome's best generals, Publius Marcellus and Lolius Urbicius, met with defeat at the hands of Bar Kokhba. These generals lost on Judean soil the glory they had previously won on other battlefields. The unexpected victories against the Romans convinced the Jewish people that their independence was assured.

3. *Death of Bar Kokhba.*

After nearly two years of relentless war, from 132 to 134 C. E., Emperor Hadrian, fearing defeat, summoned the greatest general of his time, Julius Severus, the Roman governor of

Britannia. Severus, who had suppressed the uprising of the liberty-loving Britons, was now given command of the Roman armies in Judah.

When Severus arrived in Judah, he found the Jewish army in such a favorable position that he dared not give battle at once. He therefore adopted the policy of watchful waiting. He decided to extend the line of battle, to prolong the war, to cut off the Jews' sources of supply, and to attack isolated units of the Jewish army and destroy them by means of his cavalry. He planned, in this manner, to starve the country into submission.

Severus' tactics proved successful. One by one, the fifty strongholds which the Jews had occupied were retaken by the Romans. The last stronghold which remained in Jewish hands was Bethar, not far from the Mediterranean coast. To Bethar, Bar Kokhba, after many defeats, retreated with the flower of his army. Fugitives came from all parts of the country to seek refuge in that city.

For one whole year, Severus besieged Bethar. Through the underground passages which had been prepared before the outbreak of the war, the inhabitants of Bethar were able to obtain the necessary provisions. A brook which ran through the city provided them with sufficient water. But the Samaritans betrayed the heroic defenders. They informed the Romans of the underground passages, which were thereafter carefully guarded. No longer could food be brought into the city, and the defenders, on the verge of starvation, were compelled to surrender. In 135 C. E., on the very same day on which Jerusalem had fallen sixty-five years before—the ninth day of the month of Ab—Bethar fell.

The following story, which had been handed down by the Rabbis, explains that had not Bar Kokhba committed a crime, he would have never fallen by the hands of the Romans:

"In Bethar there lived, at the time of the Roman siege, a saintly man, Rabbi Eleazar of Modin. Every day, in sackcloth and ashes, this pious sage would pray to God that Bethar might

not fall into the hands of the Romans. Everyone believed that
the prayers of the saintly man would save the city from destruction. One day a Samaritan came before the Roman Emperor
and said to him: 'O sire, as long as that hen (meaning Rabbi
Eleazar) cackles in the ashes, Bethar will not be captured. But
let not the siege be raised, and I will bring about the fall of the
city by destroying the life of its saint.' The Samaritan entered
the besieged city through a subterranean passage. He quietly
walked over to the saintly Rabbi Eleazar, who was praying in
the synagogue, and pretended to whisper some secret in his
ear. The worshipers who were present became suspicious of
the secrecy between the Samaritan and Rabbi Eleazar, and they
reported the incident to Bar Kokhba. The Messianic king immediately summoned the Samaritan spy, and inquired of him:
'What did you say to Rabbi Eleazar?' The Samaritan shrewdly
replied: 'If I tell you the truth, my Emperor will take my life;
and if I refrain from telling it to you, you will take my life;
but I would rather die by your hand than disclose the secret of
my Emperor.' Bar Kokhba, suspecting a traitorous plot between Rabbi Eleazar and the enemy, at once summoned the
Rabbi before him. 'Tell me what this spy whispered in your
ear,' demanded the Messianic king. Eleazar, who had been so
absorbed in prayer that he hardly noticed the Samaritan approaching him, replied: 'I do not know what he whispered
in my ear, for I was absorbed in prayer.' 'And what did you
say to him then?' thundered Bar Kokhba. 'I said nothing to
him,' replied the Rabbi. Bar Kokhba became enraged at the
replies of Rabbi Eleazar, for he thought the saintly man was
deceiving him. In his mad fury, he kicked the sage. Enfeebled
by long fasting and prayer, the saintly Rabbi instantly fell dead
at the feet of the Messianic king. Then a heavenly voice was
heard: 'Woe to the worthless shepherd that leaveth his flock!
Because thou hast paralyzed the arm of Israel, and hast blinded
his eye, thy arm shall be paralyzed and thine eyes shall be

blinded.' Thereupon Bethar fell into the hands of the Romans, and Bar Kokhba lost his life."

Very little is known of how the heroic Bar Kokhba really died. One legend tells that a Roman soldier brought the hero's head to the Roman Emperor, who inquired: "Who killed this man?"

"I killed him," boasted the soldier.

"Bring his body here that I may examine it," ordered the Emperor.

When the body of the revolutionary leader was brought before Hadrian, he exclaimed: "Why his body has been crushed by a snake! Had not a god killed him, no human power could have overcome him."

4. *The Aftermath of the Revolution*

The Roman soldiers massacred the inhabitants of Bethar. Blood flowed in streams into the Mediterranean, a mile away. The brains of three hundred children were found spattered on one rock, and of the entire youth of the city not one escaped. More than half a million people fell by the sword, in addition to those who perished by hunger and fire.

The Roman losses were equally great. The greater part of the Roman legions were destroyed in the battles and in the siege. Emperor Hadrian rejoiced at the victory, but he dared not, in his report to the Senate, employ the usual formula: "I and the army are well." Because of the severe losses sustained by the Romans, the Senate decreed no triumph for the Emperor. Only the victor, Julius Severus, received the mark of distinction conferred upon a conqueror.

Upon the fall of Bethar, many fugitives found shelter in the mountain caves and hollows. From these retreats, they conducted a desperate guerilla warfare against the Romans. Before long, however, these bands were destroyed.

All rebellious cities and villages were razed to the ground by the Romans, and Judah became a desert. The captives were dragged by the thousands to the slave-markets of Hebron and Gaza, where they were sold for a few coins. Most of the fugitives who had hidden in the clefts of rocks perished of hunger. Those that survived did not escape the sword of the Romans. Heralds proclaimed, in the name of the Roman Emperor, that all who would voluntarily come forth from their hiding-places would be treated with mercy. Many were lured by these promises and left their hiding-places, but they were butchered at once. Only those fugitives were saved who managed to reach the Euphrates region and Arabia, where the bloody Roman hand could not reach them.

Hadrian's cruelty was directed not only against the living, but even against the dead who had fallen in the battle of Bethar. He forbade the burying of the corpses, so that the horrible sight of the heaps of the dead bodies might serve as a warning to the living to rise no more against Rome. The Roman authorities cared little for the resultant poisoning of the air. Indeed, they were only too anxious to add the horror of pestilence to the other misfortunes of the Jews.

Tinnius Rufus, the Procurator of Judah, plowed over the city of Jerusalem to remove all traces of the ancient city. Hadrian then had the city rebuilt, and peopled it with Phoenician and Syrian soldiers. The city was built after the Greek fashion. On the site of the former Temple of God were erected a statue of Hadrian and a temple in honor of the Capitoline Jupiter. Another temple of Jupiter was built on Mount Gerizim, the sacred mountain of the Samaritans, where their temple had once stood. Statues of other Roman, Greek, and Phoenician gods were placed everywhere. The very name of the Holy City was changed. The new city was to bear the name of Aelia Capitolina, after Hadrian's surname Aelius and after the Capitoline Jupiter. The southern gate of the city, leading to Bethlehem, bore an image of a pig, as a further insult to the Jews and their God. Jews were no longer permitted within the gates of the city which they had once defended with their lives.

The cruelty of Hadrian toward the vanquished Jews is illustrated by this story preserved by the Rabbis: "Once a Jew happened to pass Hadrian and humbly saluted him. Hadrian asked: 'Who are you?' 'I am a Jew,' humbly answered the passerby. 'Remove the head of this villain!' cried out the Emperor. Another Jew, seeing his friend beheaded for having dared to salute the Emperor, passed by without saluting him. Hadrian angrily inquired: 'And who are you?' 'I am a Jew,' replied the passerby, thinking that he was safe. 'How dare a Jew pass the Emperor of Rome without saluting him!' shouted Hadrian. 'Remove the head of this villain, too.' Thereupon his councilors said to Hadrian: 'O sire, we fail to understand your actions. You kill both him who salutes you, and also him who does not.' 'Do you have to teach me how to kill off my enemies?' angrily asked Hadrian."

To crush the spirit of the Jews, Hadrian resorted to the old tactics of Antiochus, the Syrian king. He resolved to compel the Jews, by force of arms, to embrace paganism. He decreed death for all Jews who observed the Sabbath, or who occupied themselves with the teaching of the Jewish Law. Severe penalties were decreed for those who observed any Jewish custom, habit, or usage. The reading or studying of the Torah was a serious crime.

These decrees were a heavy blow to the Jewish survivors. The land of Judah was honeycombed with Roman spies. In order to escape observation, the Jews would study the Torah while hidden upon high roofs or in cellars. But every step of the Jews was watched. Anyone found observing any religious practice was punished by a fine, by corporal punishment, or even by death. Worse than death were the slow tortures to which the accused Jews were subjected.

5. *The Martyrs*

There were a great number of Jews who in spite of persecution observed all the religious laws. Many were caught wearing phylacteries (tephilin), for which they had their skulls crushed. The teachers of the Law, especially, defied death. They determined to suffer martyrdom rather than abandon their teaching. They placed the study of the Law above the observance of religious rites.

The Rabbis tell of ten great men who died for the sake of the Law. Foremost among these was Rabbi Akiba, who would openly lecture to his disciples. When one, Papus ben Judah, warned Rabbi Akiba against meeting with his disciples because of the watchfulness of the Roman spies, Rabbi Akiba declared that it was both futile and sinful to fear death. "Are you Papus," he asked, "of whom people say that he is a wise man? In reality you are a fool. Let me tell you a parable:

"A fox once walked along the bank of a river, and as he looked into the water, he saw fishes fleeing. The fox said to the fishes:'What are you running away from?' The fishes replied, 'We are running away from the nets that have been placed to trap us.' The fox said: 'Why then stay in the water and be afraid of the nets? Come upon dry land, and there we shall live in happiness and in peace, the same as your forefathers did.' Thereupon the fishes said to the fox: 'Are you the one that is reputed to be the wisest of all animals? In reality you are nothing but a fool! If we are afraid in the water, the element in which we live, then surely we will have cause to fear on dry land, where we cannot live at all.' The same is true of us. If we are afraid when we study the Law, which is our life, how much more cause shall we have to fear the enemy when we cease to study the Law."

Shortly after this incident, Rabbi Akiba was seized by the Romans and thrown into a dungeon. Later Papus ben Judah was cast into the same dungeon, and into the same cell with Rabbi Akiba.

"Papus, who brought you here?" asked Rabbi Akiba.

"Happy is your lot, Rabbi Akiba," replied Papus, "that you were imprisoned because you studied the Law of God. Woe to Papus, that he was caught and cast into prison for absurdities and vanities."

Tinnius Rufus, the Roman Procurator, regarded Rabbi Akiba as the main pillar of Judaism, and he treated him with more severity than he did the other scholars of the Law. He kept him imprisoned for a long time, hoping that, weakened by the long confinement, he would submit to the Roman decree and thus set an example to others. But Rabbi Akiba remained firm, and the cruel Procurator decided to subject him to torture. His skin was torn off by the Roman executioners with a curry-comb.

Rabbi Akiba submitted to these unbearable tortures with a smile of satisfaction on his face. Astonished at such self-control, Rufus asked: "Akiba, are you a magician that you are able to bear your pain with such indifference?" Rabbi Akiba replied: "I am no magician, but I rejoice in the opportunity to love my God with my life." Rabbi Akiba then recited: "Hear, O Israel, the Lord our God, the Lord is one." With the utterance of the last word of this verse, *ehad* (one), the martyr breathed his last. Thereupon a heavenly voice was heard: "Happy art thou, Akiba, that thy soul departed while thou wert reciting the word *ehad.*"

The following story was told by the Rabbis: "When Rabbi Akiba's flesh was torn off with the curry-comb, the ministering angels in heaven said to the Holy One, blessed be His name: 'Master of the world, is this the Torah and this its reward?'

"In reply, a heavenly voice was heard: 'Happy art thou, Akiba, for thou hast been chosen for bliss eternal.'

"The day on which Rabbi Akiba died was the day preceding *Yom Kippur,* the Day of Atonement. Rabbi Joshua, the grits-dealer, who used to wait upon Rabbi Akiba while in prison, had therefore gone home that day to prepare for the fast. The Prophet Elijah appeared at the door of Rabbi Joshua's humble hut, and greeted him: 'Peace be unto you, my teacher.'

" 'Peace be unto you, my teacher and master,' came the reply.

" 'Do you require any help?' inquired Elijah.

" 'Why, who are you?' asked Rabbi Joshua.

" 'I have come to tell you that your master Rabbi Akiba died in prison this day.'

"Elijah and the Rabbi hurried to the prison. They found the prison-gates unlocked, and the guards and the prisoners all fast asleep. Elijah at once placed the body of Rabbi Akiba on his shoulders and carried it out of prison.

"They carried the body of Rabbi Akiba for many hours, until they reached Antipatris. When they arrived there, they walked up three steps, and suddenly a cave opened for them. In the cave there was a chair, a bench, a bed, and a table upon which a candlestick was standing. They placed the mutilated body of the martyr upon the bed and left the cave. As soon as they emerged into the open, the candle in the candlestick lit of itself, and the opening of the cave closed of its own accord. When Elijah saw all this, he said: 'Happy are you, O righteous men; happy are you who study the Law of God; happy are you who are God-fearing; for a place is reserved for you in Paradise. Happy are you, Akiba, that such a pleasant abode was provided for you at your death.' "

Like Rabbi Akiba, another sage, Rabbi Hanina ben Tradion was also condemned to death because he persisted in teaching the Law to his disciples. When he was asked by his disciples why he disobeyed the edict of the Emperor, he replied simply: "Because my God so commanded me."

The following account has been preserved by the Rabbis about the death of this martyr: "When he was taken out to be executed, he was wrapped in a Scroll of the Law, and surrounded with bundles of straw which were set on fire. The executioners took tufts of wool, soaked them in water, and put them on the chest of the victim, so that he should not expire quickly but die by slow degrees.

"The daughter of the tortured Rabbi asked: 'Is this your reward for studying the Law of God?'

"The slowly dying sage said: 'If I were to burn by myself, it would be very hard. But since I am burned together with the Scroll of the Law, then He who will resent the insult heaped upon His Law, will also resent the insult heaped upon me.'

"The disciples who gathered around their dying master asked: 'Rabbi, what do you perceive now?'

" 'I see the parchment of the Scroll being consumed in the fire,' answered the sage in a very feeble voice, 'but the letters of the Scroll flying to heaven.'

"The Roman executioner then said to the Rabbi: 'If I increase the flames and remove the tufts of wet wool from your chest, so that you may die sooner, will you procure me admittance into the world to come?'

" 'Yes, I will secure you such admittance,' assured the Rabbi.

"The executioner thereupon increased the flames and removed the wet tufts of wool from the chest of the Rabbi. The soul of Rabbi Hanina at once flew heavenward, and the executioner threw himself into the flames and was consumed by them. A heavenly voice was then heard saying: 'Rabbi Hanina ben Tradion and his executioner have been chosen for bliss everlasting.' "

The Roman government forbade the ordination of Rabbis, and decreed that the ordainer and the ordained be punished by death, and that the city in which the ordination took place be destroyed.

Rabbi Judah ben Baba feared that with the execution of the eminent teachers, the Law of God would be completely forgotten. He therefore decided to ordain their surviving disciples and to authorize them to continue the teaching of the Law as independent teachers. He summoned seven of Rabbi Akiba's disciples, and in a gorge between Usha and Sefaram, he ordained them. A Roman corps surprised the Rabbi in the act of ordainment. Rabbi Judah, who was seventy years old and too feeble to flee, induced the newly ordained Rabbis to leave him and flee for their lives. The young Rabbis fled, and Rabbi Judah was immediately thereafter riddled like a sieve by the Romans' lances.

And there were many other sages who, because they remained loyal to their God and His Law, suffered death at the hands of the Roman executioners.

Shabuot (Feast of Weeks)

A TORAH FESTIVAL (SIVAN 6-7)

I. CELEBRATION OF SHABUOT

WHAT IS SHABUOT. The holiday Shabuot—the Hebrew word for "weeks"—takes its name from its date of celebration; exact-

Shabuot (Feast of Weeks)

A TORAH FESTIVAL (SIVAN 6-7)

I CELEBRATION OF SHABUOT

WHAT IS SHABUOT? The holiday *Shabuot*—the Hebrew word for "weeks"—takes its name from its date of celebration: exactly seven weeks after the second day of Passover. The *Shabuot* Festival is commonly known as Pentecost, which in Greek means "fiftieth day," because it is celebrated on the fiftieth day counting from the second day of Passover. The fiftieth day corresponds to the sixth day of the Jewish month of Sivan.

AN AGRICULTURAL FESTIVAL. It has already been noted that the Jews observed their harvest seasons as holidays. It was on the second day of Passover that the cereal harvest began in Palestine, an event which was celebrated by bringing the *omer* offering of barley, the first cereal to ripen. This harvest celebration ended with the harvesting of wheat on *Shabuot,* the wheat being the last cereal to ripen. The celebration of *Shabuot* thus marked the conclusion of the cereal festival.

On *Shabuot,* during the existence of the Temple at Jerusalem, the whole Jewish community brought a thanksgiving offering to the Almighty. This consisted of two loaves of bread baked of fine flour from the new crop of wheat, which were waved by the priest before the Lord. The sacrifice was accompanied by the Levites' singing of hymns and the playing of harps and other musical instruments.

Shabuot was celebrated also as a festival of the first ripe fruit, or, as it is known in Hebrew, *hag habikkurim.* The fruit harvest commenced on *Shabuot* and ended on *Sukkot* in the Fall. Every farmer had to bring his first ripe fruit to the Temple at Jerusalem, where he gave thanks to the Almighty for the products of his field. The Rabbis tell how the first ripe fruits for the *bikkurim* offering were selected: "Upon visiting his field and seeing a fig, or a cluster of grapes, or a pomegranate that was ripe, the owner would tie a thread around the fruit, saying, 'This shall be among the *bikkurim.*' "

THE PILGRIMAGE TO JERUSALEM. *Shabuot* was the second of the three great pilgrim feasts, when the people of Palestine, from far and near, travelled with their families in gala procession to the Holy City near the Temple of God. Before the feast of *Shabuot,* every farmer, no matter how rich or poor he may have been, was compelled by the Law of God, to put his first ripe fruit in a basket made of gold, or of silver, or of wickerwork, and to present it to the priest.

The procession of the pilgrims with their *bikkurim,* as described in the Mishnah, was very impressive:

"The people came from the villages and colonies to the chief town of each district. There they spent the night in the open squares, without going into the houses. At dawn they were awakened by the officer in charge with the call: 'Arise, let us ascend to Zion, the House of the Lord our God.'

"Those that lived near Jerusalem brought fresh figs and grapes, while those that came from distant parts brought dried figs and raisins. The bull destined for the sacrifice, his horns gilded and his head wreathed with olive leaves, led the procession. To the playing of a flute, the pilgrims marched to the gates of Jerusalem. There they were met by the Temple officers and by many artisans, who greeted them, saying: 'Our brethren from (this or that district), enter the City in peace.'

"With the flute still playing, the pilgrims proceeded to the Temple court. All pilgrims, including even the king, now carried their baskets on their shoulders to the outer court of the Temple, where they were welcomed by the Levites, singing: 'I will extol Thee, O Lord, for Thou hast raised me, and Thou hast not suffered mine enemies to rejoice over me.' Doves, which had been carried by the pilgrims in their baskets, were sacrificed as burnt-offerings on the altar.

"With his basket on his shoulder, each pilgrim recited from the Holy Scripture the prayer beginning with the words: 'This day have I proclaimed unto the Lord'; and at the words: 'A wayfaring Aramean was my father,' the pilgrim lowered his basket from his shoulder, and a priest placed his hands beneath the basket and raised it as a thanksgiving offering. The pilgrim then repeated the words: 'A wayfaring Aramean was my father,' and read to the end of the prayer: 'And now, behold, I have brought the first of the fruit of the land, which Thou, O

Lord, hast given me.' He then placed the basket with the first ripe fruit near the altar, bowed down, and left the hall. The golden, the silver, and the costly baskets were returned to their owners, but the wicker-work baskets were retained by the priests."

THE TIME OF THE FEAST. According to the Law of God, Shabuot was to be celebrated one day, the sixth day of the month of Sivan. However, for the reason given above,[1] the sages decreed that in countries outside the land of Israel, Shabuot should be observed for two days, including the seventh day of Sivan.

DAYS OF REST. The two days of Shabuot must be observed as days of rest and happiness, on which no manual labor may be performed. The only work permissible is that which is needed to supply food for human beings. And one may prepare only food needed for the same day, but one may not prepare food on one day of the Festival for use on another.[2]

On the eve of Shabuot, the men go to the Synagogue to pray the *maarib* (evening) service, while the mistress of the house, remaining home, symbolizes the joy which the Festival brings into the Jewish home, by lighting the Festival candles, and pronouncing the necessary benedictions. At the conclusion of the service the *hazan* (cantor) chants the *kiddush* (sanctification). After that greetings are exchanged, either in Yiddish, *gut yom tov* (happy holiday), and the response is, *gut yom tov, gut yohr* (happy holiday, happy year); or in Hebrew, *hag sameah* (happy holiday). Arriving home, the father greets the members of the house with a cheerful *gut yom tov,* or *hag sameah,* and everybody stands around the table which is decorated with silverware and china, and with a bottle of sparkling wine and two hallot covered with a napkin.[3] The master of the house chants the *kiddush* over a goblet of wine, then hands are washed, the *hamotzi* is said, and the family enjoys the festive

1 P. 45.
2 See p. 40, *Erub Tabshilin.*
3 See p. 11, for the reason of this custom

meal, singing Palestinian songs of soil and harvest between the courses.

A TORAH FESTIVAL. The Festival of *Shabuot* has an additional meaning. It is known as *zeman mattan toratenu*, "the season when the Law was given," because on this day God revealed Himself on Mount Sinai and gave the Israelites the Ten Commandments. For this reason the Rabbis declared *Shabuot* to be the most pleasant of all Jewish holidays.

CUSTOMS OBSERVED ON SHABUOT. Because *Shabuot* also commemorates the giving of the Law on Sinai, it is customary to spend the whole night of *Shabuot* in studying the Law. A special book has been prepared for this occasion, called *Tikun Lel Shabuot*. It contains excerpts from every book of the Bible and of the Mishnah, and is read from cover to cover by pious Jews on the night of *Shabuot*. People, however, who are learned in the Law do not read from this special book; they read directly from the Talmud or other sacred books.

A popular custom on *Shabuot* is to eat dairy food, cheesecake, and *blintzes* (fritters stuffed with cheese). This custom has developed in honor of the Law of God, which is likened to "honey and milk." The meat meal follows the dairy meal. These two meals represent the two loaves of bread which in ancient times were used in the *bikkurim* offering.

In the synagogue, the scroll containing the story of Ruth is read. That is because *Shabuot* is a festival of the harvest and of the Law, and this story which describes harvesting in Palestine tells how Ruth embraced Judaism.

On *Shabuot* it is customary to cover the floors with greens and to decorate the house and the synagogue with plants, flowers, and even with trees. The greens serve to remind one of the green mountains of Sinai; they also commemorate the harvest festival of olden times.

On the second day of *Shabuot*, during the morning services at the synagogue, Memorial Services (*yizkor*) are held for the departed. If one is unable to attend the synagogue services, one may recite the Memorial Services at home.

Because the Jewish people received the Law of God on *Shabuot* and were thus confirmed in the Covenant, the beautiful custom of confirmation has been introduced in some synagogues. Boys and girls, who have been prepared in Hebrew or Sunday schools, attend the morning service at the synagogue and are confirmed in the Jewish faith as our forefathers were on this day. It is a great event for the schoolchildren as well as for their parents and friends.

The following pages are devoted to the story of the giving of the Ten Commandments on Mount Sinai, as told both in the Bible and in the Talmud.

II. THE STORY OF SHABUOT

1. *Before the Revelation*

In the third month after the children of Israel were gone out of Egypt, they came to the wilderness of Sinai, and encamped before the mount. God called to Moses out of the mount, saying: "Thus shall you say to the house of Jacob, and tell the children of Israel: 'you have seen what I did to the Egyptians, and how I bore you on eagles' wings, and brought you to Myself. Now therefore, if you will hearken to My voice, and keep My covenant, then you shall be My own treasure from among all the people; for all the earth is Mine; and you shall be to Me a kingdom of priests, and a holy nation.' These are the words which you shall speak to the children of Israel." Moses summoned the elders of the people, and told them the words which the Lord had spoken.

Before God gave the Law to Israel, He had offered it to every tribe and nation on the earth, so that thereafter they might not excuse themselves by saying: "Had the Holy One, blessed be He, offered to give the Law to us, we should have accepted it." He had thus gone to the Edomites, the children of Esau, and said: "Will you accept the Torah?"

"What is written in your Torah?" the Edomites had asked.

"One of the commandments of the Torah is: 'Thou shalt not kill,' " replied the Almighty.

They said: "Almighty God, dost Thou desire to deprive us of the blessing which was given to our forefather Esau by his father Isaac? For he was blessed by him with the words: 'And by thy sword shalt thou live.' We dare not give up our blessing and accept Thy Torah."

Thereupon the Almighty had gone to the children of Ishmael and said: "Will you accept My Torah?"

"Acquaint us with what is written in Thy Torah," said the sons of Ishmael.

The Almighty replied: " 'Thou shalt not steal,' is one of the commandments."

"We cannot accept Thy Torah," stated the sons of Ishmael, "because our ancestor was blessed thus: 'His hand will be against every man.' We therefore dare not give up our blessing."

The Almighty then went to all the other nations of the earth and offered them the Torah, but they refused it, because its commandments were contrary to their own beliefs and customs. Finally, He went to the children of Abraham, Isaac, and Jacob and asked of them: "Will you accept My Torah?"

"What is written in Thy Torah?" inquired the children of Israel.

"The Torah I desire to give you contains six hundred and thirteen commandments," said the Almighty.

The children of Israel made no further inquiry, but all answered together: "All that the Lord has spoken we will do."

Immediately a host of one hundred and twenty myriads of

angels descended from heaven, and adorned every Israelite with a heavenly crown and a girdle of glory.

The Almighty nevertheless hesitated to entrust the children of Israel with the Torah, and He said to them: "Bring Me bondsmen who will guarantee that you will fulfill the laws contained in the Torah, and I will give it to you."

"Our ancestors, Abraham, Isaac and Jacob, will be our bondsmen," replied the children of Israel.

"They are not acceptable to Me," said the Almighty. "Bring good bondsmen, and I will give you the Torah."

"Then let our prophets be our bondsmen," said the children of Israel.

"I object to them," said God.

"We will give Thee our children as bondsmen; our little ones will be surety for us that we will observe the Torah," said the children of Israel.

"These are good bondsmen," said the Almighty; "on their bond I will give you My Torah."

On learning that the Almighty would deliver the Torah to the children of Israel from a mountaintop, the mountains fought among themselves for the honor of being chosen as the spot upon which the glory of God would reveal itself. One mountain said: "Upon me shall the Holy One give His Torah to Israel." Another mountain contended: "Nay, but upon me shall the Holy One give the Torah to Israel."

"Upon me shall God descend," said the lofty Mount Tabor to Mount Hermon, "because I am the highest of all mountains, and when in the days of Noah the flood covered all the elevated places, I alone towered above the water."

"Nay, upon me shall God descend," replied Mount Hermon, "because when the children of Israel wished to cross the Red Sea, I placed myself between the two shores, and enabled them to cross on dry land."

Mount Carmel claimed: "I alone deserve to receive the Divine Presence, because on me in after days, Elijah will make the name of God great in the eyes of the world."

Mount Sinai, which was the lowest of the mountains, never ventured to make a claim to glory. Thereupon a voice from the high heavens rang out: "In vain do you quarrel; the Divine Presence shall not descend upon any of the high mountains, who are so proud, and upon whom the heathens erect sanctuaries to their idols. I prefer Mount Sinai, the most humble of all, upon which no sanctuaries have been built by idolaters."

The Lord said to Moses: "Lo, I come to thee in a thick cloud, that the people may hear when I speak with you, and may also believe you forever. Go to the people, and sanctify them today and tomorrow, and let them wash their garments, and be ready the third day; for the third day the Lord will come down in the sight of all the people upon Mount Sinai. You shall set bounds to the people round about, saying: 'Take heed that you go not up into the mount, or touch the border of it; whosoever touches the mount shall be put to death; no hand shall touch it, but he shall surely be stoned, or shot through; whether it be beast or man, it shall not live; when the ram's horn sounds long, they shall come up to the mount.' "

Moses went down from the mount to the people, and sanctified them; and they washed their garments. It came to pass on the morning of the third day, that there were thunder and lightning and a thick cloud upon the mount, and the sound of a horn exceedingly loud; and all the people that were in the camp trembled.

Moses brought the people out of the camp to meet God; and they stood at the foot of the mount. Now Mount Sinai was altogether covered in smoke, because the Lord descended upon it in fire; and the entire mount quaked greatly. When the horn sounded louder and louder, Moses spoke, and God answered him by a voice. The Lord came down upon Mount Sinai; the Lord called Moses to the top of the mount; and Moses went up. The Lord said: "Go down, and thou shalt reascend with Aaron; but let not tne priests and the people come, lest the Lord smite them."

At noon the Israelites brought their wives and children to the mount, the men assembling in one division and the women in another. The Almighty then revealed Himself before the people. He lifted up the mountain, and holding it like a basket over the heads of the people, He said to them: "If you will accept the Torah, it shall be well with you; otherwise you shall all find your graves under the mountain." They all burst into tears, and again they declared: "All that the Lord has spoken we will do."

2. *The Revelation*

When the Almighty was about to utter the first word, nature stood still; the birds ceased chirping; wings became motionless; the billows of the seas suddenly calmed; the streams stopped flowing; the leaves of the trees ceased rustling; the angels stopped singing hymns, there was nothing but silence, in Heaven and on earth. Out of the silence came the voice of the Almighty: "I am the Lord thy God." All at once the heavens were opened; the hidden depths of the earth were revealed; so that the children of Israel might see with their own eyes that there is none like God either in the heavens above or on the earth below.

The Almighty, in His infinite wisdom, desired to give His Law not only to the generation that was worthy to behold the Revelation, but also to all generations to come. He therefore gathered around Mount Sinai all the souls of the generations to come and bade them listen to His words. The souls accepted the Torah with great joy, and bound themselves to obey His Law in generations to come for ever and ever; thus His Law became an eternal Law.

When the children of Israel heard the voice of the Almighty—few indeed are worthy of hearing God speak—they were flung back twelve miles from the mount, and their souls fled from their bodies. The Torah then presented itself before God, and asked: "Lord of the world, art Thou to give the Torah to the living or to the dead?"

"To the living," replied God.

"But they are dead," complained the Torah.

"For thy sake," said God, "I will restore them to life again." He thereupon let fall upon them the dew destined to revive the dead in time to come, at the advent of the Messiah, and they returned to life. The Almighty thereupon pronounced the Ten Commandments:

The first commandment:

"I am the Lord thy God who brought thee out of the land of Egypt, out of the house of bondage."

The second commandment:

"Thou shalt have no other gods before Me. Thou shalt not make unto thee a graven image, nor any manner of likeness, of anything that is in the heaven above, or that is in the earth beneath, or that is in the water under the earth; thou shalt not bow down to them, nor serve them; for I the Lord thy God am a jealous God, visiting the iniquity of the fathers upon the children to the third and fourth generations of them that hate Me; and showing mercy to the thousandth generation of them that love Me and keep My commandments."

The third Commandment:

"Thou shalt not take the name of the Lord thy God in vain; for the Lord will not hold him guiltless that takes His name in vain."

This commandment warns against swearing falsely. Our Rabbis say that one must abstain from taking an oath simply to strengthen a statement, even if one desires to swear to the truth. The unnecessary mention of God's name in such expressions as, "For God's sake," is also forbidden, for it leads to the abuse of the divine Name.

Concerning the third Commandment, the Rabbis tell many stories about people who were severely punished for having sworn falsely. They also tell of many who, because they refused to take an oath, suffered for it at the hands of heathen peoples, but were afterwards rewarded by Heaven.

One story tells of a woman who was entrusted with a gold piece by a friend. She put the coin for safekeeping in a jar of flour. Forgetting the gold piece, she one day used the flour to bake a loaf of bread. When the man called for the coin, she swore that she did not have it in her possession, not knowing that the coin was in the loaf she had baked. She did not intentionally swear falsely; yet she suffered a great loss because of that. Hence, say the Rabbis, never swear at all.

There is another story about a man who, before going on a journey, entrusted his money to a friend. On his return, he called upon his friend for the money. The friend refused, saying: "True, you gave me your money for safekeeping, but I have given it back to you." The man summoned his friend to appear in court. But the latter was clever: hollowing out a cane, he put the money into it and brought it to court. When the judge ordered him to take an oath that he had returned the money, he said to his former friend: "Please hold this cane for a moment, while I take the oath." After the oath had been taken the claimant became enraged, for he knew that the man had sworn falsely. In his anger he struck the floor heavily with the hollow cane. The cane broke into many pieces and the glittering coins rolled out on the floor. The judge observed the deceit and punished the man severely.

The fourth commandment:

"Remember the Sabbath day to keep it holy. Six days shalt thou labor, and do all thy work; but the seventh day is a Sabbath to the Lord thy God; in it thou shalt not do any manner of work, thou, nor thy son, nor thy daughter, nor thy manservant, nor thy maidservant, nor thy cattle, nor the stranger that is within thy gates; for in six days the Lord made heaven and earth, the sea, and all that in them is, and rested on the seventh day; wherefore the Lord blessed the Sabbath day, and hallowed it."

The fifth commandment:

"Honor thy father and thy mother, that thy days may be long upon the land which the Lord thy God giveth thee."

The Rabbis tell the following story concerning the fifth commandment. One day, one of the twelve precious stones set in the breastplate of the Jewish high priest was lost. The Israelites searched everywhere to find a precious stone to replace it. At last they were told that a non-Jew, Dima, the son of Netina, possessed the stone they desired. So the elders of the Israelites went to Dima, and offered him a very high price for the jewel. Dima was satisfied with the bargain, and went into the inner chamber to fetch it. There he found his father sleeping on the chest in which he kept the precious stone. Although the price offered was a very good one, and he was willing to sell the stone, he would not wake his father. He therefore returned to the elders of the Israelites and told them that he could not give them the jewel. The elders believed that he had reconsidered the matter, and would not sell at that price. They offered him more money for it, but he refused. After some minutes of discussion, Dima finally returned to the inner chamber, and found his father awake. He took the precious stone and gave it to the elders, who were overjoyed to find that it was exactly what they wanted, and they gladly offered to pay Dima the higher price they had last offered him. Dima, however, would accept only that amount which had been agreed upon at the beginning; and he added: "I do not accept payment for the honor I have shown my father."

Dima was rewarded by the Almighty for his deed. Among his cattle he had bred a perfectly red heifer, for which the elders of Israel paid him a very high price. It was wanted by the Jews for the preparation of the ashes of purification (*parah adumah*) and none could be found elsewhere.

The sixth commandment:

"Thou shalt not kill."

Our sages tell us that one may be guilty of transgressing the sixth commandment when not actually shedding blood or taking a man's life. For instance, they consider a person who publicly insults another as though he were guilty of bloodshed. There are many other similar analogies mentioned by the sages.

The seventh commandment.

"Thou shalt not commit adultery."

The seventh commandment requires a married man to be faithful to his wife, and a married woman to be faithful to her husband. Many are the stories told in the Talmud of how unfaithfulness in married life has led to destruction and eternal unhappiness.

The eighth commandment:

"Thou shalt not steal."

The sages tell us that the eighth commandment orders one to abstain not only from stealing property, but also from stealing a man's honor, from stealing a man's business, from stealing a man's reputation and even from "stealing a man's mind" by deceiving or misleading him.

The Rabbis tell an interesting story to prove that a thief may never benefit by stealing, but will eventually be discovered and be compelled to return what he has stolen. They say that once a wealthy merchant, in the course of his business, travelled through many lands to buy merchandise. One day, he arrived in a distant city with five hundred gold coins in his purse. Afraid to entrust the money with any of the inhabitants of the town, and not wishing to carry the money with him until the official market day, lest he be robbed, he thought the safest thing for him to do would be to bury his treasure.

He went to the outskirts of the town to look for a safe hiding-place, and found a suitable spot under a cluster of trees. Making sure that no one was near, he sat down on the

ground as if to rest, and slowly and very cautiously dug a
hole in which he buried the gold. He noticed that there was
an inhabited house nearby, but as the wall of the house facing
him had neither windows nor doors, he thought he was unperceived. He looked around for a while, marked well the
place where he had buried his treasure, and then walked
away, confident that he would find his golden coins whenever
he would have need of them.

But there was something that the merchant was not aware
of. In that seemingly solid wall, there was an opening large
enough for a person to see through. The owner of the house,
noticing a stranger roaming about the neighborhood, had
watched him steadily through the opening in the wall. He
had observed the stranger acting peculiarly and had become
suspicious. At nightfall, he went to the spot where the money
was buried, and observing fresh dirt piled up, he began digging,
until he found the bag with the glittering gold coins, and
walked away with it.

A few days later, the merchant came to the spot to take his
treasure, but to his dismay the money was not there. Heart-
broken, he rose to his feet and prayed. Suddenly a thought
flashed through his mind: some one in the nearby house must
have seen him there! But how could he prove by whom it
was taken? Arriving at the inn dejected and dismayed, another thought came to him suddenly; it was as if someone
had advised him what to do. He filled a moneybag with
pebbles, and immediately went to the owner of the house.

Upon entering, he introduced himself to the owner, and
said to him: "I am a stranger here and have brought a great
fortune with me to buy merchandise. A part of the treasure
I buried somewhere in the ground a few days ago, but the
greater part of it I still have in my possession. I was told
that you are a very wise man and can advise me well. I want
to know if it would be advisable for me to bury this very
large treasure in the same spot where I buried the smaller

part of it, or would it be safer to divide it in smaller quantities and bury it in different places; or perchance you may show me a very honest man with whom I can deposit it until I have need of it."

"Ah," thought the guilty man, "if he finds not the money in the place he buried it, he surely would not place there his great treasure." He told the stranger to wait a few minutes, on the pretext that he was very much occupied, and he went and reburied the golden coins in the same spot. Coming back, he said to the stranger: "I considered the matter very carefully, and it is my opinion that it is best to bury your treasure in one spot, so that you can watch over it very carefully." The stranger understood what had happened. He went at once to the spot: the golden coins were there.

The ninth commandment:

"Thou shalt not bear false witness against thy neighbor."

The tenth commandment:

"Thou shalt not covet thy neighbor's house; thou shalt not covet thy neighbor's wife, nor his manservant, nor his maidservant, nor his ox, nor his ass, nor anything that is thy neighbor's."

The tenth commandment forbids one to want that which belongs to another. The Bible gives a story showing how covetousness leads to perjury, theft, and even murder:

There ruled an idol-worshiping king in Israel, named Ahab, who had a very wicked wife, a heathen, whose name was Queen Jezebel. King Ahab was fond of building palaces for his pleasure. His summer residence was Samaria, but for his winter residence he built a new city in the plain of Jezreel where he erected a palace of ivory for himself. Ahab needed extensive pleasure grounds for his palace, and he desired to purchase a vineyard which adjoined his palace to add to his estate. This vineyard belonged to Naboth, one of the most respected citizens of Jezreel.

King Ahab offered to give Naboth another vineyard for
the one near his palace, or else to pay him for it in cash. But
Naboth refused to sell the vineyard, which he had inherited
from his father. Disappointed, Ahab returned to his house sullen and displeased, and he lay down upon his bed, and would
not eat bread.

But Jezebel his wife came to him and said: "Why is your
spirit so sullen, and why do you eat no bread?" And he said
to her: "Because I spoke to Naboth the Jezreelite, and asked
him to give me his vineyard for money, or else I will give
him another vineyard for it. But he refused to give me his
vineyard." And Queen Jezebel said to him: "Do you govern
the kingdom of Israel? Arise, and eat bread, and let your
heart be merry; I will give you the vineyard of Naboth."

So she wrote letters in the King's name, and sealed them
with his seal, and sent them to the elders and the nobles that
were in the city. And she wrote in the letters: "Proclaim
a fast, and set Naboth at the head of the people; and set two
men, base fellows, before him, and let them bear witness
against him, saying: 'You did curse God and the king.' Then
carry him out, and stone him to death."

The elders and the nobles did as Jezebel had written to
them in the letters which she had sent to them. They proclaimed a fast, and set Naboth at the head of the people.
The two men came before Naboth and bore witness against
him in the presence of the people, saying: "Naboth did
curse God and the king." Then they carried Naboth out of
the city and stoned him to death.

When Jezebel heard that Naboth was dead, she said to
Ahab: "Arise, take possession of the vineyard of Naboth
the Jezreelite, which he refused to give you for money; for
he is not alive, but dead." When Ahab heard that Naboth
was dead, he went down to take possession of Naboth's
vineyard. But just as he reached the spot, he was confronted
by the stern prophet Elijah, who thundered at him: "Have

you killed and also taken possession? Thus says the Lord: 'In the place where dogs licked the blood of Naboth, shall dogs lick your blood, even yours.' " And Ahab said: "Have you found me, O mine enemy?" And he answered: "I have found you. Because you have given yourself over to do that which is evil in the sight of God, behold, God will bring evil upon you, and will utterly sweep you away, and will cut off from Ahab every man-child. And of Jezebel God said: 'The dogs shall eat Jezebel in the moat of Jezreel.' "

Elijah's threat had a crushing effect upon the king. He put on sackcloth and ashes and repented of his crime. But Jezebel soon mastered the weakling again and banished his scruples.

And Elijah's prophecy came true. In his war with the Arameans Ahab was killed, and dogs licked his blood by the pool of Samaria. As for Queen Jezebel, she was thrown by her own officers from a window of her palace and trodden under the feet of horses. On the following day, when they wanted to bury her, they found of her body only the skull, the feet, and the palms of her hands; the rest of the body of Jezebel was eaten by dogs, as the prophet Elijah, the servant of the Lord, had foretold.

3. Moses in Heaven

The people, upon hearing the peals of thunder and seeing the terrible flashes of lightning, trembled and stood afar off. They called to Moses: "Speak you with us, and we will hear; but let not God speak with us, lest we die." Moses answered: "Fear not; for God is come to prove you; that His fear may be before you, and that you sin not." The people remained afar off; but Moses approached the thick darkness where God was.

The Almighty said to Moses: "Come up to Me into the mount, and be there; and I will give you the tablets of stone, the law and the commandment which I have written, that thou mayest teach them."

The Rabbis have preserved the following account:

"A cloud appeared before Moses, but he knew not whether to hold fast to it, or to ride upon it. Then suddenly the cloud divided into two parts. Moses entered between them and was carried away by the cloud to the high heavens.

"On his reaching heaven and coming close to the throne of Divine Majesty, the ministering angels surrounded the throne and said: 'Almighty God, what does he, who is born of woman, here in the abode of the Holy and the High?'

"'He has come here to receive the Torah,' the Almighty replied.

"'Why give it to the creatures of dust, why not give it to the angels in heaven?' the angels complained, and they threatened to scorch Moses with their fiery breath. But God said to Moses: 'Hold tightly to the throne of Divine Majesty and argue with them.'

"Moses obeyed, and thus encouraged, he answered the angels: 'It is written in the Torah: "I am the Lord thy God, that has led thee out of Egypt, out of the house of bondage." Were you enslaved in Egypt, and then delivered, that you are in need of the Torah? It is further written in the Torah: "Thou shalt have no other gods before Me." Are there any idolaters among you that you are in need of the Torah? It is written there: "Honor thy father and thy mother." Have you then parents that you are in need of the Torah?' It is written there: "Thou shalt not murder; thou shalt not steal." Are there any murderers among you, or is there perchance any money in Heaven that can be stolen, that you are in need of the Torah?' The angels thereupon withdrew their opposition, and acknowledged that the Torah should be given to the inhabitants of the earth, saying: 'Eternal, our Lord, how excellent is Thy name in all the earth; Thou hast set Thy glory upon the heavens.'"

Moses stayed in heaven forty days and forty nights, during which time the Almighty taught him the written law and the oral teachings, which were expounded in later generations by the Talmudic scholars. God then bestowed the Torah upon Moses, who departed from heaven with the tablets upon which the Ten Commandments were engraved. The tablets were created by God in the dusk of the first Sabbath at the close of the Creation, and were made of sapphire-like stone.

Shibeah Asar Betammuz

THE FAST OF THE SEVENTEENTH OF TAMMUZ

The seventeenth day of the month of Tammuz is observed as a fast day, because the Romans broke into the City of Jerusalem during the existence of the Second Temple.

After the destruction of the First Temple, a fast had been observed by the Jews in Babylon, on the ninth day of the month of Tammuz, as told by the prophet Zechariah, because the Babylonians had on that day made a breach in the wall of Jerusalem. (*See* page 241.) Our Rabbis, however, considered the destruction of the Second Temple a still greater national calamity, and therefore decreed that the fast be observed on the seventeenth day of Tammuz to commemorate the breach made on that day by the Romans. (See page 260.)

For a full description of these historical events, see the chapters that follow.

Tisheah Beab

THE FAST OF THE NINTH OF AB WHEN THE JEW MOURNS

I LAWS AND CUSTOMS

WHAT IS A FAST DAY? Among the Jews, fasting, as an expression of grief and extreme sorrow, is very ancient. The Jewish religion adopted it as a sign of remorse and penitence by which forgiveness might be obtained from the God against whom one has sinned. The Jew on public fast days not only commemorates his great national calamity, but also seeks forgiveness for his personal sins. Implicitly he believes that had not the Jews sinned against their God in the past, they would not have been punished by losing their sanctuary and their land. He therefore fasts in expiation of the sins of his ancient forebears and for his own sins as well; for he believes that by purging himself of sin, he will become worthy of national restoration. In other words, the Jewish fast days are national memorial days, recalling the misfortunes of the past; and at the same time they serve as a plea to God for the revival of Jewish national existence. The fast days are a means of keeping alive the hope and the courage of the Jewish people.

THE THREE WEEKS. The three weeks, between the seventeenth day of Tammuz and the ninth of Ab, are a period of mourning in remembrance of the great misfortunes that befell the Jews many centuries ago. They pray to their Father in Heaven to free them from their heartless oppressors, and to bring them back to their coveted land of Palestine. During these days the Jews observe some of the rules that apply to those who mourn the death of their next of kin: they perform no marriages; they play no musical instruments; they do not purchase new garments; and they do not have their hair cut.

THE NINE DAYS. From the first to the ninth day of the month of Ab, the grief of the Jews grows deeper, and they observe even more stringent rules of mourning to express their sorrow. Joy and merriment is avoided as much as possible: they eat no meat and drink no wine during these nine days, except on the Sabbath; they do not wash their clothes; they do not bathe even in cold water; and they take no walks for pleasure's sake.

SHABBAT HAZON. The Sabbath that occurs during the first nine days of the month of Ab, is known as *Shabbat Hazon*, because the weekly portion of the Prophets which is read in the synagogue at the Sabbath morning service—the first chapter of

Isaiah—begins with the word *hazon*, the vision of. This chapter is read with the traditional plaintive melody like that of Lamentations read on the Ninth of Ab.

In this chapter, the prophet, in scathing terms, reproaches the Jewish people for their backslidings. He prophesies that very evil days will come to punish their sins, but ends with words of consolation.

THE NINTH OF AB. The ninth day of the month of Ab is observed as a fast day, because on that day the First Temple was destroyed by the Babylonians, (page 243, below) and the Second Temple by the Romans (page 246, below).

On all other fast days food may be taken during the night preceding the fast, but no food may be had on the night preceding the ninth of Ab. The meal before this fast must be ended before sunset. At this meal some orthodox Jews eat an egg, symbolic of mourning, and add a little ashes to their food, indicating the reducing of the Temple to ashes.

On the Ninth of Ab, every Jew observes all rules of mourning. In the evening, he goes to the synagogue, removes his shoes if they are made of leather, and sits either on a low stool or on the floor, while the reader in measured, plaintive, tones chants Lamentations. This is one of the books of the Bible written by the Prophet Jeremiah who lived during the destruction of the First Temple. In beautiful and poetic words, this Prophet mourns the sad lot of the Jew.

Returning home from the synagogue, the Jew does not offer the usual greeting to his family. Sorrow, gloom, and sadness reign in the house. Even sleeping quarters are made less comfortable than on ordinary nights: some remove the pillows from under their heads, while others sleep on the floor.

In the morning, the Jew does not wash or bathe in warm water, but simply wets his fingers and eyes with cold water, not using any soap; nor does he massage himself. He does not greet the members of his family as usual, but silently goes to the synagogue to offer prayers.

The *talit* and the *tephilin* are considered holy ornaments, and therefore they are not put on at the morning service of the Ninth of Ab. In the synagogue, the worshipers again sit either on low stools or on the floor, pray, and again listen to the reading of Lamentations. The prayers ended, the Jew returns home, without greeting any one either in the synagogue or on his way home.

The Jew abstains from eating and drinking all day until after the appearance of the stars; he does not greet people, and does not wear leather shoes all day; until noon, he does not sit on regular chairs or benches, and he does not engage in any work.

After the morning service, some Jews make it a custom to visit the cemetery.

At the afternoon service (*minhah*), the *talit* and the *tephilin* are put on, and the designated portions of the Torah and of the Prophets are read.

SHABBAT NAHAMU. The Sabbath following the nine days of Ab is called *Shabbat Nahamu,* the Sabbath of comfort, because we read at the morning service in the synagogue, for the weekly reading from the Prophets, the fortieth chapter of Isaiah, commencing with the words *Nahamu, nahamu,* comfort ye, comfort ye. Thus again after the period of mourning, the Jew is imbued with words of hope for a bright future. The Jew has never lost confidence in the help of God and in the final victory of justice and truth.

I THE DESTRUCTION OF THE FIRST TEMPLE

1. *The Prophet Jeremiah*

During the reign of Jehoiakim, king of Judah, the worship of the Egyptian gods became popular in the land. Statues of

gold and silver, of wood and stone, were put up in private
homes and worshiped. The holy Temple itself was defiled by
images of idols. Worst of all, Jews sacrificed children by fire
in the Valley of Hinnom, in honor of the idol-god Moloch.
The firstborn sons were especially chosen for this purpose.
False prophets sprang up who encouraged the madness of the
people. The king made no effort to suppress the evil practices;
he himself even took part in it.

There were more true prophets of God during this period
than at any other time. These holy prophets fearlessly opposed
the immoral practices of the people. Daily they addressed
themselves to the people, the princes, and the king. They
prophesied Judah's downfall, unless the people turned from
their evil ways, and returned to the Lord their God.

The best known of these prophets was Jeremiah. When a
mere lad, he received the call from God to be a prophet in
Israel. This youthful prophet was a great patriot; he ardently
loved his country and his people. He continually announced
the doom of Israel, but his heart was bleeding within him.
The joy of life left him. He sought a solitary existence of sorrow and gloom. He often wished he were in some desert, far
away from his people, where he would not be compelled to
behold their wickedness. But he remained true to his mission.
He warned them and pleaded with them day and night, in
order that the nation might escape its sad fate, but his words
remained unheeded by the king and the nobles.

One of Jeremiah's first prophecies, in the reign of King Jehoiakim, earned him the hatred of the idolatrous priests and the
false prophets. During a festival, when a large multitude had
assembled in the Temple at Jerusalem to offer sacrifices, Jeremiah in a fiery denunciation of idol-worship and the burning
of children for Moloch, prophesied the fall of the Temple.
He had hardly finished his address when he was seized by the
priests and the false prophets. They threatened to kill him,
and cried out: "You shall die, for you have prophesied to the

people that this Temple will fall." A great uproar arose which caused several princes to hurry from the palace to the Temple. These princes made an investigation. Through the efforts of his friends, Jeremiah was this time allowed to go free because the princes found that he spoke in the name of God. After that the priests and the false prophets persecuted Jeremiah, and watched for every opportunity to do him harm.

2. *Babylon*

Assyria, the first great world empire, fell after an existence of more than six centuries, through the combined efforts of Media and Babylon. Nineveh, the Assyrian capital, fell after a siege, in the year 605 B. C. E. Thereafter Babylon ruled over the countries west of the Euphrates, among which was the land of Judah.

Shortly after this, the king of Babylon died, and the young prince Nebuchadnezzar, a great warrior, ascended the throne. The prophet Jeremiah foretold that Babylon would become a world power. He advised the Jews to break their alliance with the Egyptians, and submit to the rule of the new Babylonian king, because he had been chosen by God to carry out His judgment against the nation. But his prophecies and his threats fell upon deaf ears. The false prophets calmed the people by crying, "peace, peace," and they persecuted Jeremiah most bitterly.

The prophecies of Jeremiah now began to be fulfilled. After establishing order within his vast empire, Nebuchadnezzar undertook a campaign of conquest. Syria surrendered without resistance. The king of Phoenicia also submitted to Nebuchadnezzar. The next objective of the Babylonian king was the invasion of Egypt. To accomplish this difficult task, he had first to conquer the countries lying between Syria and Egypt, so that he might not be hindered by their hostility.

The Babylonian army, under Nebuchadnezzar's leadership, steadily advanced. An ultimatum was sent to Jehoiakim, king of Judah, to surrender peacefully, or be completely wiped out. Egypt, however, encouraged Jehoiakim to resist the Babylonian king. A decision had to be made quickly.

Expecting Egyptian aid, King Jehoiakim and his advisers postponed their decision from day to day. In the ninth month of the year 600 B. C. E. , a fast day was proclaimed, and all the people were summoned to Jerusalem, to pray to God that Judah be spared from falling into the hands of the Babylonian king. Alarmed, the people flocked to the Temple as to a place of refuge.

In the midst of the tumult, Jeremiah ordered his faithful disciple Baruch to read before the assembled multitude the prophecy which he had made years ago. In it was foretold the rise of the overwhelming power of the Babylonians. Baruch hesitated: he dared not read a prophecy to induce the people to submit to the Babylonians. Was not the nation then assembled to fast and pray in the hope of averting such a calamity? Jeremiah, however, urged him to do his duty in the name of God, and Baruch yielded. In the court of the Temple, and in the presence of all the people, he read the scroll of Jeremiah. The prophecy made a deep impression upon the assembly. There were many in the audience who had heard Jeremiah's prophetic warning before, but had disregarded it. Now the Babylonians were almost at the gate of Jerusalem, and the independence of Judah was threatened. The assembled multitude was shocked by the realization that Jeremiah's prophecies were beginning to be fulfilled.

Among the assembled people there was a young prince named Micaiah who was greatly affected by the prophecies of Jeremiah. He hurried to the palace where the princes were assembled, and told them of the reading of the prophecy. The princes invited Baruch to read the scroll in their presence, and they were deeply moved by it. They hoped that the reading of the scroll would have a similar effect upon the king, and would induce him to submit to Nebuchadnezzar without resistance.

They therefore went to the king and told him of what had happened. The king ordered that the scroll be read to him, and the princes felt hopeful. One of them read the scroll, but as the reading of a page was finished, the king took it and calmly cast it into the fire. The princes were shocked. They begged him not to tempt fate. The king, however, paid no attention, but kept on casting page after page into the fire until the entire scroll was burnt. The king then ordered that Jeremiah and Baruch be seized. Fortunately, the anxious princes had taken care to hide Jeremiah and Baruch where the king's officers could not find them, and their lives were saved.

The reading of the scroll, however, created a rift among the princes. Some of them, including the minister of war, were convinced by Jeremiah's prophecies, and urged King Jehoiakim to submit to Nebuchadnezzar. Finally Jehoiakim yielded and made peace with Nebuchadnezzar. He paid the tribute imposed upon him, and became a vassal of Babylon in the year 600 B. C. E.

But King Jehoiakim was restless under the Babylonian yoke. Moreover, the Egyptian king constantly induced him to rebel. Two years later, Phoenicia rebelled against Nebuchadnezzar, and declared its independence. The Phoenicians fortified Tyre, their capital, to enable it to withstand a long siege. King Jehoiakim used this opportunity to rebel likewise. He refused to pay tribute to Babylon, and formed an alliance with Egypt.

Nebuchadnezzar was unable to attend to Jehoiakim just then. He had to concentrate all his forces upon Phoenicia. The siege of Tyre continued for thirteen years. Now and then, however, Nebuchadnezzar sent small raiding parties into Judah.

3. *The First Conquest of Jerusalem*

In the year 597 B. C. E., King Jehoiakim died, and his eighteen-year-old son Jehoiachin succeeded him to the throne of Judah. The new ruler insisted on carrying out his father's policy of resisting Nebuchadnezzar.

At this time, Nebuchadnezzar found it possible to detach a large force from the siege of Tyre. He sent this army to oppose the Egyptians who began hostile acts against him. The Babylonians easily subdued the entire territory as far as the river of Egypt. They seized all of Judah, with the exception of a few cities in the south. But Jehoiachin relied upon the strength of Jerusalem and upon aid from Egypt, and would not surrender. Nebuchadnezzar, enraged at this unexpected resistance, sent several generals to lay siege to Jerusalem. The prophet Jeremiah again appeared on the scene. He spoke harshly and threateningly against the young king and his mother. The king, however, did not then think of submission. But when Nebuchadnezzar himself reached the camp, the king and his mother betook themselves to him to plead for mercy. The only mercy the victor showed was in sparing their lives.

Jehoiachin was dethroned after a reign of one hundred days. The entire royal family, together with ten thousand inhabitants of Jerusalem, were sent into exile to Babylon. Nebuchadnezzar plundered the treasures of the Temple and of the palace, but he did not deprive Judah of its independence as a commonwealth, and he spared Jerusalem, its walls, and its Temple. He was the first foreign counqueror of Jerusalem, after it had existed nearly five centuries.

Nebuchadnezzar placed upon the throne of Judah Jehoiachin's brother Zedekiah, who was twenty-one years old and of a mild, unwarlike nature. Such a man, Nebuchadnezzar thought, would cause him little trouble. He made Zedekiah take a solemn oath that he would be loyal to Babylon.

Judah swiftly recovered from the hard blows it had received, and returned to a state of prosperity. Jerusalem remained to the very end a rich and beautiful city, the "mistress of the countries."

In the fourth year of Zedekiah's reign, ambassadors from Edom, Moab, Ammon, Tyre, and Sidon gathered in Jerusalem to persuade King Zedekiah to join in an alliance against Babylon. Jeremiah warned the nations not to rebel against Babylon. But the false prophets of Jerusalem predicted that great salvation would come to Judah if only she dared throw off the Babylonian yoke. Jeremiah's voice went unheeded.

King Zedekiah was a man of weak character, and he soon yielded to the urgings of Egypt and of the neighboring countries. He refused to pay his tribute to Nebuchadnezzar. Most of the Jews supported the king; they believed that Jerusalem could never be destroyed. Somehow, they thought, a miracle would save it. Feverish preparations were now being made for war with Babylon.

4. *The Siege of Jerusalem*

For two years Nebuchadnezzar delayed his punishment of Zedekiah for the violation of his oath. The inhabitants of Jerusalem were extremely joyful. The predictions of the false prophets appeared to be true. But the hour of doom finally approached. At last Nebuchadnezzar started upon his expedition. The neighboring nations, who had urged Judah to rebel, submitted immediately upon the approach of the enemy. Edom, bordering on Judah, became hostile toward its neighbor. Even Egypt hesitated to send help. It was therefore an easy task for Nebuchadnezzar to capture most of the fortified cities of Judah.

On the tenth day of the month of Tebet, in the year 588 B. C. E., the Babylonian army began the siege of Jerusalem. This day therefore has been observed as a fast day by the Jews in every land to this day. The fortifications of the capital had meanwhile been strengthened. The city had been supplied with provisions and water to withstand a long siege. The population of Jerusalem was greatly swelled by the arrival of villagers. The residents of the country districts fled for protection to the capital with their families and their cattle upon the approach of the enemy. The people of Jerusalem defended themselves heroically against the Babylonian army.

After the siege had lasted a year, Apries, the king of Egypt,

finally decided to keep his promise to the Jews. He sent a
large army against Nebuchadnezzar. The Babylonians were
compelled to raise the siege of Jerusalem, and to advance
against the Egyptians. The joy of Jerusalem was boundless.
The people streamed out from the gates of the city to enjoy a
taste of freedom once more after their long confinement. They
wished to see how their fields and vineyards had fared, and
also to lay in a fresh supply of provisions in case the siege was
renewed. The nobles and the rich soon resumed their sinful
ways. The prophet Jeremiah protested. In the presence of the
king and the nobles, he rebuked them and announced that the
Babylonians would return to capture Jerusalem, and fire, sword,
pestilence, and famine would rage in the city. The king sent
courtiers to ask the prophet to pray to God that the Babylonians
might not return. The prophet replied: "Even if the entire
Babylonian army were destroyed and only two wounded soldiers remained, even they would rise and set the city on fire."

The nobles of Judah had long been unfriendly to Jeremiah.
Now they turned with a deadly hatred against him when he
delivered this last bold address. They had long been waiting
for an opportunity to seize the prophet, and that opportunity
at last came. One day, Jeremiah desired to leave Jerusalem to
visit his native village Anathoth. As he was about to pass
through the gate, he was seized by the guard who accused him
of trying to desert to the Babylonians. He was forcibly taken
before the nobles, who were glad of the opportunity to avenge
themselves upon him. They treated him like a traitor and spy.
They struck him and cast him into a cistern in the dungeon
which was under the command of Johanan, the royal secretary,
a cruel, heartless man.

In the narrow, filthy cell, Jeremiah remained for many days
in solitary confinement. Not even his family was permitted to
see him.

The joy of Jerusalem was of short duration. The Babylonians
routed the Egyptian army, and Judah was left to fight her battle

alone. The neighboring nations, her former allies, now scorned Judah, and anxiously awaited the fall of Jerusalem. The Babylonians returned to besiege the city. The people began to lose courage. Many stole out and went over to the Babylonians or fled to Egypt. King Zedekiah realized too late the folly of the rebellion against the mighty Babylonians. Secretly he had Jeremiah brought into an inner chamber of the palace, and asked him if he had a prophecy concerning the outcome of the war. "Surely," replied the prophet, "you shall fall into the hands of the king of Babylonia."

King Zedekiah did not punish the prophet for his boldness. He even granted Jeremiah's petition that he be removed from Johanan's prison. Jeremiah was placed now under guard in the palace, and supplied daily with a loaf of bread from the royal bakery. He remained there several months. He was allowed to see his friends, and his faithful disciple Baruch was again near him.

Meanwhile the siege of Jerusalem became more horrible from day to day. The sword without and famine within took victims by the thousands. The streets of Jerusalem were strewn with the dead that lay unburied in the heat of summer. Children died of hunger and pestilence in the arms of their helpless mothers. The rich, in their despair, gave their treasures away in vain attempts to obtain a piece of bread.

The Rabbis have preserved a few tragic stories about these terrible days. One of them tells: "Once a very rich woman said to her husband: 'Pick out one of my best precious stones, go through the streets of Jerusalem, and see if you cannot find someone to give you a morsel of bread for it.' For hours and hours the husband walked through the streets of Jerusalem, and whomever he met he offered to give a precious stone in exchange for a morsel of bread, but there was no bread to be had. Exhausted with hunger and fatigue, the husband fell dead in the street.

"Towards evening, the rich woman said to her only son.

'My child, I am greatly worried about the fate of your father. Pray go out and look for him.' The son was very much weakened from lack of food, nevertheless he went, and after a long search, found his father's dead body in the mud of the streets. 'Oh, would that I had died in your stead, my dear father!' exclaimed the unfortunate son. And prostrating himself on the corpse of his father, he embraced it, and there he, too, breathed his last."

In the midst of this suffering, Jeremiah boldly told the people that to save their lives they must surrender to the Babylonians. When the nobles heard this, they demanded that the king put the prophet to death because he was discouraging the defenders of the city. Kind Zedekiah replied with his usual weakness: "He is in your hands; I can do naught against you."

The nobles seized Jeremiah. Not daring to kill the man of God by their own hands, they cast him into a slimy pit, from which they did not expect him to escape alive.

Jeremiah would certainly have perished in the pit had it not been for an Ethiopian servant of the king, named Ebed-melech. Outraged at the treatment the prophet had received, Ebed-melech appeared before the king and said: "O sire, the holy prophet of God will surely perish in the slimy dungeon. Why not save his life?" The king consented to save the prophet, and he said to Ebed-melech: "Take thirty men with you, and take up Jeremiah the prophet out of the slimy pit, before he dies." So Ebed-melech took the men with him and some ropes, and went to the pit. Ebed-melech called out to Jeremiah: "Put these ropes under your arms." And when Jeremiah did so, they pulled him up out of the pit.

The prophet, however, was even now not given his freedom. He was kept under guard in the court, but the king now protected him from any attack by the nobles. King Zedekiah himself now thought of surrendering to the Babylonians. The king one day summoned the prophet to a secret chamber of the palace, and said to him: "I will ask you a thing; hide nothing from me." Then Jeremiah said to the king: "If I tell it to you, will you not put me to death? and if I give you counsel, you will not hearken to me." The king swore secretly to Jeremiah: "As the Lord lives, I will not put you to death, neither will I give you into the hands of these men that seek your life."

Then said the prophet to the king: "Thus says the Lord God of Israel: 'If you go forth to the Babylonian king, then you shall live, and your family shall live, and this city shall not be burned with fire; but if you will not go forth to the Babylonian king, then this city shall be given into the hand of the Babylonians, and you shall not escape out of their hand!' " The king then expressed his fear that if he would surrender, the Jews in the Babylonian camp would mock him and put him to death for such an act. The prophet assured him that no harm would befall him in the Babylonian camp. But King Zedekiah lacked courage to take such a step.

5. *The Destruction of Jerusalem*

Meanwhile, death by famine, pestilence, and the sword, struck the inhabitants of Jerusalem. The number of fighting men kept decreasing, until hardly any were left to defend the walls. On the ninth day of the month of Tammuz, June, 586 B. C. E., the bread supply gave out. The defenders of the city were so exhausted that they could no longer offer any resistance. The Babylonians succeeded in making a wide breach in the wall and entered the city. They killed youths and men who appeared to them to be able to offer resistance, and threw the rest of the population into chains as captives. They entered the Temple, and killed the priests and the prophets who sought protection there. The neighboring nations, the Philistines, Edomites, and Moabites who had joined Nebuchadnezzar, also entered with the Babylonians, and plundered the treasures of the holy place.

King Zedekiah, in the meantime, escaped with a few followers through a secret underground passage. He hoped to cross the Jordan, and escape the vengeance of the Babylonian king.

But Zedekiah and his men, faint with hunger, made slow progress in their flight. They were soon overtaken by the Babylonian horsemen and taken captive. King Zedekiah and his sons, together with the rest of the captives, were taken to Riblah to await the pleasure of Nebuchadnezzar. Among the chained captives was the Prophet Jeremiah, who was found by the Babylonians in the king's court and was taken for a servant of the palace. The Babylonian king punished Zedekiah in a most cruel manner. Zedekiah's sons and relatives were slain in his presence. After that Zedekiah himself was blinded. In chains he was sent a captive to Babylon. There he did not survive his sorrows long.

The Rabbis have handed down a peculiar story: "When the Babylonian commander forced his way into the Temple, he found the priests engaged in the services, and the Levites singing Psalms and playing their harps. 'Cease all these ceremonies, or you shall meet with a horrible death,' ordered the commander. The singing stopped at once, and the commander, looking about the Temple, cried out in astonishment: 'What is the meaning of this blood seething on the floor of the Temple?'

" 'It is nothing but the blood of the sacrifices we offer to God,' replied the priests, terror-stricken.

" 'I can distinguish human blood from that of oxen,' said the Babylonian commander. 'Murder has been committed in this very holy place. Slaughter oxen in this spot, and see if the blood will cease seething.' A great number of oxen were slaughtered and their blood mingled with the blood on the floor of the Temple, but the seething did not cease.

" 'Tell the truth,' thundered the commander; 'else, you shall die by torture.'

"The priests then narrated the truth: 'There once lived among our people a prophet of God, named Zechariah. He prophesied in the name of God that the Temple would be destroyed if the Jews continued to do evil. For his candor, he was slain by the people of the Temple. His blood was shed in this very spot, and since then it has not stopped seething.'

" 'I, I will stop the seething of the blood,' said the haughty commander. He then ordered that the members of the Sanhedrin, the highest court in Jerusalem, be slain on the bloody spot, but the blood of the prophet continued to seethe. He massacred many learned men, thousands of young priests, and thousands of school children on the bloody spot, but the blood of Zechariah still seethed. Finally, the Babylonian commander exclaimed: 'Zechariah, Zechariah, the best in Israel have I slaughtered for your sake. Do you desire that I destroy all the people?' Only then did the blood of the prophet stop seething.

"This incident startled the heartless commander. A thought flashed through his mind: 'If the Jews have been punished so cruelly for having taken the life of a single man, what then shall be my fate, who have killed people by the thousands?' "

Nebuchadnezzar was at first undecided whether to spare Jerusalem or destroy it. Finally, he decided to destroy it together with the Temple. He sent Nebuzaradan, the commander of his guard, with orders to destroy the city. The Edomite nobles, who had always hated Judah, goaded Nebuzaradan on to destroy Jerusalem without mercy. The order was issued by Nebuzaradan; the walls of the city were razed to the ground. On the ninth day of the month of Ab, August, 586 B. C. E., the palaces and the Temple were set on fire. The few treasures of the Temple, the sacred vessels of gold and silver, and the musical instruments were shattered and carried away to Babylon.

Because of the great calamity that befell the Jewish people, they observe to this very day the ninth of Ab as a day of fasting, mourning, and prayer. It is strange that also on the very same date, the ninth of Ab, a few centuries later, the Second Temple was destroyed by the Romans. So the ninth of Ab brings to mind a twofold calamity of the Jewish people.

6. *Last Rays of Hope dimmed*

Nebuchadnezzar did not wish to destroy Judah altogether. He needed it as an open highway in his war with Egypt. He determined, therefore, to allow it to exist as a small community, under the rule of Gedaliah, a man of noble birth, a mild and peace-loving man, and a disciple of the prophet Jeremiah. Gedaliah gathered around him the remnant of the nation. He encouraged the cultivation of the fields and the gardens, that the country might not be turned into a desert. The people that were allowed to remain in Judah by the Babylonian king were the common people, the farmers, and the vintners. Land was assigned to them for cultivation. Gedaliah became the governor, and established his residence at Mizpah, about four and one-half miles northeast of Jerusalem. The harmless captives, the daughter of King Zedekiah, many women and children, and the farmers—about a thousand souls all told—were placed in his care.

The Prophet Jeremiah was treated by Nebuchadnezzar with great respect. Nebuzaradan, the general in charge of the captives, removed his chains. Jeremiah was now free to go to Babylon or wherever he chose. The choice was a difficult one. Jeremiah had witnessed the heart-rending scenes when the chained captives were being led away to Babylon. His heart went out to them in their great despair. He comforted them with the hope that at least their children or their grandchildren would return to their former home. He longed to share their captivity with them and strengthen and encourage them on the road. The captives themselves desired his presence, hoping that by his influence with the Babylonian king, he would be able to lessen their misery. At the same time, Jeremiah hesitated to leave his native land. But in a prophetic vision he was finally told to join Gedaliah, and to continue as a teacher and a guide to his people. His faithful disciple Baruch accompanied him. And, indeed, the presence of Jeremiah inspired the remnant of Israel with renewed hope and courage for the future.

The new governor erected a sanctuary at Mizpah. A large number of the scattered fugitives returned to Mizpah, and took an oath of allegiance to the Babylonian king. They settled down to cultivate the land, and the fields and the vineyards yielded an abundant harvest. A few cities rose again from their ruins.

Finally, some chiefs who had been leading a wild adventurous life in the mountains, also decided to join Gedaliah. These adventurous men laid aside their arms, and began to cultivate the fields. They helped rebuild the ruined cities, which had formerly served as hiding places. These brave, bold men added an element of strength and security to the feeble "remnant of Judah."

But Judah was not destined to remain a commonwealth. A certain chief, Ishmael, the son of a royal prince, plotted to avenge himself against Gedaliah. Outwardly he made peace with Gedaliah and the Babylonians, but in his heart he harbored a bitter hatred against both. Another chief, named Johanan, meanwhile received secret information about Ishmael's treacherous intention of killing Gedaliah. He warned Gedaliah of the danger, and begged his permission to put Ishmael out of the way. Gedaliah, however, paid no heed to the warning. Ishmael arrived in Mizpah with ten companions, on the occasion of a festival, feigning friendship. Gedaliah invited them to a banquet. While the guests were making merry, unconscious of danger, Ishmael and his men suddenly fell upon them and killed Gedaliah, his men, and the Babylonians that were present. The murderers escaped.

Johanan and the other chiefs soon heard of Ishmael's outrage, and started in swift pursuit. Ishmael was overtaken near the lake of Gibeon and a fight followed. Two of his men fell, but Ishmael himself with eight of his companions fled across the Jordan and went to the land of Ammon. There he was safe from the vengeance of Nebuchadnezzar.

The little commonwealth was shattered by the death of

Gedaliah. The remnant that was left feared that Nebuchadnezzar, in his wrath at the murder of his governor and of his garrison, would destroy the innocent as well as the guilty, and they decided to flee to Egypt. Jeremiah assembled all the chiefs and the people and ordered them, in the name of God, to remain where they were. He told them they need not fear Nebuchadnezzar, for he would treat them mercifully. But the leaders would not listen to the prophet, and decided to emigrate. They started upon their way to Egypt, and drew all the rest with them, including the Prophet Jeremiah and his disciple Baruch. They arrived in Egypt and were received kindly by Pharaoh Hophra.

When Nebuchadnezzar became aware of what happened in Mizpah, he again sent Nebuzaradan to Judah. The Babylonian general did not find even one man of prominence. Only a few farmers stayed behind. This last remnant of Judah, seven hundred and forty-five persons in all, Nebuzaradan carried into captivity to Babylon in the year 582 B. C. E. Thus Judah became a desert, the abode of wild beasts, as the prophet had foretold.

Gedaliah's memory has remained sacred, and the anniversary of his death, the third day of Tishri, is still observed every year as a day of fasting and mourning, and is known as "Gedaliah's fast day."

II THE DESTRUCTION OF THE SECOND TEMPLE

1. *Rebellion*

Forty-nine years after the destruction of the First Temple, Cyrus, the Persian emperor, proclaimed throughout his empire that the exiles of Judah might return to their former home and rebuild Jerusalem and the Temple. After many years of hardship, the Jews again established themselves in their homeland, and enjoyed varying degrees of independence for over six centuries. But about the year 63 B. C. E., two brothers, Hyrcan and Aristobolus, were fighting over the crown of Judah. Unable to defeat his brother, Hyrcan invited Rome to decide whether he or his brother should be recognized as the king of Judah. Pompey, then emperor of Rome, ordered the brothers to appear before him at Damascus. Both brothers appeared before Pompey and pleaded their case. Pompey was determined to bring Judah under the Roman yoke, and he therefore decided that the weakling Hyrcan should retain the title of king over Judah, and not the ambitious Aristobolus.

From that time on, the Romans treated Judah as a conquered province. Soon after, the Roman emperor Augustus dethroned Archelaus, then king of Judah, and banished him to Vienna in Gaul, and the Romans sent their representatives to govern Judah. These representatives bore the title *procurator*. Most of these procurators were cruel men and treated the Jews as conquered subjects. There were many men in Judah who loved their country, and were ready to give up their lives for its freedom. These patriots were known as the "Zealots." They hated Rome and her harsh rulers. Forming into bands, they withdrew into the clefts of the mountains, and from there they would attack the Romans, and plunder and murder without mercy. The number of the Zealots, though small at first, steadily grew, until they became a mighty power.

The last Roman procurator of Judah, Gessius Florus, was also the cruelest. He was a creature to whom nothing was sacred, and whose oath was worthless. Under Florus, conditions became unbearable for the Jews. But whom could they ask for help? They could expect none from the Roman Emperor Nero, who was committing one insane crime after another. Neither could they rely upon the weakling Agrippa, who was king, in name only, over Judah; for he was busy heaping flatteries upon Nero, and he trembled before the cruel Florus. What other means of deliverance was left but self-defense!

Cestius Gallus, then governor of Syria, was aware of the conditions in Judah. He warned the Roman Emperor of the restlessness there and of the rebellion that was brewing. But Nero was too busy playing the guitar and issuing murderous instructions to pay attention to such trifles.

With conditions steadily growing worse, the patience of the Jews became exhausted. Men and youths throughout the land of Judah, and particularly in Jerusalem, grew more and more anxious to throw off the Roman yoke, and awaited a favorable opportunity to revolt openly against Rome. The cruel Florus soon furnished the occasion. He issued an order to the Temple treasurer to send him seventeen talents of gold out of the treasury of the Temple for the use of the Roman Emperor. When this order became known to the inhabitants of Jerusalem, they rushed to the Temple, ready to protect the sanctuary with their lives. Some broke out in wailing, while others cursed the name of Florus. Meanwhile, they passed a box around as though they were taking up a collection for Florus.

Florus came to Jerusalem, and demanded that the gold be delivered to him in person. When the Temple treasurer refused, Florus ordered the Roman soldiers to plunder the residential quarter of the rich in Jerusalem. The savage soldiers entered the houses, and murdered more than three thousand men, women, and children in the course of their plunder. The next day a large multitude gathered in the ruined part of the city. They mourned the dead, and cursed the cruel Florus. Only with great difficulty did the leading men of Jerusalem succeed in restraining the people from attacking the Romans.

Florus, with his customary impudence, demanded that the entire population of Jerusalem go forth to greet the Roman troops as a token of friendship and peace. At first, the Jews refused; but after hearing the pleas of the Temple officials, spoken in the name of God and peace, they reluctantly went forth to receive the soldiers with friendly greetings. In return the Romans met the Jews with frowns and gloomy silence. At the first murmur of discontent that the Jews uttered, the soldiers fell upon them and dispersed them, their cavalry trampling upon the fleeing Jews. A fearful crush took place at the gates. The road from the suburb of Bezetha to the city was strewn with the bodies of the crushed and the slain.

Florus ordered his soldiers to take possession of the Temple treasury by force. The people of Jerusalem in their fury threw stones at the soldiers, killing many of them. When Florus saw that the Jews were determined to give battle, he lost courage. He announced to the representatives of Jerusalem that, in order to restore peace, he was willing to withdraw most of his troops, and to leave only a small garrison behind.

With the departure of Florus, calm was restored in Judah. But peace was of short duration. Some of the inhabitants of Jerusalem favored war with Rome, while others preferred peace. The people as a whole divided into two parties. The party in favor of war was composed mainly of brave young men who were ready to give their lives for the freedom of their people. These brave revolutionists, or Zealots, were determined to break the Roman yoke once and for all. At their head in Jerusalem was Eleazar ben Ananias, a man of high priestly descent. He was a scholar and belonged to the School of Shammai, whose members had always been sympathizers of the Zealots.

The peace party was composed of the moderate students of the School of Hillel, who hated war on principle, and of the rich who feared for their possessions. The members of the peace party tried in vain to quench the flame of rebellion. But the leaders of the revolutionary party induced the people to stop paying taxes to the Roman government. The Zealots attacked the fortress of Masada, slew the Roman garrison, and took possession of the arsenal. They persuaded the priests to discontinue the daily sacrifice in behalf of the Roman Emperor. This step alone would have been a declaration of war, for it signified that the people had renounced their allegiance to the Roman Emperor. The Temple henceforth became the center of the revolution.

The strength of the revolutionary party steadily grew, until the entire nation had become Zealots. The number of courageous fighters increased day by day. Not a single Roman was left in all the land of Judah.

2. *Victory Over the Romans*

The Romans entrusted the task of suppressing the revolution in Judah to Cestius Gallus, the governor of Syria. Cestius gathered his legions and led an army of over thirty thousand veteran warriors from Antioch against the Jews. Certain that he would be able to crush the revolution at one blow, he marched along the Mediterranean shore and in every city he left traces of blood and fire.

When the Zealots of Jerusalem learned of the approach of the Roman army, they rose up in arms. When Cestius halted his forces one mile from Jerusalem, the Zealots suddenly attacked with such fierceness that they broke through the Roman lines and killed over five hundred in the first sally, while they themselves lost only twenty-three men. The Roman cavalry, coming to the rescue of their infantry, saved them from complete rout on that day. Laden with rich booty, the victorious Zealots returned to Jerusalem, while Cestius remained inactive in his camp for three days.

On the fourth day the Roman army again approached the capital. For five days they assaulted the walls, but were driven back by a hail of arrows. On the sixth day, the Romans succeeded in partly undermining the northern wall facing the Temple. But Cestius failed to press this advantage, and retreated. He did not consider it advisable to continue a struggle with such desperate heroes, a struggle which was bound to be of long duration.

As soon as the Zealots saw the retreat of the enemy, they

followed in hot pursuit. They attacked the Roman rear and flanks from the mountain ridges. The Roman army had to keep to the highway of the valleys and passes, and proved an easy target for the arrows of the pursuers. Caught in a narrow pass between walls of rock, the Romans could not defend themselves against the Zealots' arrows. Night, however, put an end to the rout.

To prevent the repetition of a similar attack at the break of day, Cestius resorted to a ruse. He left four hundred of his bravest troops in camp, and he himself, together with his main army, stole away in the dark of night. At dawn, the Jewish warriors perceived the ruse, but it was too late to follow. The Zealots fell upon the four hundred Romans, killed them, and then pursued the Roman army, but were unable to overtake it. They found booty of weapons and instruments of siege which were abandoned by the Romans in their haste. Cestius' military chest also fell into their hands. The Romans lost about six thousand men in this expedition. The legion of picked troops which Cestius brought with him from Antioch lost its eagle—a loss which the Romans regarded as a supreme disgrace.

The Zealots returned in triumph to Jerusalem. The army of almighty Rome had been put to rout. The brave Zealots felt no anxiety about the future. "As we have defeated two generals," they said, "so shall we defeat their successors." The members of the peace party no longer dared to oppose them. Even the Samaritans forgot their old enmity toward the Jews, and joined their ranks.

Unusual activity was now displayed in Jerusalem. Everyone was preparing for war with Rome. Everywhere weapons were being forged and war engines were being constructed. The walls of Jerusalem were strengthened to withstand a long siege. Young men engaged daily in military exercises. The enemies of Rome rose up not only in the Jewish capital, but in all parts of Judah, and organized committees to take charge of the preparations for the conflict. Foreign Jews also zealously participated in the revolution.

3. *The Fall of Galilee*

For nine months, the Romans took no action against Judah. Nero, who was in Greece when the news of the rebellion of Judah and the defeat of the Roman army under Cestius Gallus reached him, was thunderstruck. What if the example of the Jews should be followed by other nations? The news that Cestius Gallus, the defeated general, had died by his own hand, added to Nero's terror. Nero therefore sent Flavius Vespasian, the best general of his time, to crush the rebellion. Vespasian was the general who had gained his laurels in the triumphant campaign against the Britons.

Vespasian left Greece for Judah in the winter of the year 67 C. E. His son Titus joined them with two legions. Neighboring princes rushed to Vespasian's headquarters to pay him homage. Agrippa, king of Judah, was among them. They placed their troops at the Roman general's disposal in order to prove their loyalty to Rome. Vespasian's army consisted of picked Roman troops and allies, exceeding fifty thousand men.

In the spring all preparations for the impending war were completed. Vespasian, more cautious than Cestius, conducted the war with slow and careful deliberation. It was Vespasian's plan to subdue Galilee first, so that there would be no desperate enemy at his rear on his march against Jerusalem. After many stubborn and bloody battles, the Romans took possession of all the fortresses in Galilee and destroyed them. All Galilee was now conquered, but the Romans were worn out with their bloody work, and their ranks were greatly depleted. General Vespasian was compelled to give his army a rest, and he had to fill the gaps made by the brave warriors of Galilee.

One of the Jewish commanders in Galilee was the sickly but courageous Johanan of Gishala. After the fall of Galilee, Johanan led several thousand Galileans to Jerusalem, where thousands of fugitives had already arrived. The Jewish capital was never so crowded, so strong. The strong fortifications made Jerusalem almost invincible. On three sides, south, east, and west, the hill on which the city was situated consisted of crevices and steep rocky walls. In addition, the city was protected by a wall. The north side, which was more open to attack, was fortified by a triple wall.

4. *Civil War*

Unfortunately, civil strife broke out among the defenders of Jerusalem, a prelude to civil war. Several parties arose in the city, under ambitious leaders, who were hostile to one another. The bitter hatred betwen the Zealots and the moderates finally led to bloodshed. The Zealots seized and killed all persons whom they regarded as secret friends of Rome. They removed a high priest, who was secretly a supporter of Rome, and selected a new high priest by lot.

The moderates who were headed by the Sanhedrin, the highest court in Judah, regarded the election of a high priest as an insult to the holy office. Anan, a former high priest and a very forceful orator, persuaded the moderates to avenge the insult by an armed attack upon the Zealots. Led by Anan, the moderates, who were now in the majority, drove the Zealots step by step from all parts of the city to the Temple Mount. The Zealots were forced to entrench themselves in the Temple halls, where they were besieged.

Meanwhile the report spread in Jerusalem that Anan and his companions had opened negotiations with the Romans and were about to surrender the city to them. This rumor induced the brave Johanan of Gishala, the Galilean warrior, to come to the aid of the besieged Zealots. He agreed with them to call upon a foreign tribe, the Indumeans, to come to the rescue of the capital which was in the hands of traitors. Twenty thousand Indumeans, warlike and bloodthirsty, thereupon advanced upon Jerusalem. But Anan learned of their coming, and he ordered the gates of the city to be locked and well guarded. The Indumeans pitched their camps at the gates of the capital.

That night a fearful storm broke over the city, and many of the guards of the city left their posts and sought shelter in the houses. While the storm was raging, several Zealots sawed through the iron bars of the unguarded gates, and admitted the Idumeans. The Idumeans attacked from one side, and the Zealots from the other. The moderates soon laid down their arms, and the maddened Idumeans scattered through the city, murdering all those whom they suspected of disloyalty to the revolution. On the following day the victorious Zealots sought out and murdered all who had participated in the attack. Anan was the first victim.

Johanan of Gishala, with the support of numerous Galilean fugitives, now set himself up as the revolutionary chief. His heroism and his contempt of death attracted many loyal followers, for Johanan was a born leader.

The Romans did nothing while the civil war raged in Jerusalem. The cautious Vespasian dared not attack the lions in their den, but he permitted his army to remain quietly in winter quarters. In the spring, Vespasian began a campaign not against Jerusalem, but against other districts in Judah which he soon conquered. In the meantime word came to him that the legions of Gaul and Spain had rebelled against Nero and had elected Galba as his successor. Vespasian was anxious to be in Rome to profit by the changes which would take place there. Nevertheless, he did not dare approach Jerusalem to lay siege to it, but he invested it at a distance from the west and south. In spite of his desire to end the campaign quickly, Vespasian left Jerusalem unmolested for two years.

During that time a new civil war was stirred up in the capital by the savage leader Simon bar Giora, who had been in possession of the fortress of Massada. Ambitious and energetic, Simon bar Giora left the fortress and gathered about him a band of adventurers and slaves to whom he promised liberty. His followers increased day by day until his forces numbered twenty thousand men.

The Zealots of Jerusalem feared Simon bar Giora, and tried to do away with him. Unsuccessful in this, they captured his wife and part of his band. They expected that he would now humble himself before them. But instead Simon bar Giora was driven to fury. He murdered all who went outside the gates of Jerusalem to gather provisions or wood. Bar Giora's wife was finally released, and her release softened him somewhat. Not for a moment, however, did he give up the idea of entering Jerusalem to take part in its affairs. Day and night he lay in wait before the gates of the capital.

In the meantime the moderate party secretly kept up their activities. They succeeded in winning over a large portion of the people. Upon an agreed signal, these moderates arose suddenly and fell upon the Zealots, killing many of them. But the Zealots soon recovered from their surprise, and assembling on the Temple Mount, they prepared for a counter-attack. The moderates, in their despair, opened the gates of Jerusalem, and invited Simon bar Giora into the city. They hoped with his aid to avenge themselves upon the Zealots. The Temple Mount once again became a battle ground.

Vespasian continued to postpone his attack upon Jerusalem, hoping that the defeated party would open the gates to him and enable him to gain an easy victory. He wished also to have his hands free when the time came to take advantage of the upheaval in Rome. He had sent his son Titus and the Judean king Agrippa to greet Galba, the new emperor of Rome. But Titus returned to Judah with the news that Galba had been murdered, and that two rival emperors had been proclaimed, Otho in Rome, and Vitellius in lower Germany.

In the course of the war between Otho and Vitellius, Vespasian began to think of taking the imperial power into his own hands. The prefect of Egypt, Tiberius Alexander, a Jew who had renounced his Judaism and had embraced the pagan belief, was the first to declare his allegiance to Vespasian. Vespasian left his generals in charge of the Roman army in Judah, and together with his son Titus proceeded to Egypt, where he remained until word was brought of Vitellius' death.

Jerusalem had another respite for two years, during which civil war raged. There were five parties in the city, each trying to crush the other. The members of these parties numbered twenty-four thousand warriors. Had these twenty-four thousand reckless men acted in harmony, they might have performed wondrous feats of valor on the battlefield. But each party claimed supremacy over the other. Bloody encounters between the hostile parties frequently took place in the streets of Jerusalem. No party dared leave the city and attack the Romans, for they feared that, once outside the city gates, their opponents would not permit them to re-enter. In the course of the struggle between the factions, many buildings were destroyed, and, far worse, stores of provisions, sufficient for several years, were burnt.

5. *Rabban Johanan ben Zakkai*

There then lived in Jerusalem a great sage, Rabban Johanan ben Zakkai, a disciple of Hillel the Elder. This sage belonged to the peace party because on principle he hated war. The Rabbis in the Talmud have preserved a beautiful story about this great man.

"One day, as Rabban Johanan walked through the market place, he saw people drinking water in which straw had been boiled to satisfy their hunger. 'Alas,' exclaimed the Rabbi, very much grieved at the sight, 'will people who drink a soup of straw be able to withstand the attack of the mighty armies of Vespasian? They are fighting a hopeless war. I must leave the besieged city, and make an attempt to bring salvation to my suffering people. But how can I leave the city when its gates are so closely guarded?' He thought and thought, and finally hit upon a scheme.

"One of the chief leaders of the war party in Jerusalem was a man named Abba Sikra ben Bettiah, a nephew of Rabban Johanan. That same day, Rabban Johanan sent a secret message to his nephew: 'Pay me a visit, but take care that no one knows aught of it.'

"Abba Sikra, although he belonged to a party that was hostile to his uncle, obeyed the summons, and paid him the required visit. Thereupon Rabban Johanan said to him: 'How long will the terrorists of your party be so obstinate and uselessly kill by famine all the inhabitants of this city? Do they not realize that they vainly oppose the more numerous and the more powerful Romans?'

" 'I am helpless,' answered the leader of the rebels. 'Should I utter one word in favor of surrender and peace, I would be instantly killed by my fellow leaders of the war party.'

" 'If you are unable to do anything yourself, then find a way for me to get out of the city,' pleaded the venerable sage. 'Maybe I will be able to bring some relief to our suffering people.' "

" 'We have agreed among us,' stated Abba Sikra, 'that no living soul shall pass through the gates of the city.'

" 'Then carry me out in a coffin as a dead man,' pleaded Rabban Johanan.

"Abba Sikra hit upon a plan. 'Pretend that you are sick,' he suggested to his uncle, 'and lie in bed for a few days. Then tell your friends and disciples to visit you, and to put some decayed matter in your bed, so that people may take you for dead. Let your friends then pass the word: "Our great teacher Rabban Johanan is dead." Then let them carry you out of the city in a coffin. Let no strangers be permitted to carry you, lest they feel that your body is too light for a corpse.'

"Rabban Johanan followed the advice of his nephew. When the rumor was spread that Rabban Johanan had died, some of his disciples lifted the coffin containing Rabban Johanan in order to carry him out of the city. They marched all day until they reached the gates of the City at sunset. 'Who goes there?' shouted one of the armed guards at the gates.

" 'It is the corpse of our beloved teacher Rabban Johanan,' said the bearers of the coffin. 'Verily, you are familiar with the rules that no dead person may remain within the walls of Jerusalem overnight.'

"The rebels were about to stab through the body with their spears, but Abba Sikra held them back, saying: 'Why arouse the indignation of the people, for they will say: "The rebels have stabbed the dead body of a great teacher." ' The rebels then wanted to thrust him down, but Abba Sikra said to them: 'You will arouse the anger of the people, for they will say: "The rebels have thrust a great master down." '

"At last the gate-keepers unlocked the gates, and permitted the coffin to be carried out. The disciples carried their master until they reached the Roman camp. When they obtained permission to see Vespasian, the commander of the Roman army, they opened the lid of the coffin, and out came the living Rabban Johanan ben Zakkai.

" 'Peace be unto you, O king! Peace be unto you, O king!' cried out the venerable sage to the Roman general.

" 'You deserve death twice,' said the general somewhat surprised and flattered. 'First, I am no king, and you called me king; second, if I am a king, why did you fail to come until now?'

" 'I am convinced that you are a king, O sire,' said Rabban Johanan; 'for had you not enjoyed such high rank, Jerusalem would not have been delivered into your hands. And the reason I have not come out to you until this day is because the members of the war party would not let me.'

"Said Vespasian to Rabban Johanan: 'If there is a barrel full of wine, and a serpent is wound around the barrel, would not one break the barrel to get rid of the serpent?'

"At the very moment Rabban Johanan was conversing with Vespasian, a herald came to the Roman commander with the message: 'The Roman emperor is no more, and the Senate has appointed you emperor.'

"Elated, Vespasian said to Rabban Johanan: 'Your prophecy has come true. Tell me what is your wish, and I shall fulfill it, for I must leave at once for Rome and appoint someone else to take charge of the army in my stead.'

" 'My only wish is,' replied the venerable sage, 'that you spare Jebneh (Jamnia) and her scholars.' "

6. *Jerusalem Is Besieged*

Vespasian and his son Titus left the battlefield for Rome where the former was proclaimed emperor and the latter heir to the imperial throne. Titus then decided to return to Judah, vowing to subdue Jerusalem. He considered it a blot upon Rome that after nearly four years the rebellious city was still able to resist. He knew, too, that the prestige of the imperial family depended upon the conquest of Jerusalem.

Titus was impatient to be done with the conquest of Judah, for he wished to be in Rome. He assembled an army of more than eighty thousand men and a very great number of siege engines. The Jewish traitors, King Agrippa of Judah, and the convert Tiberius Alexander, assisted Titus in the difficult task of capturing Jerusalem. Titus, as yet inexperienced in the art of war himself, promoted Tiberius Alexander to the rank of commander-in-chief in the war against the Jews, his own people.

At the approach of the enemy, the parties in Jerusalem forgot their quarrels and united their forces. Zealots from all over Judah and from foreign countries flocked to Jerusalem to defend the Holy City. The walls of Jerusalem were fortified still more strongly to resist the force of the Roman siege engines.

Titus finally concentrated his large army, and encamped about a mile from Jerusalem. Before beginning the siege, he called upon the people of Jerusalem to open the gates to him in peace. All he demanded was submission, the recognition of Rome, and the payment of taxes. He wanted the Jews to surrender peacefully because he was eager to return to Rome. Besides, he was in love with the Jewish princess Bernice, sister of King Agrippa, who did not wish to see the destruction of the Holy City. But the heroic defenders of Jerusalem refused to listen to his promises. They had sworn to defend the city with their lives.

Thereupon the Romans began their assault in earnest. Titus, with a few companions, approached the northern wall of the city. The Jews rushed upon them suddenly from one of the gates. They separated Titus from his men and almost succeeded in making him prisoner, but his companions redoubled their efforts and rescued him. On the following day, the Tenth Legion of the Romans, while making its camp on the Mount of Olives, was surprised by Jewish warriors and fled in panic. These bold attacks convinced the Romans that they had a difficult task before them. The Romans, however, succeeded in placing their engines against the outer walls.

The Romans put up high ramparts to the level of the walls, on which they placed the siege engines. From these ramparts the enemy hurled arrows, heavy blocks of wood, and stones upon the defenders of the walls and into the city. On three sides battering rams were driven against the walls in an attempt to make breaches in them.

The Romans had no sooner erected the siege engines than the Jews rushed out of the city like demons, destroying the works and scattering the workmen. They spread terror and confusion among the enemy, and withdrew again behind the walls. Not only the Zealots but all men capable of bearing arms took part in the combat. Even the women showed an unparalleled courage. The defenders hurled blocks of stones at the enemy and poured boiling oil upon their heads. They soon learned the handling of war engines, and turned the machines which they had captured upon their former owners.

The Romans, after repairing the damage done to their equipment, finally made a breach in the outer wall, on the seventeenth day of the month of Tammuz. After a battle of fifteen days, they compelled the defenders to withdraw from the outer wall. The seventeenth day of Tammuz is therefore observed by all Jews as a day of fasting and mourning, because it marked the beginning of the fall of the Holy City and of the Temple.

A desperate struggle between the Romans and the Jews now began about the new wall which the defenders had erected between the first and second walls. After four days of fierce fighting, the Romans made themselves masters of the new wall.

But this did not mark the end of the struggle. Fierce combats were fought daily, the Jewish warriors not yielding an inch without struggle. After seventeen days, the Romans threw up four dikes against the second wall. They were about to begin an assault when Johanan of Gishala with his band rushed upon the Romans from a subterranean passage, set fire to the works placed by the Romans against the second wall, and destroyed them. Two days later, three courageous men of the Bar Giora's party set fire to the other Roman siege works, disregarding the showers of missiles that fell upon them.

The nearer the danger approached, the greater grew the courage of the besieged. In fact there was no choice left for them but victory or death. At the very beginning of the siege, they realized that they could expect no mercy at the hands of the Romans. Captured Jews were crucified, at times five hundred in one day, upon the order of Titus. By this he meant to show the stubborn defenders the fate that awaited them.

7. *Jerusalem Is Captured*

Titus, having given up hope of a speedy end of the war, determined to prolong the siege until the city was starved into submission. To prevent the besieged from leaving Jerusalem by secret passages, he surrounded the entire city with a wall more than four miles in circumference. As a result of this blockade, famine began to rage in the city. The meagre food

supply gave out, and the houses and the streets were filled with
corpses. Living skeletons stalked through the streets of the
city. The wealthiest people could obtain no food at any price.

The Rabbis have recorded in the Talmud a tragic story of
those days of suffering: "Martha, the daughter of Boethus,
was the richest woman in Jerusalem. During the siege, when
food became scarce, she sent one of her servants to the market
place to buy fine flour for her. But by the time the servant
arrived there, all the fine flour had been sold. He came back
and said: 'Mistress, there is no more fine flour to be obtained,
but bread baked of fine flour can be purchased.'

" 'Get me bread of fine flour,' Martha said to the servant.

"By the time he arrived in the market place, the bread baked
of fine flour had been sold. He returned to his mistress and
reported: 'There is no more bread of fine flour to be had, but
bread of coarse flour can be bought.'

" 'Go then and get me black bread,' said Martha.

"By the time the servant got there, the black bread too had
been sold. He came back to his mistress and said: 'There is no
more black bread to be had; all that is left is barley flour.'

"Martha then expressed her willingness to buy barley flour,
but by the time the servant got there, the barley flour too had
been sold, and he came back and reported: 'Alas, even the barley flour is gone, and there is no food at all to be bought.'

"Martha took off her shoes, for they were too heavy for her
weakened feet, and said: 'I will go out in the streets myself;
perhaps I will be able to get something to eat.' Weakly she
staggered along the streets, when some ordure clung to her
naked feet. Her refined and delicate body could not bear the
contact of ordure, and she fell dead in the street."

In spite of the famine, the Zealots performed heroic feats
in their efforts to hinder the work of the Romans, but the
enemy proved too powerful for them. After twenty-seven days
of stubborn combat, the Romans succeeded in throwing up a
new dike against the second wall. Johanan of Gishala again

rushed out of the city to set the work on fire, but this time he failed. The second wall caved in under the violent assault from without. The Romans were amazed to find another wall behind the one that had just fallen. They attempted in vain to take it by storm. The Jews bravely repulsed a night attack, and the struggle continued till morning.

Now, Titus made another attempt to induce the people to surrender the city, and he promised to spare the Temple. Johanan of Gishala replied that the city of God could not fall, and that the final outcome depended upon God alone.

Even the Romans admired the courage and bravery of the Zealots and their devotion to the Temple and to the cause of their people. Many of them began to regard the Zealots as invincible. Individual Romans forsook their standards and their faith and accepted Judaism. They also were convinced that the Holy City would never fall into the power of the enemy. The inhabitants of Jerusalem were proud of the conversion to Judaism of a few Romans in the hour of the greatest danger, and they provided the converts with food, although they themselves were gradually starving to death.

The Romans had meanwhile erected siege engines against the outer works of the Temple. They labored ceaselessly for six days, but did not succeed in making any breach in the wall. Thereupon, Titus gave up the plan of sparing the Temple, and ordered the gates of the outer Temple wall to be set on fire. After the fire had raged for an entire day and night, he ordered that the flames be extinquished, and that the legions clear a way for an assault.

At the same time he called a council of war to decide upon the fate of the Temple. Some of his advisers were of the opinion that the Temple must be destroyed, because it would remain a hotbed of revolt. Others, including Tiberius Alexander, the converted Jewish commander-in-chief, were in favor of sparing the Temple. It was finally decided to capture but not to destroy the Temple.

The Jewish warriors meanwhile made another sally against the Romans, but were driven back and pursued. In the confusion that followed, a Roman soldier seized a burning brand and hurled it through a window of the Temple. The woodwork of the Temple halls caught fire. It spread rapidly to the adjoining halls, and the entire structure was soon in flames. At the sight of the burning Temple, even the most courageous of the Jewish warriors lost heart. Titus rushed in with his troops, ordering them to extinguish the flames, but his voice was not heard; the maddened soldiers were bent on plunder. They scattered through the chambers of the Temple, set fire to many places, and murdered all the Jews who had not escaped from the burning structure.

The Jewish warriors rallied once more, and on the scene of the fire a new battle raged. In their despair, many Jews threw themselves into the flames, for they cared not to survive the Temple. Many thousands of men, women, and children remained in the southern colonnades, disregarding the approaching enemy and the consuming flames. The bloodthirsty Romans threw themselves upon the masses and butchered them. The Temple burned to the ground; only the foundation and a few ruins of the western wall remained. This wall stands to this day, and is known as "the wailing wall." For many centuries Jews have stood before it, and shed tears of sorrow and grief over the destruction of their holy Temple.

Several priests had found refuge on the wall for a few days. Finally, driven by hunger and thirst, they pleaded for mercy. "Priests," said Titus, "must perish with their Temple," and ordered them killed. The victorious Roman legions offered sacrifices to their gods on the Temple site, as though they had conquered the God of Israel. They planted their eagles there, and hailed Titus as emperor of Rome. By a strange coincidence, the Second Temple was reduced to ashes in the year 70 C. E., on the very day that the First Temple had fallen by the hand of the Babylonian king, the ninth day of the month of Ab

Grieving over the loss of both Temples, the Jews to this very day observe the ninth of Ab as a day of fasting and mourning.

The struggle was not yet over. The leaders of the revolution retreated with the remnants of the army to the Upper City, known as Zion. Titus invited the Jewish revolutionary leaders to a peace conference, but Johanan of Gishala and Simon bar Giora declared that they had taken an oath to die rather than surrender. They demanded that they be given free withdrawal and be permitted to retain their arms; on that condition they would deliver the Upper City to the Romans. Titus, however, insisted upon unconditional surrender, and the struggle broke out afresh. After eighteen days of hard work, the Romans succeeded in erecting new dikes against the walls of the Upper City. The Jewish warriors became exhausted from their exertions and from hunger, and were no longer able to repel the enemy. The Romans climbed the walls, occupied the towers, and entered the Upper City. On the following day, they set fire to the only remaining quarter of the city, the Upper City, or Zion. The walls were completely destroyed, and thus the Holy City, together with the Temple, was razed to the ground.

The brave Johanan of Gishala, sick and starving, was captured by the Romans. Simon bar Giora, with a few companions, escaped to one of the subterranean passages of Jerusalem. Provided with tools, they hoped to bore their way through into the open and escape capture, but they struck solid rock, and all their efforts were in vain. The meagre provisions soon gave out, and Bar Giora determined to die like a hero. In a white undergarment and wrapped in a purple cloak, he suddenly stepped forth from the ground upon the former site of the Temple. He asked the Roman sentinels, who became frightened at this strange apparition, to lead him to their commander. When the officer arrived, the leader of the Zealots said: "I am Simon bar Giora." He was immediately cast into chains, and was dragged to Rome for the triumph.

8. *"Judaea Devicta"; "Judaea Capta"*

Over nine hundred thousand persons were taken prisoner in the course of the war. The residents of Jerusalem Titus penned up in the Temple area, and left them to the mercy of his friend Fronto. Fronto crucified on the spot everyone who was recognized or denounced as a warrior. Of those who remained, seventeen thousand died of starvation, because the Roman conquerors failed to provide them with sufficient food. Others deliberately starved themselves rather than accept food from the blood-stained hands of the Romans.

Seven hundred of the most handsome and vigorous youths Fronto selected to grace Titus' triumphal entry into Rome. Male captives over the age of seventeen were doomed as imperial slaves in the Egyptian mines; a still greater number of young men were donated to the provinces to fight wild beasts in the arenas for the amusement of pagan onlookers. The weaker captives were sold for a trifle as slaves. Their only hope was to be sold into a city that contained a Jewish community, for their brethren would ransom them at any cost, and would receive them with sympathy.

All the Jews of the Roman empire came perilously close to sharing the fate of their brethren of Judah. The hatred of the heathens for the Jews had been intensified by the war. Bernice, the Jewish princess, however, stayed the hand of her lover Titus, shielding her people in this tragic hour of their history.

Upon Titus' arrival at Rome, the triumph over Judah was celebrated with great pomp and magnificence. In the procession organized for Vespasian and his sons Titus and Domitian, there were carried the Temple vessels, the golden candelabrum, the golden table, and a scroll of the Law. The captives were led in chains. Simon bar Giora was dragged with a rope through the streets of Rome and afterwards hurled down from the Tarpeian rock. Johanan of Gishala died in a dungeon.

The Jewish convert Tiberius Alexander, the real victor of the war, participated in the triumph over his brethren, and a statue of him was erected in the Roman forum. The splendid procession marked the great joy of the Romans at the victory over Judah; it had been a long time since the Roman legions had been called upon to fight so stubborn a foe. So important did they consider the victory that for several successive years memorial coins of gold, silver, and bronze were struck in honor of the event. These coins represented Judah as a woman beneath a palm tree in an attitude of despair, either sitting or standing, with bound hands. The legend on these coins, either in Greek or in Latin read: *"Judaea Devicta"* (the conquered Judah), or *"Judaea Capta"* (the captured Judah).

The plundered Temple treasures remained for a long time in the Temple of Janus in Rome, and the scroll of the Law taken from the Temple remained in the emperor's palace. A triumphal arch was erected in honor of Titus, on which the images of the vessels taken from the Temple may be seen to this very day.

New Celebrations

THE REBIRTH OF ISRAEL

THE LONG JEWISH EXILE. Throughout the long and painful centuries, during which the Jews were dispersed among the nations of the world, they at no time gave up hope of returning to their ancient home, Eretz Yisrael, or Palestine. The Jews have always longed to return to their homeland where they might once more become a free and independent people.

Almost every prayer in Jewish liturgy was devoted to Zion and Jerusalem. In their daily prayers, offered three times every day, and in their Grace, offered after every meal, the Jews prayed that the glory of God might once again return to reign over Zion and the Holy City Jerusalem. Every day at midnight, pious Jews woke up to offer special prayers to their God that He might restore Zion and Jerusalem to their ancient glory.

Jews all over the world proclaimed their right to their ancient homeland. They never gave up their claim to the land, and they continually hoped that some day God would send a deliverer who would bring the Jews to their land from every corner of the earth. They hoped and looked for a Messiah to bring them salvation from their sufferings, and take them back to the land of their ancestors and their Prophets.

The merciless persecution of the Jews in all lands was instrumental in awakening Jewry to the realization that they must turn their longing for a national home into deeds. The daily Hebrew papers that once used to appear in Russia, were given over primarily to the fostering of the national spirit, as it was known by its Hebrew name, *Hibbat Zion* (Love of Zion). And this propaganda had a tremendous effect upon the European Jews.

THE FIRST PALESTINIAN COLONIES. The first attempt at establishing colonies in Palestine, was made in 1878. A colony was founded in the vicinity of Jaffa, named Petah Tikvah (the Beginning of Hope). It is now one of the largest colonies in Palestine.

With the spread of the *Hibbat Zion* movement among the Jews, many of the Russian Jews styled themselves *Hoveve Zion* (Lovers of Zion), and formed clubs for the purpose of migrating to Palestine and of building a homeland where they and their persecuted brethren might live in peace. The majority of the Lovers of Zion were young men, mostly university students, who organized themselves into several immigrant groups.

The first group that arrived in Palestine, in 1882, established the Rishon Lezion (First in Zion) colony. Without any funds, without proper implements or tools, these young idealists threw themselves upon the sacred soil, which they broke with their bare hands. They endured all possible hardships and displayed the spirit of the determined pioneer. A number of them died of malaria and undernourishment. Nevertheless, this colony is today the pride of the entire new settlement, and from it have come many of the founders of other colonies.

Pioneers from other lands immigrated into Palestine and established colonies there. From these colonies minor settlements soon branched out under different names. Most of these had to go through a period of hard struggles before they could become self-supporting, though nearly all of them were in a flourishing condition at the time of the outbreak of the First World War.

THEODORE HERZL. Little by little the *hibbat zion* cause grew weaker and weaker. Finally, when the movement was almost dead, an unusual man made his appearance. This man was Theodore Herzl. Herzl came to his lofty position in the Jewish world from the outside, after spending nearly all his life in non-Jewish circles. He was born in Budapest, Hungary, on the eleventh day of the month of Iyar, 1860. He was a lawyer by training, a journalist by profession, and a member of the editorial staff of Vienna's leading paper, the *Neue Freie Press.*

This strikingly handsome young man, with the manners and bearing of a nobleman, was admired in the "best" non-Jewish circles and seldom had occasion to associate with his brethren. Commissioned by his paper to go as correspondent to Paris, he became acquainted with the notorious and sensational Dreyfus affair in 1894. The infamous accusation leveled against an innocent and honorable man, solely because of his Jewish origin, was to Herzl's noble and justice-loving soul a revelation of the tragedy of a whole people—his people. He set himself to thinking about the position of the Jew in all lands and his helplessness in the face of prejudice and hatred. As a result he wrote his famous *Judenstaat.*

His plan, as outlined in that book, is that a state in Palestine be formed by the Jews with the sanction and under the protection of European powers. Following his suggestion, the Zionist Organization came into being, the Jewish Colonial Trust was established in London, and the Jewish National Fund was organized for the purpose of redeeming the soil of Palestine and turning it over to the Jewish people.

HERZL DAY. Theodore Herzl became a popular hero whose influence reached out to every part of the globe. He now decided to call a Congress of representatives of all Zionist groups. The object of this Congress was to lay before the world the many grievances of the Jew and to show his true national hopes and plans. Herzl and his advisers decided that the Congress should meet in Basle, Switzerland.

It met in August, 1897. For the first time since the downfall of the ancient Jewish State, nineteen hundred years ago, Jews from all parts of the world came together as representatives of a Jewish nation. The Congress adopted a program which declared that "the object of Zionism is to establish for the Jewish people a publicly and legally secured home in Palestine."

After this Congress, Dr. Herzl and his associates set out to win the consent of the nations of the world to the Zionist cause. Wherever they went they established clubs to raise funds and gain supporters for their cause. Thousands joined the Zionist ranks, among them many prominent persons like Max Nordau and Israel Zangwill.

But Herzl was destined to die without seeing the realization of his hopes. Slandered by his foes and misunderstood by his friends, he found the burden too heavy for his shoulders. He died at the age of forty-four, on the twentieth day of the month of Tammuz, 1904, more of a broken heart than of the physical malady which overtook him. Herzl gave his life for his people. He was the father of modern Zionism, and the real founder of the State of Israel. His slogan: "If you will it, it is no dream," has given hope and inspiration to the builders of Israel in all lands. To the memory of this great man, the Jews pay tribute each year, on the anniversary of his death.

THE BALFOUR DECLARATION. During the First World War, England declared war on Turkey and set out to wrest the Holy Land from the Turks. Her armies invaded Palestine and captured many important cities.

On the second day of November, 1917, a very important declaration was made by the English Government. This declaration was made in a letter addressed by Arthur J. Balfour, British Secretary of State for Foreign Affairs, to Lord Rothschild, which read: "His Majesty's Government views with favor the establishment in Palestine of a national home for the Jewish people, and will use its best endeavors to facilitate the achievement of this object."

This declaration was made possible because of the efforts of noted Zionist leaders, Nahum Sokolow, Dr. Tschlenow, and Dr. Haim Weizmann. It is the latter to whom most of the credit is ascribed.

Weizmann had left Russia and gone to Switzerland to study chemistry. After some time he received an appointment as professor of chemistry in the university of Manchester, England. He first won fame among the Zionists because he advanced the project of establishing a Hebrew University in Jerusalem.

During the First World War, Weizmann invented an explosive which was successfully used by the British Government in its prosecution of the war. It is said that he refused to accept any reward for his invention, but requested that the English Government show good will towards the Zionist aim of establishing a Jewish home in Palestine.

Zionists the world over have since celebrated the anniversary of this great event, the issuance of the "Balfour Declaration," with mass meetings, lectures, and festivities. But this day was turned from a day of celebration into a day of protest, when Great Britian issued its White Paper in 1939, practically retracting the promises made in the Balfour Declaration. The day became a holiday of renewed struggle, with the Jews pledging to increase their efforts to establish a Jewish homeland in Palestine.

HALUZIM—PIONEERS. The Balfour Declaration proved to be a turning point in the history of Zionism. The Jews all over the world now took an active interest in the rebuilding of Palestine as a homeland for their persecuted brethren.

Jewish pioneers from many European countries, ambitious young men and women, known as *haluzim* in Hebrew, began to flock to Palestine. Without adequate tools and equipment, they tirelessly tilled the soil. For many years these pioneers suffered severe hardships; they met with many disappointments; they suffered from malaria in their attempt to cultivate the swamplands; but these brave young people were not to be turned from their task. With superhuman effort and courage, they drained the swamplands and turned the once barren Palestinian soil into green gardens and blooming orchards.

Many colonies, villages, and towns sprang up, inhabited by Jewish peasants and workers. The most noted of these settlements is the city of Tel Aviv (Mound of Spring). In 1909, a small group of Jewish teachers, merchants, and physicians conceived the idea of building a settlement on the Mediterranean shore near Jaffa, naming it Tel Aviv. Forty years later, in 1949, Tel Aviv boasted a population of over 200,000, consisting only of Jews, most of whom speak Hebrew.

THE HEBREW UNIVERITY. Jewish culture in Palestine developed as rapidly as the material growth of the region. Many Hebrew periodicals and dailies were published. Hebrew once more began to flourish as a living language of the Holy Land. The Holy Tongue, as in time of old, was used in everyday life by young and old—in the streets, at play, in markets, homes, schools and theatres. All subjects in elementary and high schools were taught in Hebrew.

On the first day of April, 1925, a great event took place in the cultural life of the Jews in Palestine. A Hebrew University, dedicated to higher Hebrew and secular learning, was opened, a project that had been advocated by Dr. Haim Weizmann. It was built on Mount Scopus, overlooking the ancient Temple site. This edifice of learning was dedicated by the world famous scientist, Professor Albert Einstein. Lord Balfour, author of the Balfour Declaration, presided at the dedication, and greeted the representatives of the world governments and learned bodies who were present. Lord Balfour concluded his address with the old Hebrew prayer: "Blessed be He who kept us alive to reach this day."

THE WHITE PAPER. From the very beginning, the Arabs strongly opposed the idea of a Jewish settlement in Palestine, and there had been friction between Jews and Arabs right from the start. In 1929, the Arabs brazenly attacked the defenseless young students at the Hebrew Academy in Hebron, killing some and severely wounding many. Old men, praying at Safed, were slaughtered by the enraged Arabs. Attacks on Jews continued in spite of the fact that England had promised and undertaken to protect the Jews in their Homeland.

Arab riots took place frequently in the period of 1936 to 1939. During that period, the *Haganah* (Defenders), a Jewish force, was organized for the purpose of self-defense. This organization was destined later on to play the major role in establishing an independent Palestine for the Jewish people.

In February, 1939, the British Government invited Jewish and Arab leaders to a conference to be held in London to discuss the future of Palestine. During the conference, Prime Minister Chamberlain submitted a plan calling for an independent Arab State in Palestine, with the Jews constituting a permanent minority. Dr. Haim Weizmann, President of the World Zionist Organization, and other Jewish leaders were opposed to such a move. They felt that they had been misled by Britain. They claimed that, relying upon the Balfour Declaration, the Jews had made great sacrifices in rebuilding Palestine. They accused Britain of bad faith. And on March 16, 1939, the Jewish delegation to the conference officially rejected the British plan.

Then on May 18, 1939, the British Government issued its White Paper on Palestine. In this document it was proposed to create an independent Arab State in Palestine at the end of the next five years; during these five years only 75,000 Jews would be allowed to enter Palestine; that after the five years, no Jews at all would be allowed to enter Palestine. According to the terms of the White Paper, the Jews would remain a permanent minority, and the Arabs a permanent majority.

The White Paper was severely condemned by many honest men all over the world. Winston Churchill described it as "a plain breach of promise, a repudiation of the mandate." When, however, a few months later, Churchill became Prime Minister of England, he made no effort to rescind the White Paper, but on the contrary saw to it that its provisions were rigidly enforced.

In 1945, elections were held in Britain, and the Labour Party during the election Campaign adopted a plank stating that it would wholeheartedly support the plan for a Jewish commonwealth. The Jews now hoped that with the success of the Labour Party at the polls, their aspirations for a Jewish homeland would be realized. But their hopes were shattered again. When the Labour Party came out victorious, the Labour Government immediately forgot the promise made during the campaign, made by the very men who were now appointed to government office. Indeed, the lot of the Jews in Palestine became much worse than it had been under Churchill.

Prime Minister Attlee appointed as his Foreign Secretary an outspoken anti-Semite, Ernest Bevin. The latter brought his anti-Semitism into the British Foreign Office. In his speeches

on the Palestine problem, he cast aspersions upon the Jews
of every land. The hostile attitude of the British toward the
Jews, which hitherto had been under cover, now came out in
the open. The British officers launched unreasonable restric-
tions, repressions, and legal prosecutions upon the Jewish population of Palestine.

The Jews suffered endless humiliation and hardship under
the British rule. Their hopes were shattered by the brutal conduct of the British officials who received their orders from the
Colonial Office in London. But one particular act of horror
was committed by the British officials which brought down upon
them the condemnation of the entire civilized world.

THE EXODUS 47. The *Haganah* had now gone underground.
They sought to prevent violence, and undertook to bring in
Jewish displaced persons from all lands into Palestine, against
the will of the British officials. The *Haganah* took the position that it was not the Jews who were acting illegally in
trying to settle their unfortunate brethren in Palestine, but that
it was the British Government who acted illegally in trying
to prevent the Jews from entering their own country. It organized a vast system of underground transportation of Jews
who boarded vessels at ports in Italy, France, and Roumania.

The British, however, were on the alert, and whenever they
spotted such vessels they would send their warships to board
and seize them, and the unhappy passengers would then be
confined to detention camps. Later on the British officials
ordered all these "illegal" immigrants to detention camps on
Cyprus. At times the immigrants would resist, many at the
cost of their lives.

One of the refugee-carrying vessels, the *Exodus* 47, had
more than 4,000 men, women, and children crowded on board.
The British seized the ship, and this time they decided not to
send the Jews to Cyprus, but to return them to France, from
which country they had started on their Mediterranean voyage.
Upon arriving in France, the passengers of the *Exodus* refused

to disembark, and the French authorities refused to use force against them. The British now committed one of the most savage and inhuman acts of their entire Palestine record: they took the immigrants to Germany and forcibly removed them to the soil that had been drenched with the blood of hundreds of thousands of Jewish martyrs. This brought down upon the British the condemnation of the entire civilized world, and the Jews were thereafter sent to Cyprus again and not to European ports.

THE UNDERGROUND GROUP. The Jews of Palestine were thus forced by the British to resort to terrorism. There soon sprang up groups of fighters who resolved to take more drastic action against the British to redress the grievances of their people. They struck violent blows in the dark. Two groups of such character were the *Irgun Zvai Leumi* (People's Army), consisting of about 5,000 members, and the *Lohame Herut Yisrael* (Fighters for the Freedom of Israel), known chiefly as the "Stern Group," after its founder, which consisted of less than a thousand members.

Both groups were well organized and very efficiently carried out their tasks of harassing the British military and civil officials. They blew up installations; they derailed trains; and often they took many British lives for each member of their group who was executed by the order of the British courts. They held the British to be illegal intruders in the land, and as such conceded them no right to sit in judgment over the fate of their members.

Many acts of terrorism and violence were committed during those trying and restless days. On November 6, 1944, Lord Moyne, the British resident Minister in the Middle East, was assassinated in Cairo, Egypt. The King David Hotel in Jerusalem was blown up in the summer of 1946, and many died. In the same summer, an attack on the Acre prison was made, and prisoners confined there by the British were let loose. A number of these fighters bravely and fearlessly faced death. An outstanding example of such bravery was provided by Dov Gruner, who was hanged by the British.

The civilized world and world Jewry strongly condemned these acts of terrorism and horror. But neither public opinion nor British violence could stop those fighters who had vowed not to lay down their arms until the hated British were expelled from Palestine.

A crucial period now began for the Jews in Palestine. Curfews, arrests, court-martials, and executions became the order of the day. At one time the entire population of Tel Aviv, over 200,000 inhabitants, were kept under house arrest for several days. This situation occurred in many other places. Hundreds of persons suspected of terrorism were seized and kept without trial, and many of them were deported to Kenya where they were kept as prisoners without a hearing. The terrorists retaliated. If one of their members was flogged by the British, they kidnapped and flogged British officials. They derailed trains, and often killed soldiers and officers. And the British kept on answering in kind: they met terror with terror.

The British also did their best to influence United States diplomats in their favor. And the Middle Eastern oil came to their assistance. British and American oil companies were exploiting the rich oil fields in Iran, Iraq, and Saudi Arabia, amassing great wealth and paying high royalties to the Arab countries. These companies persuaded high government officials in the State Department of the United States to favor the Arabs in preference to the Jews.

A JEWISH STATE IN PALESTINE. Now the British Government hatched an evil plot against the Jews. On February 18, 1947, Ernest Bevin told the House of Commons that the Cabinet had decided to relinquish the British Mandate, evacuate the British troops from Palestine, and throw the entire problem into the lap of the United Nations. But the real objective of the British was vengeance. They aimed to throw Palestine into a state of chaos, deprive it of its financial assets, denude it of all raw materials, and make sure that there would be friction between the Jews and the Arabs. They hoped to prove to the world that the Palestine situation was hopeless, and force the United Nations to ask them to remain in the land on their own terms in order to maintain law and order.

In the spring of 1947, the United Nations took up the Palestine problem and decided to make a thorough investigation before tackling the matter for a final solution. It appointed a special committee of its own. The emissaries went to Palestine, and upon their return submitted a report favoring a partition of the land between the Jews and the Arabs with an economic union between the two states. They also suggested that Jerusalem be placed under an international regime in order to safeguard the sacred places of the city.

The General Assembly took up the resolution submitted by the committee, and spent many weeks in discussing the problem. The seven Arab States who were members of the General Assembly strongly opposed the partition plan, and they were aided by the delegations of other countries. But the Jewish Agency, too, had a delegation there, and they gave their side of the case. The cause of the Jews was ably defended by Dr. Abba Hillel Silver, Major Aubrey Eban, Dr. Emanuel Neumann, Moshe Shertok, and Dr. Haim Weizmann.

For days and days, voices were raised in the General Assembly arguing for and against the partition plan, and tens of thousands of Jews listened breathlessly at their radios, wondering what the outcome of this debated question would be. At last, on November 29, 1947, the General Assembly of the United Nations put the question to a vote. Thirty-nine nations voted in favor of partition, to establish a Jewish State in Palestine. Only thirteen votes were cast against partition, and this of course included the vote of the seven Arab nations. After almost nineteen hundred years of wandering, suffering, persecution, humiliation, torture, and death, there was created a Jewish State, a home for the persecuted remnant of Israel.

Jews everywhere, and especially in Palestine, rejoiced at this great victory of the Jewish cause. But soon their joy was turned into sadness, for the hope of peacefully implementing the partition of Palestine vanished.

THE ROAD IS BESET WITH DIFFICULTIES. The delegates of six Arab nations rose in a body and walked out of the Assembly after the partition vote was taken. The Council of the Arab League recommended that the Arab States send military forces to invade Palestine as soon as the British withdrew from the country.

According to the resolution of the United Nations, the British were to evacuate a seaport, not later than February 1, 1948, for Jewish immigration. But the British refused to do so. The British navy continued its blockade of Palestine, seizing Jewish immigrants for internment on Cyprus, and interfering with Jewish attempts to import military supplies. At the same time the British supplied arms to the Arab States, under the pretext of having to fulfill existing contracts.

On the day after the United Nations adopted the partition plan, the Arabs began their attack upon the Jews, and before long it developed into a full-fledged war, in which thousands of soldiers were killed on both sides. The British continued to help the Arabs and to hinder the Jews from offering effective resistance. The British still had a large army in Palestine and the Mandate was still in force; thus it was easy for them to disarm those Jews who were compelled to fight for their lives as an underground force.

The State Department of the United States, six days after partition was voted, announced that it would refuse to license any arms shipments to the area where fighting had broken out between the Arabs and the Jews. This announcement shut off arms for the Jews and left the Arabs free to obtain arms from the British. It was an invitation to the Arabs to destroy the new Jewish state at birth.

The Arab Legion of Transjordan, financed, armed and officered by the British, was invited to help the British to preserve order in Palestine. But it began almost at once to engage in battle against the Jews. Travel had become very dangerous, and trucks and buses had to move in convoys, with armed guards.

In Damascus and Beirut, recruiting stations were opened for a "Liberation Army" to fight against the Jews, under the leadership of notorious Nazi Arabs. German Nazis, Polish reactionaries, and reactionary elements from many lands flocked in for a struggle against the Jews.

By March, 1948, the situation looked discouraging for the Jews on every front, military as well as diplomatic. The Jewish Agency headquarters in Jerusalem was bombed. In the north a convoy taking supplies to the isolated colony of Yehiam, near the Lebanese border, was attacked by 2,000 Arabs and wiped out. The systematic Arab campaign against Jewish truck convoys on the road from Tel Aviv to Jerusalem, cut off the Holy City from supplies. On March 31, bread rationing was ordered in Jewish Jerusalem.

Meanwhile something happened in Washington which shook the whole world as if by an earthquake. President Truman, under the influence of the pro-Arab clique in his State Department, suddenly reversed himself on the Palestine partition plan. Instructions went out to the United States delegation at the United Nations to ask for a special session of that body to take up once more the Palestine question. Suddenly, the Jews found themselves deserted by one whom they had regarded as their most powerful friend. It was with considerable anxiety and bitterness that the representatives of the Jewish Agency went again before the United Nations to renew their fight for the life of the Jewish State. Moshe Shertok of the Jewish Agency told the Security Council of the United Nations: "We have passed the threshold of statehood; we refuse to be thrown back." This was the bitter voice of a people struggling for its very existence.

THE JEWS IMPLEMENT PARTITION FOR THEMSELVES. The special session of the United Nations was called for April 16, 1948. In the discussion which dragged on for weeks, the United States delegation joined the British Foreign Office in an effort to upset the decision of November 29, which had favored partition. The hostile members of the State Department thought that they had dealt at last a fatal blow to Jewish aspirations, for little did the enemies of the Jews expect that the new Jewish State, although weak and betrayed by its friends, would be able to implement partition for itself.

On April 3, the *Haganah* forces captured Kastel, an Arab mountaintop village just outside Jerusalem on the road to Tel Aviv. Two days later another important victory was gained by the Jews near the other end of the road. *Haganah* demolition squads blew up the 150-room British Army Staff College near Rehovoth. This had become the headquarters of Hassan Bey Salama, commander of the Arab forces in that area. Its demolition was a serious blow to the Arab forces which had been preying on Jewish road traffic. The Arabs fought hard to regain Kastel. It changed hands several times, but after April 9 it remained firmly in the hands of the Jews. The road from Tel Aviv to Jerusalem was thus opened, and a food convoy of 179 trucks safely reached Jerusalem on April 13. This victory gave the Jews renewed hope and courage.

THE BATTLE AT MISHMAR HAEMEK. In the meantime, Fawzi el Kaukji, commander of the Arab Liberation Army, launched an attack in the north. On April 4, Kaukji, at the head of 1,500 Syrian and Iraqi troops, attacked Mishmar Haemek, a Jewish colony of 500 which was founded in 1926, and which lies in the heart of the Emek, the Vale of Jesreel. For four days the Arabs battered at the colony with cannons and mortars. Mishmar was almost entirely surrounded, but the *Haganah* managed to get through reinforcements on the third day. A four-hour truce was declared on April 8. Before the truce expired, a British colonel drove up to the gates of Mishmar, and told the local *Haganah* commander that he would like to arrange a truce for an indefinite period. When he was told that the defenders of Mishmar had no authority to extend the truce, he said: "I'm afraid you are in no position to reject such a generous peace offer." The local commander simply replied: "We shall see."

At dawn of April 9, Kaukji opened a new attack, and this time the Arabs were completely routed. Two days later Kaukji received reinforcements, and in a strong counter-attack he succeeded in driving a wedge into the Jewish defenses with his heavy guns. But the *Palmach*, Jewish Commandos, opened their attacks, and the Arabs were forced to withdraw their heavy guns to avoid having them fall into the hands of the Jews. Heavy fighting continued till the seventeenth, with both sides receiving more and more reinforcements. By the time the battle ended, all the Arab villages in the area had been occupied by the Jews, and the Arab population was in flight. Kaukji's army had been smashed. This was the first large-scale battle, ending in the defeat of the most experienced commander and the biggest army the Arabs had yet mustered.

This was the news that reached the United Nations' second Special Assembly on Palestine as it got under way after April 16.

THE BATTLE FOR TIBERIAS AND HAIFA. The Arab population had started to run away early in the battle of Palestine. First about 20,000 of the richer families left the country. Then, in the first six weeks of the battle—from April 1 to May 15— the entire population of Tiberias, Haifa, Jaffa, Jerusalem, and Safed fled the country.

Tiberias, an Arab city of 14,000, is the capital city of Lower Galilee. A truce had been declared in this city, but it was broken on April 8, when Arab Legion troops opened fire on Jews in the Streets. *Haganah* forces fought for ten days against the Arab Legion and foreign volunteers. By April 18, every Arab soldier and civilian had fled the city. Six thousand people fled without any apparent reason. An inexplicable flight on a much larger scale was to take place in Haifa, the third largest city in Palestine and the main seaport of the land.

Haifa was a city of 130,000, almost equally divided between Jews and Arabs. On April 22, the British gave up control of the city, and withdrew all their troops into the port area. Soon an all-out battle between Jews and Arabs started. Many Jews were killed by Arab snipers while travelling in buses and other vehicles.

At dawn of April 21, twenty-five boys of the *Haganah* made a daring surprise attack. Crowded into two armored cars, they sped into the heavily populated Arab quarter of the city. The Nejada, the Palestinian Arab youth organization, had its headquarters in a three-story stone building, and had built a special eight-foot cement wall in front of the building to protect it from attack. The Haganah fighters broke through the wall with explosives and took the headquarters room by room with grenades and Sten guns. In the meantime snipers shot at the twenty-five Jewish heroes from nearby roofs and walls. The small band held out against hundreds of Arabs until they were freed the next day when the main attack began.

On April 22, at one o'clock in the morning, the Jews began a mortar bombardment upon the Arab quarter of Haifa, known as the Old City, at the foot of Mount Carmel. Two columns of Jewish fighters struck down Mount Carmel in the early hours of the morning. Another force moved up from the business section of the city along the docks into the Old City.

The Old City was taken house by house. By eleven o'clock of the morning of April 22, the fight was over, and a mass exodus of Arabs from Haifa had begun by road and water—an unexpected, almost miraculous occurrence. Palestine's main seaport and third largest city was in Jewish hands.

THE FALL OF JAFFA. The port of Jaffa was the largest all-Arab city in Palestine, close to the all-Jewish city of Tel Aviv. From Jaffa, snipers had for months fired on the neighboring

Jewish city. On April 25, the *Irgun Zvai Leumi* fighters launched an attack from Tel Aviv on Jaffa. Two thousand Irgunists with armored cars and mortars captured the slum districts of Manschich. But at this point the British joined the battle against the Irgunists with fighter planes and artillery, and thus prevented the Jewish fighters from advancing to the center of the city and taking the harbor.

In the meantime, on April 27, the *Haganah* reached an agreement with the Irgunists, and both fighting groups joined one command under the *Haganah*. Jointly they renewed their attack on Jaffa and seized the eastern and southern suburbs of the city, thus threatening to cut off all retreat from Jaffa. On April 29, the city was almost encircled, and its inhabitants began to flee. Of the 70,000 Arabs in Jaffa, only about 2,000 remained in the city. Thus the largest all-Arab city and port remained in the hands of the Jewish fighters.

THE BRITISH INTERFERE IN JERUSALEM. By the end of April, the Jews took over most of Jerusalem outside of the Old City walls. The *Haganah* seized the Central Post Office, the largest public building in Jerusalem, and the old Russian compound adjoining it, which had been occupied by the Criminal Investigating Division of the British Government. On the same day, the *Haganah* forces also captured the Greek Monastery of St. Simeon, an Arab military strongpoint which had been a base for Iraqi troops. The Haganah also advanced into Katamon, the wealthy Arab quarter of Jerusalem.

When it looked as though the *Haganah* would soon take the whole of Jerusalem, the British intervened. The High Commissioner threatened to send the Royal Air Force against the Jewish positions unless the advance halted. A thousand British Commandos were sent from Cyprus and Malta to Palestine. Tanks from Egypt and Marines from Haifa poured into Jerusalem. A cease-fire was imposed, which was observed for three days. But during these three days the Arabs had time to bring up reinforcements under cover of British guns. Thus the Jewish offensive in Jerusalem was stalled.

The Arab legion was entrenched in the Old City of Jerusalem where 1,500 Jews were besieged. The legion also took possession of the Sheik Jarrah quarter which dominated the approaches to the Hadassah Hospital. From this quarter, the Arabs had for weeks assaulted convoys on their way to the hospital. On April 25, the *Haganah* troops drove the Arabs out of this quarter. But the British intervened and forced the *Haganah* out. Thus, thanks to the British, the Arab occupation of Sheik Jarrah made it impossible for the Jews to use the Hadassah hospital during the war.

In the meantime, virtually the entire Arab population of Jerusalem had fled, and when the British Mandate ended, the Jews were in control of nine-tenths of Jerusalem.

THE BATTLE FOR GALILEE. In the Safed district in Eastern Galilee, the Jews were greatly outnumbered by the Arabs, and the Jewish settlements lay wide open to attack. Seven thousand Jews lived among some 47,000 Arabs, and were scattered among twenty-nine farming settlements and the city of Safed. In the city itself, 1,500 Jews were outnumbered by more than 12,000 Arabs.

The commander of Eastern Galilee was the twenty-nine-year-old Yigal Alon, who had been second-in-command of the *Palmach,* the Jewish Commandos, and the hero of the battle at Mishmar Haemek where the army headed by Kaukji was defeated. At his command, Yigal had only about 3,000 men consisting of two battalions of *Palmach* Commandos and one battalion of infantry. He was greatly outnumbered by the Arabs, who had about 3,000 troops in Safed alone.

Tiberias, which had fallen before to the Jews, had opened the main road north as far as the colony Genosar, halfway to Lake Tiberias. But from there on, the road was under Arab fire and the bridges had been destroyed. On the night of May 2, Yigal placed fighting units to cover the mountains on both sides, while others worked all night repairing the bridges. The next day military supplies were rushed north in preparation for the offensive. The Haganah forces, striking out from Rosh Pinah, cleared the entire territory between Lake Tiberias and Lake Hula. Then striking eastward, the Haganah forces drove all the fighting Arabs between the two lakes over the border into Syria. The population of all the villages in that area fled in panic with their armed forces.

Now the Jews proceeded to break the ring around Safed. All the roads leading into Safed were in Arab hands. But on the night of May 10, *Haganah* troops came over mountain foot-paths from the Jewish colony of Ein Zeitim, four kilometers to the north, and made a surprise attack on the Arab forces. There was a house-to-house fight in the center of the city, and the Arabs fought bravely and well. The fortunes of the battle turned in favor of the *Haganah* after a flank attack was launched by the Jewish fighters. That same night a detachment of sixty boys of the *Palmach* came over the mountains from Rosh Pinah and attacked the Arab village of Akbara, two kilometers south of Safed. The news spread among the Arab defenders and struck terror among them. They feared that a major striking force had come down from the mountains to encircle the city from the south. The Arabs began to flee south and west into Arab-held Central Galilee, through a corridor which had been purposely left open by the *Haganah.* The Arab population of Safed, together with the Arab soldiers, fled down through this corridor. Thus ended the campaign for Eastern Galilee.

Western Galilee had been assigned to the Arab State. In this Arab territory there were seven isolated settlements and the seaside town of Nahariyah. These colonies were entirely cut off from the rest of the Jewish settlements, and their inhabitants feared massacre at the hands of the Arabs. Quick action was necessary.

The Jewish commander of Western Galilee was Moshe Carmeli. On the night of May 13, Carmeli struck. A *Palmach* unit with mortars and machine guns dislodged 300 Iraqi troops stationed on Givat Napoleon and took possession of the hill. Now an armored column of about forty cars with enough supplies for three months reached Nahariyah. This was the first convoy to reach Nahariyah in six months. By noon of May 14, the Jews held all of Western Galilee, except Acre, its capital, and this too was soon to fall.

Thus the Jews had done the job for themselves; partition became an accomplished fact.

JEWISH DECLARATION OF INDEPENDENCE. In this chaotic state of affairs, the British served notice on the United Nations that they would surrender their mandate on May 15, earlier than had been originally arranged, and that they would remove their troops from Palestine as soon as possible. The object of the British was obvious: to let loose the Arab forces against the Jews of Palestine who were poorly equipped. But the Jews were not to be caught napping by this act of British intrigue.

On the third day of Nisan (April 12, 1948), a month before the Mandate ended, the General Council, highest organ of the World Zionist movement, adopted a resolution declaring: "After twenty-seven years of an oppressive foreign regime. . . the Jewish nation will establish its own State of Independence in its homeland." On April 26, the Vaad Leumi (People's Council), as the elected representative of the Jewish people of Palestine, announced the formation of a provisional cabinet with David Ben-Gurion as Prime Minister and Moshe Shertok as Foreign Minister.

On Friday, May 14, the greatest event in Jewish history in more than nineteen hundred years took place. In the Art Museum of Tel Aviv, at 4 o'clock in the afternoon, David Ben-Gurion rose and read the Jewish Declaration of Independence. He then declared: "We . . . hereby proclaim the establishment of the Jewish State in Palestine, to be called Israel."

The news of a reborn State of Israel was flashed over the wires and cables of every land. The United Nations General

Assembly was then in session at Lake Success, and twenty minutes later news came from Washington that President Truman had granted *de facto* recognition to the new State. Then the U. S. S. R. granted the new state *de jure* recognition, and this was followed by similar action on the part of many other members of the United Nations. The Arab delegations at the United Nations were thunderstruck at this sudden change in their political fortunes; they threatened war against the Jews. This was no idle threat, for the very next day the armies of the seven Arab States began an attack on Israel with the intention of wiping out the new nation.

A tiny nation of less than 700,000 souls was now forced to fight against the combined strength of 30 million Arabs. In addition, the Jews were in great need of arms because of the embargo that had been imposed against the Middle East by the American Government. And President Truman, despite his *de facto* recognition of Israel, had failed to remove the embargo. At the same time, the Arabs could get all the arms they needed from British and other sources.

ISRAEL BRACES ITSELF FOR THE STRUGGLE. The Arabs began their attack from Transjordan, whose Legion was trained and led by British Brigadier General John Bagot Glubb Pasha. The British had allowed the Legion to entrench in the old walled-city of Jerusalem months before. The Egyptians were in Gaza, and the Arab Legion was already in Lydda and Ramlah, about fifteen miles southeast of Tel Aviv. The Iraqis were at Ras el-Ein, fifteen miles to the northeast. The Lebanese and the Syrians were ready to invade Eastern Galilee. The British planned that Abdullah, King of Transjordan, would rule over Palestine and Transjordan, and they in turn would control Abdullah. The situation looked hopeless for the infant State of Israel, but the leaders made ready for the struggle.

Yaakov Dori, long the secret *Haganah's* chief of staff, and Yigal Alon, the youthful chief of the *Palmach* Commandos, undertook the task of unifying the various elements that com-

posed the Jewish Army. But an American Jew, Colonel David
Marcus, did more than any single man in helping to unify the
Jewish army. By his valor, courage, and teaching he helped
shape the Jewish army which so valiantly fought against superior forces. Up to the day of his tragic death, this Jewish
colonel was loved, obeyed, and respected by the Palestinians.

The residents of Tel Aviv took the daily bombing by the
Egyptians without showing signs of alarm. Work, produc-
tion, and transport went on in the normal manner. People became indifferent to danger everywhere. The settlers of the fron-
tier colonies and villages, although outnumbered by the enemy
and poorly equipped, fought stubbornly and heroically and
helped keep the enemy out of Palestine. The brave 5,000 Commandos of the Palmach spread through the border areas and
managed to hold off and defeat forces many times their number
and far better equipped than they.

THE FIRST FOUR WEEKS OF BATTLE. The Arabs held Latrun,
the bottleneck of the Jerusalem-Tel Aviv road, and cut off all
supplies from Tel Aviv to Jerusalem. Little food and water
could reach the 100,000 besieged Jewish inhabitants of Jerusalem. The Arabs also had possession of Ras el-Ein where the
pumping station was located, controlling Jerusalem's water
supply, and water had to be brought in by carriers. But the Jews
of Jerusalem were determined to hold on to their homes and
their city despite hunger, thirst, and death.

A human mule train of volunteers was organized, each with
a gun and a pack on his back, to carry supplies—including a
daily water ration of two gallons per person—nightly across
the mountains around Latrun to Jewish trucks waiting on the
other side at Bab el-Wad, to be transported to Jerusalem.
Workers from factories of Tel Aviv and the docks of Haifa
went to risk their lives nightly in this train of volunteers.
Finally, the Jews succeeded in building a road around Latrun
under the fire of the enemy and over rugged hills, and the
situation was greatly improved.

The first four weeks of battle passed, and Abdullah did not take Jerusalem as had been planned by the British. The Egyptian armies never succeeded in joining the Legion forces, for they were stopped at Ramat Rachel. The Egyptians moving north to Tel Aviv were caught in a circling vise at the Arab town of Isdud in Arab territory, twenty-three miles south of Tel Aviv, and were vainly struggling to get out. The Lebanese and Syrian armies failed to break into Israel. The Iraqi forces never got beyond Tulkarm and Ras el-Ein. Between 350,000 and 400,000 Arabs fled their homes, most of them without being attacked by the Jewish army. The Jews, on the other hand, took 700 square kilometers of territory originally assigned to the Arab State, and controlled all ports except Gaza.

At the end of four weeks of battle a truce was imposed.

AFTER THE FIRST TRUCE. This truce expired after four weeks, on July 9. The Jewish army then emerged with surprisingly heavy fire power and armor, using heavy tanks for the first time. The troops showed the effects of intensive training, and the course of the campaign was mapped out by an able staff.

In swift enveloping actions, the Israeli army took Lydda, Ramleh, and Ras el-Ein on the central front, and Nazareth in the north. The capture of Nazareth gave Israel the road junction which controls Central Galilee. They had already taken Eastern and Western Galilee.

At Lydda, the Israeli forces captured Palestine's largest airport in a sudden, violent night attack. This airport had been given to the Legion by the British when they left Palestine. At Ras el-Ein, the Jews recovered the pumping station which controls Jerusalem's water supply. The capture of Ramleh cleared the Arabs from the coastal plain near Tel Aviv, and gave the Jews control of the main Jerusalem road as far as Latrun. Now the Legion left at Latrun controlled only three miles along the Tel Aviv-Jerusalem road. All this was accomplished in but ten days of renewed fighting.

Now, when the aggressors were in danger, the machinery of

the United Nations was set in motion very hastily. Acting on a resolution offered by a delegate of the United States, the United Nations ordered a truce within three days.

THE BERNADOTTE PLAN. Two days before the Jewish State was declared, the United States proposed in the General Assembly of the United Nations that a mediator be appointed to iron out the Palestinian dispute. The United Nations accordingly appointed Count Folke Bernadotte of Sweden to serve as mediator.

Bernadotte's proposals, which were made public on July 4, called for a drastic revision of the November 29 decision in favor of the Arabs at the expense of the Jews. He proposed to give Jerusalem and the Negev to the Arabs, and to allow Abdullah, the tool of Britain, to add Arab Palestine to Transjordan, with Jerusalem as his capital. Israel was to be granted statehood, but in name only, for it was to be deprived of self-rule over immigration, foreign policy, and defense. It was a plan to return all power in Palestine to the British.

The truce ordered by the United Nations was without a set term. In the meantime the aggressive Arabs kept on violating the truce on every front, and the mediator, openly pro-British and hostile to the Israeli government, refused to say a word against the Arab violations of the truce. The Jews begged the United Nations to set a time limit for the truce and to permit them to resume war if the Arabs refused peace talks. But no time limit was set. The enemies of Israel, the Anglo-American bloc in the United Nations, were determined to weaken the new state economically, if not on the battlefield. The cost of keeping the infant state fully mobilized would so weaken it economically that the Jews would be willing to compromise.

The State Department at Washington indicated that it would use pressure on Israel to accept the Bernadotte plan. But the Jews would not be coerced into national suicide. They needed the Negev for resettlement of the homeless Jews who were waiting in Europe. By the partition plan, Israel was allotted

5,000 square miles, and the Bernadotte plan would reduce it to less than half of that, about 2,100 square miles. But Marshall and Bevin favored this plan because the British needed the Negev as a military base, and to the "Geopoliticians" this was more important.

On September 17, Count Bernadotte was assassinated in Jerusalem, and Dr. Ralph J. Bunche, Bernadotte's chief aide, was appointed Acting Mediator on September 18.

THE BATTLE FOR THE NEGEV. George C. Marshall, Secretary of State of the United States, declared before the United Nations General Assembly, on September 21, that the United States considered the Bernadotte plan a fair and sound settlement of the Palestine question, saying he "strongly urged the parties to it and the General Assembly to accept it in its entirety." General approval of the plan was also voiced by Foreign Secretary Ernest Bevin of Britain, and the Foreign Minister of France.

On October 3, 1948, the Israeli Government declared its opposition to "any plan separating the Negev or any part of it from the territory of the State of Israel."

A few days later, the Egyptians opened a heavy assault on the northern approaches to the Negev. The Israeli army, after heavy engagements, repulsed the Egyptian attacks. When the Egyptian planes strafed convoys carrying food to the Jewish settlements in the Negev, the Israeli forces advanced against the Egyptian positions. After a week of heavy fighting, the Israeli army occupied Beersheba, astride the main Egyptian supply lines. By capturing Beersheba, the Jews severed the Egyptian supply lines, and opened the road to the Jewish settlements which had been virtually cut off from supplies for six months.

A few weeks later, the Israeli forces advanced from Beersheba to the Egyptian border, overrunning Bir Asluj and el-Auja. An Israeli armored column advanced thirty-five miles into Egyptian territory, destroyed many planes in the Egyptian airfields, and three days later returned, according to plan, with several Egyptian Spitfires, a considerable quantity of war material, and many prisoners.

On January 7, 1949, the Israelis and the Egyptians reached a cease-fire agreement, and hostilities in the Negev ceased at 2 P. M. that same day. The Israeli troops were then in actual possession of the entire area, except the Faluja pocket and a small coastal strip from Gazah to Rafah.

The Egyptians and the Israelis signed an armistice agreement on February 24, 1949, thus ending nine months of hostilities. By the terms of this agreement, the Egyptians were permitted to withdraw their forces trapped at Faluja under United Nations supervision. When the withdrawal was completed on February 28, Israel assumed control of the area.

On March 23, Lebanon and Israel signed an armistice agreement. Thus ended the battle in the north, with Israel in control of all Galilee.

ELECTIONS IN ISRAEL. The State Council of Israel met in Tel Aviv, on November 25, 1948, and unanimously decided to hold the first general elections on January 25, 1949. On that day, general elections for the Constituent Assembly were held all over Israel. Not one single unpleasant occurrence was reported among the voters of Israel. Everybody voted: men, and women, including Arabs residing in Israel. The voters elected 120 representatives of all parties, among them two of the Arab parties, to the Constituent Assembly.

On February 14, 1949, the Constituent Assembly opened in Jerusalem amidst tears and songs. After a stirring address by Dr. Haim Weizmann, the Provisional President of Israel, the 120 members took an oath of allegiance. And two days later, on February 16, Dr. Haim Weizmann was elected first President of Israel by the Constituent Assembly. Thus was the Government of Israel formed anew, after a lapse of almost 2,000 years.

MIGRATION INTO ISRAEL. On January 18, 1949, Ernest Bevin announced in the House of Commons, to the pleasant surprise of the Jews all over the world, that his Government would permit the Jews held in Cyprus camps "to leave as soon as the Jews provide transportation for them." And the Jews did immediately set out to provide them with transportation. When the first shipload of the Jews held at Cyprus arrived at the Israeli port of Haifa, they were met by the happy faces of Israeli officials and by the joyous crowds watching from the shore, and no longer by the guns of British officials. In a very short time, all the Jews detained in Cyprus were brought to Israel.

Tens of thousands of Jews were brought into Israel from many European lands: Roumania, Poland, Hungary, Czechoslovakia, and others. Thousands of displaced Jews were brought from detention camps in Germany and Austria, and still more thousands from China, South Africa, and North Africa. From very distant lands, the children of Israel were flown by plane, as "on eagle's wings." Almost the entire Jewish population of Yemen was brought to Israel by plane.

And on Hanukkah, 1949, the Palestinian Jews celebrated the arrival of the one-millionth immigrant into Israel.

ISRAEL—THE FIFTY-NINTH NATION OF THE UNITED NATIONS. On May 12, 1949, the application filed by Israel for membership in the United Nations was taken up for consideration. After much discussion by the delegations of various countries in favor and against the application, it was finally taken to a vote in the General Assembly of the United Nations. To the great disappointment of the enemies of Israel, Israel was elected as the fifty-ninth member of the United Nations by a vote of 37-12, with 9 abstentions.

Israel's Foreign Minister, Moshe Shertok, made the first Israeli speech in the General Assembly of the United Nations. He was congratulated by many United Nations delegates, and was then escorted to his country's seat, bearing the plaque "Israel."

Amidst the great joy of thousands of Jews and Gentiles, the Israeli flag, the White and Blue, was finally raised at United

Nations headquarters at Lake Success—a flag waving proudly among the flags of the nations of the world.

May it wave in glory forever. Amen.

Index

A.

Aaron, appointed priest and spokesman, 165; meets Moses, 165; in Pharaoh's palace, 167; ordered to smite Egyptian streams, 172

Ab, nine days in month of, 229. *See also*: Ninth of Ab

Abba Sikra, revolutionary chief, 257

Abdullah, king of Transjordan, 289

Abiram, denounces Moses, 156-57

Abodah. See: Sacred Service

Acra, fortress of, 70; held by Hellenists and Syrians, 84

Adar, month of, chosen by Haman, 11

Additional service. *See*: *Musaf* service

Afternoon Service, on *Yom Kippur,* 38

Agrippa, king over Judah, 247; pays homage to Vespasian, 252; helped Titus in siege of Jerusalem, 259

Ahab (King), obtains Naboth's vineyard, 222-23

Ahasuerus (King), agrees to destroy Jews, 99, 112; feasts made by, 104; orders Queen Vashti to appear, 105; has restless night, 119; learns that Mordecai was not rewarded, 110; orders Haman to honor Mordecai, 120; orders Haman to be hanged, 123; recalls Haman's decree, 123-24

Akiba (Rabbi), supports revolution of Bar Kokhba, 193; his fable of the fishes, 200; martyrdom of, 201; burial of, 201-2

Alcimus, appointed high priest, 89; orders Bacchides to slay 60 pious men, 90

Alexander the Great, in Jerusalem, 59

Al het. See: Confession, prayer of

Alkabiz, Solomon, author of *Lekah Dodi,* 7

Almighty, on trial, 185

Alon, Yigal, commander of Eastern Galilee, 286; hero of battle of Mishmar Haemek, 286; commander of Palmach, 286, 289

Amnon, Rabbi of Mayence, martyrdom of, 21

Amram, marries Jochebed, 150; kisses and strikes Miriam, 150, 151

Anaitis, goddess, 86

Anan, head of moderate party, 253

Andronicus, sentenced to death, 66

Antiochus Epiphanes, becomes king of Syria, 64; in Egypt, 65-6; robs the Temple, 66; spreads lies about the Temple and Jews, 68; wreaks vengeance upon Jews, 70; decides to conquer God of Israel, 70-71; forces Jews to worship Greek gods, 71; decides to destroy Jews, 76; robs temple at Susa, 85; death of, 86

Aphikoman, on *seder* nights, 141

Apollonius, informs Seleucus of Temple treasury, 62; killed, 80

Appelles, at Modin, 78; killed, 78

Apries, king of Egypt, sends army against Nebuchadnezzar, 237-38

Arab Legion, invited by Britain, 281

Arab nations, attack Jews, 280; begin war against Jews, 289; flee their homes, 291

Arbor Day, Jewish, 94-5

Arch of Titus, 267

Aristobulus, contender for crown of Judah, 247

Armenia, rebels against Antiochus, 86

Asarah Betebet, fast day of, 93